BOMB DOORS OPEN

The memoirs of
Flight Lieutenant Ken Trent DFC*

Seeker
Publishing & Distribution
in the Channel Islands

Published in 2016 by
SEEKER PUBLISHING
Units 1 & 2 Elms Farm
La Route de la Hougue Mauger
St Mary
Jersey   JE3 3BA

www.seekerpublishing.com

Origination by
SEAFLOWER BOOKS
www.ex-librisbooks.co.uk

Printed by
CPI Anthony Rowe
Chippenham, Wiltshire

ISBN 978-0-9955644-0-4

© 2016 Ken Trent

CONTENTS

DEDICATION

This book is dedicated to the 55,573 Bomber Command
crew who lost their lives in the Second World War

All of Ken's proceeds from the sale of this book
will be donated to
The Royal Air Force Benevolent Fund & Holidays for Heroes Jersey

ABOUT THE AUTHOR

Ken Trent was born in London in 1922. After leaving school he served in the RAF in Bomber Command. He won the DFC and Bar for his bravery and devotion to duty. Demobbed in 1946, he became a successful businessman. In his spare time, he has been a passionate sailor and horse rider. He lives in Jersey with his wife Ann.

Flt/Lt Tim Dunlop is the Bomber Leader of the Battle of Britain Memorial Flight, which operates the only flying Lancaster bomber in Europe. He has also seen active service in Iraq, Afghanistan and the Congo. As a pilot of the A400M Atlas, he is lucky to fly both the oldest and the newest aircraft in the RAF. He has served with the BBMF for eight years, and is responsible for training crews of the Flight's bomber aircraft.

Chris Stone is a writer and BBC journalist who lives and works in Jersey. He first met Ken Trent in the cockpit of a Lancaster at the Island's International Air Display, and was immediately struck with the stories he had to tell, and the modesty with which they were told. He is very proud to have helped to put them into print.

FOREWORD

by Flt/Lt Tim 'Twigs' Dunlop
Bomber Leader
Battle of Britain Memorial Flight

The story of Flt Lt Ken Trent, and the tales of derringdo which won him a DFC and Bar, are exciting, inspiring, and connect with me on a very personal level;

many reminded me of my own upbringing.

It is his experiences as a Lancaster bomber pilot that I can relate to the most. In particular, his early time progressing through the RAF training system, his first solo, the passion, nerves and general camaraderie; they are still the same today. What is very evident throughout Ken's book is the need for teamwork, lots of rehearsals and a great crew, comprising of people you can rely upon in the direst of situations. The way he and his crew trained together is very similar to us in the Battle of Britain Memorial Flight, and the Lancaster's smell, a mixture of oil and rubber, is still the same. The hours of sorties he flew over enemy territory are frightening to think of now, but his ever present motto 'Just Do It' is truly inspirational. Whilst my flying in the BBMF Lancaster is relatively benign, being responsible for the rest of the crew is very similar. Thankfully I don't take us into the dangers of battle (it is only ever a camera shooting at us!), but we do have the responsibility and privilege of preserving one of only two remaining airworthy Lancasters.

Every time I safely return her to RAF Coningsby I breathe a small sigh of relief, a feeling Ken and all the members of 617 Sqn must have felt returning to the Petwood at Woodhall Spa. Ken's time with the famous Dambusters involved dropping the largest conventional weapons of that time: Tallboy and Grand Slam. Designed by Barnes Wallis, along with an improved bomb sight they paved the way for precision bombing attacks, a role the future 617 Sqn will continue, using the latest laser guided weapons such as Paveway IV with Lightning II aircraft.

I have realised reading Ken's story how close it is to my own; from his love of flying, dislike of desk jobs and the 'filing' of his paperwork. Many men influenced me to join the Royal Air Force: my father with his love of aviation, my grandfather who served as an Officer in the Army; but it is men like Ken who inspired me and the younger generation to serve our country.

An extraordinary voyage, written by an incredible pilot, this book made me laugh out loud in so many places and feel humbled the next. It is so important that Ken's experiences are written down for us all to enjoy. One of the highlights of serving with the BBMF is listening to veterans' tales or reacquainting them with the old girls; this book allows future generations to enjoy those same stories and experiences too.

Lest we Forget

ACKNOWLEDGEMENTS

Ken Trent would like to thank:

Barry and Judith Taylor who helped right from the start
His co-author Chris Stone
His publisher Simon Watkins
Tim Dunlop of the BBMF for the foreword
John Nettles for the narration of the audio book of this title

Chris Stone would like to thank:

Simon for his support and encouragement
Gary Godel for sharing his knowledge
Caroline for her understanding
Ann for the tea and biscuits!

The publishers would like to thank Vicky Aldus for proofreading, Roger Jones of Seaflower Books for origination and the following for permission to reproduce the photographs in this publication:

Ken Trent; The Imperial War Museum
The *Jersey Evening Post*; Graeme Delanoe
Alan J. Barrow (LM658 website)
John Ward (President, 49 Sqn Association)
Colin from Aces High

INTRODUCTION

My family, my kids and grandchildren all seem to think that I have had an extraordinary voyage through life. Pressure from all of them to record some of my life experiences, coupled with an unsuccessful attempt at trying to put it all on a dictaphone, has left me at the age of 93 putting this journey into print. I was partly inspired by reading the stories of some friends of mine who served with the ground forces during the war, facing terrible sights which, high up in my bomber, I never had to endure. After the war ended, it was considered 'bad form' to brag about one's exploits, and a whole generation of us waited decades to tell our stories.

It was an unremarkable start. From a paper shop in the East End, I went to a boarding school where I managed to laze my way through my studies, achieving nothing of merit save keeping the other boys supplied with illicit beer and cigarettes. Had the war not started just as I left school goodness knows how my life would have turned out.

The war was a time of mixed fortunes for my family. My distant cousin Leonard Trent VC was involved right from the start in the Battle of France, before being shot down in 1943 during a bombing raid over Amsterdam in which nearly all the bombers were lost. He survived bailing out, and was imprisoned in Stalag Luft III from where he took part in The Great Escape only to be quickly recaptured. He was lucky to survive the war.

My cousin Bernard (Frederick) Trent was not so lucky, and lost his life on his very first trip.

It was my good fortune that all the gunners and fighters I encountered in more than forty missions failed to do any serious damage.

When it ended, believing that the past was history and tomorrow the future, I pushed the war behind me as I pushed ahead with my life, still unconsciously craving the thrill and excitement of life in a Lancaster bomber. That craving led me to some very dodgy business deals, some exhilarating moments racing yachts in the high seas, and a series of accidents jumping horses over high hedges.

All through my life, my motto has been 'Just Do It'. Whether it was getting over a thrashing at school for some petty misdemeanour, flying into flak over night-time Germany, or sailing my boat into the teeth of a storm, it has served me well. It also helped me to forget the war; not just the danger, the death, the wail of sirens and crash of bombs, but unfortunately also the comradeship, the fun, and the united spirit of doing something because it was right.

I'd like to thank Gary Godel, RAF historian, for finding it for me again. His phone call, out of the blue fifty years after the war, re-awakened memories and feelings in me which I had long forgotten, and most of all a sense of pride in what I and my comrades achieved in those dark days and nights. I remember the fun and laughter we shared in the mess and in the bars of Lincolnshire, and of course most of all I remember those who never came home. This book is for them.

Ken Trent DFC*
July 2016

13 JULY 1944. BARNETBY LE WOLD, LINCOLNSHIRE

It was a beautiful English summer day, warm and with few clouds. The base which was to be my first operational posting was three miles away across the fields. With nothing to do but walk and think, my mind started wandering and suddenly I was gripped with a feeling which until now had never troubled me.

Fear.

It came down on me like a black curtain. How does one cope with it? In a few days I would be flying high above enemy Germany, hundreds of miles away, amid guns and searchlights in the dark, with the lives of six other men depending on me. The terror of what could happen was suddenly very real, there in that English summer lane. The heavy kitbag weighed me down, my feet began to drag, and the confidence which had buoyed me up until now seemed to drain away into the dust. I forced my feet to continue – left, right, left, right, left, right – but as I walked the fear walked with me. The kitbag got heavier, I was hot, shaking and had now completely lost my nerve. 'Will I ever walk back down this lane again, or is this a one way journey? For God's sake, pull yourself together. You have a good crew; you can't just let them down, and yourself down. What's wrong with you? JUST DO IT!'

But it was no good. I stopped and turned. All around me was typically quaint, English beauty. The enormity of what I was about to do was terrifying.

This is what I had striven for, worked and trained for, for years. This is what I so badly wanted. Or was it?

I knew I had come too far to back out. Hitching my kitbag higher on my shoulder, I gritted my teeth and forced my feet onwards. The gates of the base finally appeared and, after a final look back down the lane, I presented myself at the Guard House. I was in, and there was to be no turning back.

CHAPTER ONE

A DESPERATE WRETCH

My earliest recollection is of sitting in a London taxi with my father and my sister Janet, known as JJ. It was a warm, sunny day. The pram hood on the taxi was open, exposing us to a lovely warm breeze. However this was no pleasure trip, as we were on our way to the Woolavington Wing of the Middlesex Hospital, where my mother lay seriously ill. These cannot have been easy times for my parents, who had only recently purchased a sub-post office and general store. My mother's illness meant that responsibility for the running of the shop, along with the care of two small children, lay with my father, who during the First World War had suffered a wound to his ankle which was never to heal throughout his long life. Fortunately my mother recovered – God, she believed, had looked kindly upon her. She was to live for another nineteen years.

I was born on the Becontree Estate in the east of London. A council development, it had been thrown up to clear some of the old Victorian slums and rehouse not only their inhabitants, but also returning First World War veterans. I arrived in this world at home, 35 Farm Way, where my parents rented their council house. It was 1922, just four years after the First World War had ended. Thousands of men had returned from that war with terrible injuries to their minds and bodies, not just my father. His life's adventures had begun long before that though.

Lionel Walter Trent was born in 1880, but his mother, my grandmother, died very soon afterwards. His father married again, and had eleven more children. Grandfather Walter Trent worked as a fitter of pubs; his speciality was to fit the bars and tables with all their pumps and fixings. He was highly regarded, and quite a perfectionist in his profession; he even used to build complete pub interiors to export around the world. He built them for exhibitions which were seen from Moscow to New York. Because of his skill and craftsmanship he also received commissions to work on other projects, and could boast that he had fitted out the carriages of the Royal Train. His obsession with detail and work didn't sit well with my father, who ran away from home when he was just seventeen years old to join the army, where he served for six years before emigrating to Canada. That country was just starting to be developed, and the government offered cheap 'quarters' of land on condition that it was improved in some way, either by building or farming. Back in London, my grandfather's business was failing because he wouldn't offer the discount prices of his rivals. It didn't take long for him to follow my father to Canada, along with four of my father's brothers and sisters. In the cold and snowy winter wastes of Canada they built a home together, using wood which they cut themselves from the forests all around them.

Back in Europe though, the winds of war were blowing, and in 1914 the British Army was mobilised to fight the Germans. My father, Gunner Trent, was a deeply patriotic man and took the boat back to England to join the colours again at the age of thirty-four. The army welcomed him as an experienced soldier, and he was soon in action as part of a Royal Field Artillery gun team. He was one of the people responsible for the team of horses which pulled the gun into position. The Germans would always try to work out where the artillery was, and send over shells of their own to disrupt their work. My father explained to me years later what happened to him. Their sector was fairly quiet, and so, typically, he had gone a short distance away from the gun to tidy up the emplacement. He always spent more of his life tidying than thinking. Suddenly the Germans sent over some counter battery fire, and a shell burst right in the emplacement. A big piece of shrapnel hit him above the ankle, and almost severed his leg. It was the end of his war. He never elaborated about it much, but we were always aware of his injury. While they managed to save his leg, it never healed properly and was constantly infected. I learned very young how to fold bandages, because every time his wound burst it would leak smelly liquid and we had to help to clean it up. Despite the discomfort, he put up with it all his life.

The wound was the reason why he never returned to Canada. While his father and some brothers and sisters stayed out there in the home they had built, he stayed in London to try to rebuild his life. Eventually, one of his brothers was married, my father fell for the bridesmaid ... and two brothers married two sisters! Alice Mabel Anderson was six years younger than my father, and she was very intelligent too. They made a good team when they bought their little shop, as she kept all the books.

Funnily enough, by coincidence my grandfathers were both firm friends and businessmen, and both had the same bad luck. Grandpa Anderson owned a business in Poplar which hit hard times, and the receivers were called in to confiscate his belongings. Before they could arrive though, Grandpa Trent came to the rescue with his van. He pulled up at the shop in Crisp Street, which was always busy because it was a market street, full of barrows and bustling with activity. The two of them loaded up the van with all of Grandpa Anderson's furniture and other things, and drove off before the bailiffs arrived. As they drove around the corner, congratulating themselves on a clean getaway, the edge of the van caught the corner of one of the street stalls - which specialised in fresh eggs. Crash! The whole lot went smashing all over the street, making a sticky mess which the stall owners were less than happy about, to put it mildly. The stall was actually a part of Perks Stores, which owned the building it had been put next to. Perks decided to sue Grandpa Trent because he had been the one driving, and took him to court for the cost of the eggs. Grandpa stuck it out though, and eventually won the case when the court ruled that it hadn't been a proper market stall because it didn't have wheels.

I must have been about four years old when my mother took JJ and me across Goodmayes Park to St Steven's Church School. In those days children played safely in the streets and parks and went for walks with their friends, without the need to be accompanied by their parents. So after a few days, when my mother felt that we knew the way to school, we were left to go there on our own. Eventually, the inevitable happened and we played truant. I don't think it was because I was particularly naughty, but I wanted a change, I wanted to do something a bit different. It was a simple matter to wave goodbye every morning, and then simply wander off, usually to the park. Unfortunately for me, the school found it strange that we hadn't attended for a few days, and called my mother to ask where we were. My mother came straight to the park and found us there, and oh boy was she cross! She never shouted at us but you always knew when you were in big trouble, and the hot water in which we found ourselves on this occasion ensured the offence was never repeated. I don't really know how we thought we would get away with staying away from school anyway. It was a very small place, a church school with maybe twenty children. Two missing would have been easy to notice!

It can't have been easy for my mother and father to look after the two of us, because they were working so hard. They had to be up first thing in the morning to prepare all the papers for delivery, then Father would look after the shop all day. He sold all kinds of things: papers, confectionery, cigarettes, tobacco, lead soldiers, farm animals and other toys. Mother managed the sub-post office, doling out stamps and posting letters, as well as keeping the books for the whole shop. She was clever and quick, and could arrange the figures far more quickly and accurately than my father. He used to go to the bank every week after they had worked out the takings, and always asked the cashier 'Could I have my photograph, please?', meaning could he see the balance of his account. He never made a lot of money though, and I know that a lot of it went on me and Janet. The fees of the schools I wasted my time in weren't cheap. While they were both working-class people, they wanted me to rise above their social level and would spare no expense to help me. So after a brief term at Becontree Council School, I was withdrawn because they didn't like the behaviour, or the accent, I was acquiring from the snotty-nosed local kids who attended it.

Most of the Easter and summer holidays from 1930 until leaving school were spent on the beach at St Osyth near Clacton, pronounced 'Ozzith'. We and the locals knew it as Toosey. My parents purchased a beach hut which was situated fifty feet above the highest tide and which was named Sol Lux (Sunshine). Sol Lux was the name of a dog we had acquired when I was a very young child. When my parents tried to return it to its owners, I made such a song and dance they decided to give it to me!

What a wonderful contrast it was for us, to leave the grimy red brick streets of East London and play in the clean clear air of the seaside. Golden sand, warm red lino, and the smell of seaweed all come back to me as though it were yesterday. There was a long line of these huts along the sea wall. Some were quite palatial, others little more than a cramped space in which to change and perhaps leave your towels. None of them had running water, and we relied on a shared pipe to get enough to drink or clean ourselves in. We heated it up on an oil stove. The toilets were primitive affairs, with a simple bucket sufficing for every call of nature. I clearly remember the old country gentleman who used to come and empty them for a penny a time. He wore clothes which must have been made in the previous century, and brought his horse and cart along the line of huts with a slow sad shuffle. No one wanted to be downwind of him, or his dripping, fragrant cart with its ominous tank on top. While his mother had christened him Cecil, he was known to all and sundry, not unkindly or unreasonably, as the Shit Man.

The bunk beds for us children were in the same room as the paraffin cooking stove; a narrow room along one side of the hut contained a double bed, and in the largest of the rooms there was a put-u-up settee. The toilet was at the back, down some steps and through a door. I woke up in that toilet one night, screaming, after sleepwalking from my bunk. In my panic, I couldn't open the door and my howls must have woken the whole village. Despite that episode they were wonderful times for me.

I should point out that most of the time I was there with my sister and my cousin – no parents. The lady who was paid to look after us had been sacked after a disagreement, and our parents wanted to take us home. Our protestations were so noisy, however, that they relented and allowed us to stay, given that there were other families they knew close by who might be trusted to keep an eye out for us.

Three kids, aged about eleven, left to fend for themselves in a big hut on the sea. Of course, they left us food and provisions but we were very much the masters of our own destiny. We even had a few pennies to spend at the fish and chip shack at the end of the sea wall. My parents had the shop to run!

I remember meeting one of my first loves there. The family in a hut down the wall had a very attractive daughter. We would wait until the tide went right out, then walk out to the water's edge to 'inspect' each other. At that age, it was all very innocent. It was going well until I realised her father was watching us from the hut with his binoculars, and I beat a hasty retreat.

It was these golden days at the beach which inspired another, longer lasting love: sailing. Among my possessions was a book named *Dinghy Sailing for Boys and Girls*, and I had no idea what an important part this book was going to play in my life. I had already read it from cover to cover many times when we discovered a small dinghy buried in the sand not far from the hut on one of our first walks along the beach. We took our buckets and spades to clear the sand from the boat, dragged it down to the sea, pushed it home along the water's edge and concealed it under our hut.

I was thrilled to find that every part of a sailing dinghy was listed in my book – exotic terms such as masthead, gudgeon pin, shelf and lodging knee. I still have that book, and can remember every single part of the diagram of a sailing boat. In addition, the book gave very good advice on safe sailing practices, even explaining how to sail up a tidal river, giving descriptions of where the shallows and deep water would be. Most importantly, one of the things it clearly stated never to do was to go out in off-shore wind conditions: invaluable advice for a novice sailor. We were children, we were at the seaside, and we rarely had any adults telling us what to do, which meant we quickly learned to measure up and take risks and become independent without even realising it.

Following the book's advice, we obtained an anchor and cable, oars and rollocks. We painted the dinghy a different colour and tarred below the water line – and then we were in business. JJ used to row out, drop anchor and peel the vegetables, throwing the peelings over the side; it was great fun for kids. It took a couple of years but we eventually got the centreboard working and with the addition of a small gaff sail, we were sailors. My time spent with this little craft was to cultivate a life-long love of the sea.

The Thames barges used to beach themselves on the shore at half tide, and use a huge mechanical digger to dig up sand to take back to London. They would work until the tide came in high enough to float them off again. I managed to talk myself on board one, and had a marvellous ride all the way there and back.

Unfortunately, my parents were keen that I should also have a more traditional education, and so it was that JJ went to St Winifred's College, Goodmayes, and I went initially to the Loughton School for Boys and then, at the age of twelve, to Framlingham College. Aged eight, I was one of only four boarders at the Loughton School. I don't remember missing my mother or father because I hardly saw them anyway, as they were so busy with the shop and post office. We all ate together with the headmaster Mr Johnson (known as Oggie), his wife, and their daughter, Cynthia. A strict watch was kept on our general deportment and table manners, and every Sunday we attended matins in the town church. We were encouraged to play sport at every opportunity, and I became quite proficient at tennis and table tennis to the extent that I was regularly asked to make up a four with the masters. For more traditional team games we had to march down a path, then across a little bridge and over a railway line to the sports field. On one occasion I went to play a game of cricket, resplendent in my whites, when a chugging steam train came by and *whoosh!* I was left covered in sooty black powder!

I enjoyed my time at Loughton, and the people who I came into contact with were by and large very pleasant. One of them in particular was very pleasant indeed, and nearly got me expelled. Cynthia, as I've mentioned, was the headmaster's daughter. She was gingerish, slim, and a little shorter than me. Her mother dressed her in nice clothes, but she thankfully hadn't inherited her mother's bossiness. She was just a nice girl, who was a good sport and a lot of fun to be with. One day we started, as boy and girl, to discuss what Mother Nature had given us. The school grounds had a playground on one side and a long drive on the other, and in between were wonderful thick rhododendron bushes. We decided to go into said bushes to examine further what differences there were between us. Again, at that age, it was all quite innocent, but to our regret the rhododendron bushes weren't quite as thick as we had imagined, and it wasn't long before disaster struck. We were spotted by the headmaster – her father – himself. He came storming out of the school building towards us and she made a very fast escape, leaving me to face his wrath. He followed me into his study and proceeded to give me a bloody good hiding with his cane. I was terrified that he would throw me out of the school, and cast about desperately for something to say that would mitigate my undoubted sin. 'I'm sorry,' I said, 'and I deserved that, Sir.' Whether it was my sorrowful admission of guilt, or the fact that he probably needed the money my parents paid him to further my education, he allowed me to escape without being expelled. I didn't tell my parents that Cynthia had done just as much for my education as his lessons ever had!

I was supposed to write to my parents every week to let them know how I was faring. But in between games, Cynthia, and my feeble attempts at study, somehow I rarely found the time. On one occasion I received a letter from my mother. Inside was a postcard, stamped ready for my reply, with several questions written on it. The first was 'Are you well?', soon followed by 'Do you want any money?' The answers required were simply 'yes' or 'no', and I was invited to tick the appropriate box. It shows what a desperate wretch I had become, and what a wonderful woman she was.

On another occasion, there were high jinks on the last day of a school term. Playing 'I'm the king of the castle' resulted in my being pushed off a bench, trapping my feet and falling onto my head. As if this wasn't bad enough, a boy running past accidentally kicked me in the head, rendering me unconscious before I even hit the ground. I was taken up to the school building by some other boys and, having recovered consciousness, was able to return home the next day as it was the end of term. However, a couple of days later, I began to suffer nosebleeds; the doctor diagnosed a brain haemorrhage and prescribed bed rest for several weeks. I can remember having to go to a doctor's house for an X-ray, and being given a penny to hold while they passed the rays through me. I was very miffed to find that I had to give the penny back! I spent six weeks in bed, so bored that I offered to do all my mother's darning for her. She told me that I made a beautiful job of it, and in due course I made a complete recovery.

In 1933, at the age of eleven, my time at Loughton came to an end. My parents had made a decision to send me to a public school – Framlingham College in Suffolk.

So it was that I found myself in Ipswich, prior to the commencement of the autumn term at Framlingham, being kitted out for both the school sports uniform and the all-important tuck box. I remember my father singing out, 'This switch for Ipswich!' as we drove there in the car. The uniform was a herringbone suit, and every boy had to get them from the same supplier. The school was situated a few miles north of the town, out in the country – a whole new experience for me. Smartly dressed in my new suit, I felt somewhat overwhelmed by the large statue of Prince Albert surveying the green lawns and gardens in front of what seemed to me a massive school building. There was a sweeping expanse of lawn, a long driveway, and an imposing chapel. I got to know that statue of Prince Albert very well, as one of the punishments at Framlingham was to 'walk up and down', which meant just that. You had to walk on the gravel – never the grass – up and down the front of the main building under the prince's stern gaze.

Since I was to be twelve in the November of that year, I was put straight into the Senior School – and into Garrett House, whose colour was green. The school buildings consisted of a classroom block to house 300 boys, complete with science laboratory; the chapel, which housed a wind organ, and a large room named the Set Room. The Set Room was where both masters and boys ate, where school meetings were held, and where the Sunday evening film was shown. It was also used for the administration of punishments, as we shall see. My house master was Mr Stevens, who was nicknamed The Colonel.

As a newcomer I was the lowest of the low, and sat at the far end of the dining table at mealtimes. If you wanted something from the elevated beings further up, you had to ask, in a suitably submissive voice, 'Excuse me, would you be kind enough to pass the salt/jam, please?' and if you were lucky you might be passed what you were hoping for. That politeness didn't work in the opposite direction though. 'SALT UP!', 'JAM UP!' meant that we lower mortals had to scrabble hurriedly to supply our impatient elders. If the requested condiment wasn't on the table, we had to rush to the cupboard to find it, and pass it on with suitable deference. Many was the time that I ended up with carelessly dribbled jam rubbed into my new herringbone.

The days followed a set pattern: rising bell at 7 a.m., prayers and breakfast in the Set Room, morning lessons until 1 p.m., lunch. Games in the afternoon from 2 to 4 p.m., evening school until 6 p.m., followed by chapel and dinner from 7 p.m. until 9 p.m.; preparation (homework), bed and lights out by 9.30 p.m. Sport took up two hours of every school day with cricket being played in the summer, rugby in the autumn and hockey in the winter term. Squash, tennis, fives, horse riding and swimming in the school pool in summer were also featured in the curriculum. Unsurprisingly I enjoyed games far more than academic work, and because I was small I made quite an effective hooker in the rugby team, being able to stay on my feet when taller boys might have collapsed the scrum.

At Framlingham, all of a sudden I, an East London estate boy, was mixing with boys who had very wealthy parents. I was deeply affected by the fact that they had so much and I had so little. When you're a child, things like that are very simple, black and white. My mum and dad had a little tuppenny paper shop in the East End, while here it was 'Mater' and 'Pater' and all that nonsense. Some of the senior boys, once they had passed their driving tests, would turn up at school at the beginning of term in a sports car, which would then be driven home by the family chauffeur. Yes, yes, I definitely wanted some of that! (The beginning of ambition? Maybe …)

Each boy was allowed a certain amount of pocket money, a pound a term I think, to spend in the tuck shop, which in theory kept us all financially equal. But of course the affluent boys simply set up accounts at the local shops which their parents would settle at the end of every term, and so their tuck boxes were always full of the latest delicacies. Mine was often empty, and I resolved to try to do something to resolve the balance. The answer came from my best friend at Framlingham, Barry Grant. He was an outstanding natural musician, who played the piano and the organ and was in demand during the school holidays to play between films at the local cinemas.

When there was no organist for chapel services, Barry played the organ and I took responsibility for the blowing – which is what Barry normally did. Let me explain that 'blowing' meant taking a turn on the big pumping handle which stuck out of the side of the organ. Behind the pipes there was a section which looked like an enormous set of bellows. Down the side of the bellows was a piece of string with a weight on the end. You had to pump until the bellows were full, which would then keep a supply of air going into the organ pipes. The little weight would move upwards as the air started to run out, so we always knew how hard we had to pump to keep it inflated. It was a dare to us to see just how high we could let the little weight go before we started pumping again. If you left it too late the instrument would literally run out of puff, and the beautiful hymn being played would reach an ignominious end with a sigh and a raspberry.

On the occasions that Barry was blowing and I was in my place in the choir, he would cheekily smile at me, as he either took a sneaky swig of communion wine or sipped from one of the hidden cache of beer bottles we had secreted in the organ – but more about that in a minute. Directly the masters had left the chapel, Barry would alter the stops and blast out all the modern numbers he played at the cinemas.

On Sunday afternoons we were allowed to walk in the local countryside. Barry and I would head off with empty pockets, admiring the quaint small farms which dotted the county of Suffolk: the cows and sheep in the fields and the hens running round the farmyards. While walking, we would be thinking hard about how we could exploit the wealthier, snootier boys at school to make a few bob. Finally a scheme suggested itself. After some careful discussion and preparation, the plan was agreed. We, fourteen-year-old schoolboys, were to move into the booze and fags business. We came up with a plan worthy of master criminals, which we set about executing without delay.

Spare keys for the school's back doors, which were locked at night, were kept in glass cases on the wall, the glass to be broken only in case of fire. Just before my next trip home, with a certain degree of guile, I achieved the first phase of our plan by unscrewing the front of one of the boxes and pinching a key. I took it home and went to visit Uncle Dick, who had a shop just next door to ours. One of his specialities was key cutting, and in moments he had made me a duplicate using the series of special files he kept for the purpose. Luckily he didn't ask what the copy was for. I went back to school, and managed to replace the missing key undetected. All we needed then was a large case and a modest amount of starting capital which we managed to acquire and keep topped up to enable us to buy more 'stock'.

Whenever we were feeling in need of some extra cash, we would plan an expedition. We would wait patiently for lights out, and creep down to meet at the bottom of the stairs next to the back door. Using my carefully copied key, we would quietly let ourselves out, then take a deep breath and lock the door behind us. We couldn't leave it open because a caretaker would go around the building every night to make sure everything was properly locked. Carrying the big two-handled case full of empty bottles which would sometimes clink alarmingly, we tiptoed our way out to the right of the tuck shop, past the chapel, and across the playing field. At the other side was a stile, then we were on a road which led, three-quarters of a mile later, to Framlingham Castle – and the pub which was nestled in its shadow. The landlord and regulars knew us well, and were tickled pink at our little venture. We would present all the empty bottles, which were on a penny deposit each, and receive in return a whole case of full ones. We always asked for clean new bottles with fresh labels on so they would be easier to sell, but never cared what beer actually went into them! We also picked up as many packets of cigarettes as we could afford. We could sell them all on at a handsome profit to the rich boys at school, even charging tuppence a bottle deposit to boost our earnings. We had to charge for the bottles so that we would get them back, and they wouldn't be left lying around to be found by the masters.

After a quick drink and a fag to calm our nerves we headed back down the road, over the stile, across the field and to the school door, carrying the case full of booze and fags. That was always a sticky moment, as you could never be sure that the caretaker wouldn't be waiting for you. We would let ourselves in with the pilfered key, lock the door behind us, and then head down the corridor to the chapel. It was here, in the organ loft, that we stashed our ill-gotten gains. The next day we would be surrounded by rich kids, furtively offering us their money for a bottle of beer or packet of cigarettes. We had to tell them to be extremely careful with those in particular, because a carelessly discarded fag butt could leave a trail. We made plenty of money on every bottle or packet for a modest amount of risk, and we started to do very nicely thank you. In fact, once the contraband was inside the school, the risk was much less, because of old public school traditions. You could get away with most things, but it was DEATH to sneak on someone – really more than your life was worth. So unless a master or the priest actually caught us red-handed, it was very unlikely we would ever be caught. And we never were! On the occasions when we were afraid we were going to be intercepted, we secreted our goods in a cellar beneath the chapel which was accessible from the outside.

All these late-night dealings may have enhanced my wallet, but they did nothing to bolster my flagging academic achievements. The teachers at Framlingham were enthusiastic, and encouraged every one of us to do his best in every subject. I did tolerably in maths, algebra and geometry, which were my best subjects, but I'm afraid in the others I let myself slide dreadfully. My reports were invariably a lament on how I 'could try harder'. I stayed resolutely in the lowest form, together with my friend John Lowe. He was a tall, gangly bloke who shared my inattention to academic exercise. Neither of us progressed at all well, and the form was generally regarded as a load of dunces.

The only teacher I really tried hard for was the headmaster, Mr Whitworth, known as Whitty. The reason? He was a sailor. I knew that if I did my best he would take me out on his eighteen-foot sailing boat, which he did several times. I looked up to him because of his mastery of wind, wave and tide, and I always tried to concentrate hard in his maths lessons. What little I learned stood me in good stead later when I went on to join the RAF.

Throughout my life, the best way for me to learn has been by practical activity, and the one respectable occupation I took part in was the school military cadets; the Officer Training Unit or OTU. It was known as 'The Corps'. Nearly all the boys at school were members, and we learned all the basics of military life. We wore old-fashioned uniforms with puttees around our legs, and were regularly inspected to make sure we were well turned-out. We marched up and down over the school grounds, and learned how to respond quickly to words of command. 'Quick march! Left right, left right, halt! Present arms!' Funnily enough, while I didn't really like being told what to do at school, I liked the order of marching and army drill. Every now and again we would go into the local woods for a little war with kids from a nearby school: lots of rushing about and throwing yourself flat in the mud on your tummy. I remember we were taught to fall so that we could bring our rifles to bear straight away. On occasion they were extravagant enough to provide us with blank cartridges so we could get used to the sound of the guns being fired. I enjoyed learning how to strip, clean, oil and rebuild my rifle. It was a very practical existence, and a very welcome diversion from the dullness of lessons. It led me to join the RAF Cadet Corps when I left school, but alas, it didn't prompt me to greater efforts in the classroom.

Military activity wasn't just limited to school of course, and while we were playing with our rifles, the world was heading towards war. In 1938, when Hitler invaded the Sudetenland, there were fears of imminent attack and the order came that the school was to be blacked out. Black paper was stuck to all the windows, and we had to be careful not to show a light. Fortunately, at the time there was no further aggression from Herr Hitler, and we were able to continue to live unmolested.

As well as being made to 'walk up and down', a punishment for more serious scholastic misdemeanours was to 'get the stick', which was essentially a good going over with a cane by one of the prefects. I had the stick several times, once even on the day before I was due to leave. I had been caught smoking: a very serious offence. I was apprehended by a prefect, who reported me to a house master. I can't remember which, but it would either have been the Colonel or the one we called Pop, who was a physics master. The house master would hear the prefect's report of your wrongdoing then come up with a suitable punishment. On this occasion it was to be six strokes. You would be called to his study to be notified of your fate, and told to report to the Set Room after evening prayers, where the prefects would be waiting for you, often rubbing their hands with anticipation. They would have long canes with pieces of rubber on the end. 'Bend over!' was the command, and then they would take a ten-yard run up before *SMACK*! The cane would come down hard across your bottom. I remember one of them was a First Eleven bowler called Bellamy, who could really lay it on. The important thing, always, was never to show any pain or emotion. You had to bite your lip, prepare yourself not to make any noise, turn off your feelings and think, 'Just do it.' Soon it would be over. I hated to show any weakness, even though they sometimes drew blood. Looking back, I feel sorry for those prefects. It can't have been good for them, but it did me a lot of good in that it made me ready to accept unpleasant things without complaint, and to press on regardless. When I was flying towards a hail of flak over Germany several years later, I called on that same strength.

My last report was fair but I must say that it could have been much better. Academically there is no doubt that I let my parents and myself down and yes, I do regret the waste of their hard-earned money and the fact that I threw away those years when I had a chance for academic learning. I also let down the school, which had done its level best to help me. However I did learn something – valuable ambition and the desire to have the life enjoyed by many of the boys. Most important of all was the character, self discipline and courage that was installed by the strict regime I experienced at Framlingham. It was not easy living through the day knowing you had to appear in the Set Room at 9.30 p.m. after prayers, in your pyjamas, for four or six of the best. I wanted to succeed, and I wanted to earn my own money my own way.

As I prepared to leave school, I remember the unsettling atmosphere of blackout blinds and speculation. Everyone seemed to believe that another war was imminent. Despite the threat, we went on our usual holiday to the coast, which I managed to enjoy very much despite the knowledge that I would soon have to start making a living and fending for myself.

CHAPTER TWO

REACHING FOR THE SKY

I entered the big wide world, aged sixteen, in the summer of 1939. While I had been on holiday the world had been in crisis, but until now it hadn't really affected my cosy existence. Everyone knew the war was coming though, as Churchill had warned us about the threat from Germany. He was already a hero to me. He had made a bad mistake in the Dardanelles in the First World War, but we heard him all the time on the wireless talking about Hitler and his ruthless intentions. Sure enough, not long before my seventeenth birthday, at ten o'clock on a Sunday morning, I listened to the wireless at home and heard Chamberlain the appeaser telling the world that his piece of paper had failed, and that 'this country is at war with Germany'. Huddled around the radio, we couldn't believe we were at war again. 'That bloody two-bit painter!' Dad said, meaning Adolf Hitler. Invasion fever gripped everyone, and I remember all the sirens sounding and people rushing to air raid shelters, even though there was no sign of any enemy aircraft!

With the help of my father, I managed to get a job at the sales office of John Knight Limited, Silvertown, East London, who were part of Lever Brothers, the soap manufacturers, and it was there that I worked while Europe descended into war. I worked in the Sales Forwarding department, occupying myself with documents, receipts and paperwork. The introduction of conscription had an immediate and noticeable effect on the company, and the men at John Knight had suddenly disappeared, as they joined up and went away. Our section was left with only very young or very old men, and a lady took charge. She was wonderful, very kind, and I would have done anything for her. She evidently taught me well, because in very short order I was running the London forwarding section of the company. Women ran most of the other managerial posts, and what a good job they did.

The company soon decided it would move its offices from Silvertown to somewhere safer, and with a wonderful irony set up its wartime offices in Loughton, just down the road from where I had been at school. The offices were established in the outbuildings of a very large house, complete with housekeeper. In the evenings I would often work late, and as it was too far to cycle home I used to sleep, by arrangement, in the big house. I would make my own breakfast and supper, and the housemaid would tidy up after me. It was here that I really discovered my ability to work when I thought it was worthwhile. There was a war on, and everyone had a real strength of purpose. I was proud to be good at my job, even though it wasn't directly involved in fighting, and I spent hours and hours working overtime. You couldn't afford to be ill, and there was very much a feeling that one had to get on and 'do one's bit'. Since those first days at John Knight, I've never wanted to take time off because of being ill. I would much prefer to be working.

I couldn't spend every night in the big house though, and had to make a regular commute back home to my mother and father's shop in Becontree. It was fourteen miles each way. The easiest way to do that was to find myself a bicycle, so I managed to get hold of a racing machine which would go quite fast. The only problem was that I enjoyed the speed too much! On one occasion I came flying down the road and didn't see the baker's van which was unloading right in front of me. I crashed into it at full pelt, through the open doors, and ended up sitting inside the van covered in bread but otherwise unhurt. The bike hadn't come out of the ordeal quite so well, as the forks had been bent back by the impact so far that the front wheel rubbed against the down tube. I whipped the wheel out and poked the end of the forks down a metal drain cover. A sharp tug, and the forks were straight enough for me to pedal off before the baker, who was delivering, could notice what had happened. It got me home, but the damage was too much and the bike and I had to part company.

Since I had been working, I had been paying my parents part of my wages as keep. What I hadn't realised was that they had saved up my little donations, and with typical generosity they used this fund to help me buy a replacement bicycle. It was a delightful machine, quite fancy and much faster than the previous one, and I loved the sensation of speed that it gave me. In no time I was a member of the East Anglian Road Cycle Club, and training for all I was worth. I began to race, and joined about twenty other enthusiasts for their rides every Sunday. Because of my age, the older members insisted that I shouldn't race for any further than twenty-five miles, which I thought ludicrous. I regularly rode much further than that, from work at Loughton out to the 32nd mile marker on the Newmarket Road, before I headed back towards home. That added about an extra fifteen miles to the journey, so the total ride home was about forty miles. I used to head straight for the larder when I got back, and consume a whole pint of milk in one go. After a couple of months I was pretty good on the bike, and on one occasion completed a twenty-five-mile time trial in one hour three minutes and eleven seconds. Mind you, it was very flat where we lived, so I probably had it easy!

Cycling quickly became a very important hobby for me. I raced against a lot of older men, and often managed to beat them. I was young and quite silly though, and my love of speed often got me into trouble. Pedalling furiously at the front of the peloton one day, I leaned on another chap who was next to me, shoulder to shoulder, just for fun. It all came to an abrupt halt when the pedal of my fixed wheel bike hit the ground, and suddenly, *WHAM!* We were on the floor and the rest of the group piled straight into us. Needless to say we were relegated to the back for a while. It was a very friendly club though, and every Sunday we would meet at a particular junction next to an old hollowed-out tree. When we set off they would leave a rolled up piece of paper in the hollow, with details of which way we were going and where we expected to stop for a quick cup of tea or coffee. It was friendly, but fast and competitive, and I liked that. We even went on a cycling holiday, going to ride the hills in Devon and

Cornwall. I remember a friend of mine screaming down the Countisbury Hill on a fixed gear bike, with his legs spinning like crazy and unable to stop. There was a man with a horse at the bottom of the hill, which was clearly spooked by us coming down towards it. My friend went right underneath the horse's neck, somehow avoiding the reins.

This was all during what became known as the 'Phoney War', when it seemed nothing much was happening. War had been declared and everyone was ready for an invasion, but nothing much occurred to disturb our otherwise simple way of life.

The invasion of France was a shock, though, and everyone watched in disbelief as the French Army and the British Expeditionary Force was swept aside by the well trained *Wehrmacht* machine. In June 1940 the Channel Islands were occupied by the German Army. John Knight had customers in the Channel Islands, as well as some outstanding orders, and I well remember his sense of panic.

The Germans didn't wait long before beginning their dreadful attacks on our country. We knew they were bombing the RAF airfields, as some of them were quite close to where we lived, but nothing came too close to us while the raids were carried out in daylight. You would see the trails of condensation high up in the blue sky, as the British fighters and German bombers and escorts duelled to the death, and sometimes a parachute would float lazily down. You never knew whether it was one of theirs or one of our own. Churchill quickly had enough of us being attacked without retaliation though, and in a daring raid some RAF bombers were sent to attack Berlin. On 25 August 1940 about a hundred bombers flew all the way to the German capital and let them have it. We heard all about it on the news and were delighted that at last we were striking back at the hated Hun, but inevitably there were serious consequences. Even though he was gaining ground by smashing up the RAF airfields and radar stations, Hitler decided he would rather go after London. It meant that I, in my own little world of work and cycle racing, and my parents and their little shop, became a target.

I clearly remember the first daylight raid I saw. The unsynchronised throb of the bombers' engines as they lumbered towards the City, a high-pitched screaming sound as I saw an aircraft plummeting towards the ground, a single engined fighter which could have been ours or theirs. The sound ended in abrupt, sudden silence. I was on my bike when I saw someone coming down on a parachute, and I pedalled furiously to get to where he was going to land. As I got closer, a convertible car came haring past me with the roof down, a young man hanging out of the top brandishing a rifle. His determination to get to grips with the Hun really summed up the mood of the time for me; everyone wanted to get their own back on the men who had bombed our homes. Unfortunately I never found where the parachutist landed, so I never found what became of him.

Every day on the wireless and the cinema news reels there would be exhilarating reports of what had happened. Fearful numbers of German planes seemed to have been shot down, but I think we realised even then that the figures were exaggerated for the sake of our morale. I was lucky that no bombs came near me during the daylight raids, even though I saw the bombers and heard the explosions. The closest I came to danger was when I saw a man walking across the park towards my parents' shop. Two bombs came whistling down and buried themselves in the ground on either side of him, making huge explosions as they went off, but he somehow survived. He came into the shop with his ears still ringing.

The daylight raids didn't last long because they proved too expensive for the Germans. Our splendid young men in their Spitfires and Hurricanes were doing a marvellous job in breaking up the waves of attackers, and winning the Battle of Britain. Unfortunately they switched to night-time bombing instead, which proved far more dangerous. Some of my father's customers were killed, other people nearby simply didn't turn up for work one day because they had bought it or were bombed out. When I close my eyes and think of those times, I always hear the *brrrmmm brrrmmm* of the engines, the wail of the sirens, the all-pervading smell of the dust and dirt which was thrown up by the bombs, and people coming out of their shelters in the morning in wonderment that they were still alive. We didn't have a proper shelter, just a reinforced metal table with strong legs, issued by the government, which you were supposed to hide under if there was an attack. Janet and I usually slept under it, with my parents under the stairs. My father was having none of it. He was a true Brit, a man who thought Churchill the greatest living Englishman, and I remember him saying, 'We're not going to move for that bastard Hitler!' Then the first time the windows were blown in we were all under that table in a flash! Having fought the Germans in the First World War, Father was in no mood to appease the 'bloody Krauts'. He would have fought them to the last bullet if he had to, and then chased them down the road with a stick. He called Hitler a failed painter, and had nothing but contempt for him. It was only his age and his wound which stopped him from signing up again and chasing him across Europe single handed. My mother was a little more frail, and I can remember helping her across the street in the blackout, as she hooked her arm through mine and I warned her of the potholes and kerbs to make sure she stayed upright.

The bombing campaign ground relentlessly on to become known as the Blitz, and all around me the people of London were having to come to terms with the fear and desperation which comes out when you are under such unremitting attack. I was caught in the open on one occasion when I went next door to see my Uncle Dick. A bomb landed close to me and the blast blew me down the road. Luckily I wasn't badly hurt, and managed to get up and get inside quickly. Lots of families sent their children out to the country to escape, which led to at least one terrible tragedy. At Silvertown there was a reception centre for these children, where they were gathered before being sent away to safety. During one particularly vicious night-time raid, the centre had a direct hit and was destroyed with all those little ones in it. We all heard about it because it was very close to us, and it only fuelled the anger we felt towards the Germans. As far as I was concerned, and this was a view shared by many at the time, the only good German was a dead German. I hated them, and wanted to get back at them in any way I could. Later in the war, when I was dropping bombs on German cities, I felt no remorse at all. I completely agreed with our commander Bomber Harris, who said, 'They have sown the wind. Now they shall reap the whirlwind.'

As a young man approaching the age when he could be called up, I was very keen to guide my destiny and choose where I might 'do my bit'. I had joined the Air Defence Cadet Corps almost as soon as I left school, and my youthful experience in the Officer Cadets stood me in good stead. What finally convinced me to get on with it and volunteer were the trips I used to make out to Epping. At High Beech there was a beautiful old pub which had a great view to the west and the setting sun, and this was where all the fighter pilots used to take their girlfriends. They would turn up in their sports cars, revving the engines and showing off their impossibly glamorous companions. Their uniforms were immaculate; they were clean-cut, smashing kids with wings on their breasts who flew the Spitfires and Hurricanes which defended our skies. Of course I wanted to be one of them, as did virtually every other young man of my age.

I volunteered for the RAF, in the capacity of UT (untrained) pilot. Not long afterwards, on 7 February 1941, I was called up. The night before I was due to go for my first tests, I went to the Rio cinema, known to us all as the R-Ten. Although I forget what film we saw, I remember what followed very clearly. I was walking home with my friend Doug West when the sirens went for a raid, and of course all the lights were out because of the blackout. There were anti-aircraft guns firing in Barking Park, and in their flash I suddenly saw an object coming down on a parachute. I yelled above the roar of the guns to Dougie, who saw it too, but he thought it was a man who had bailed out and started to run towards it. I had recognised it as something far worse though. It was a land mine, a huge container like an oil barrel, filled with explosives which could demolish a whole row of houses. They came down on parachutes because they were quite fragile and could have blown up before they reached the ground. I screamed at Dougie and ran as fast as my legs would take me away from where the dreadful device was going to land, before throwing myself flat next to another house. Dougie arrived moments later, flung himself down next to me and we both put our hands over our heads, opened our mouths and closed our eyes, just as we had been taught to do. Even though my eyes were closed I saw the brilliant flash of the explosion, and felt the roar of hot air and debris as it flew over us. The wooden fence next to where we had landed crashed down on top of us, and then a large part of the house came crashing down on top of that. The fence protected us from the bricks, slates and debris which fell, and when it became quieter we managed to get out from underneath it all relatively unscathed. There's no doubt that fence saved us that night, and in the true Blitz spirit we simply shrugged and carried on walking home. When I got there I saw in the mirror that I was filthy dirty, and covered in dust and goodness knows what.

But if I was worried at the possibility of being killed by Hitler's bombs, I was far more concerned at the possibility of being rejected by the RAF. It was now that my lack of diligence in academic work at school hit home. I felt stressed and worried that I would not be deemed suitable at the interview, nor pass the necessary tests, and I so much wanted to be a pilot. I arrived at Uxbridge with a number of young men similar to myself, all of whom thought they might be the next Douglas Bader or Bob Stanford-Tuck. We were given a rudimentary medical assessment, which I found to be a simple affair after my summer of bike racing. We were sworn in, and given a number which we had to remember. They asked a little about our educations, then it was time for the part I had been dreading – the tests! As luck would have it, they were mainly quite simple mathematics questions, and I thanked my stars that old Whitty had kept me interested at school. That was it for the first day of assessment, and I came away hoping I had done well enough to be asked for an interview. I was petrified that they would use the intervening week to examine my old school reports, in which case I was sure I would be sunk!

I must have impressed them enough though, because I was called back for an interview. If anything, this set my nerves on edge even more. Three or four of us waited outside the interview rooms, into which candidates were called for their moment of truth. I remember being convinced I had no chance; that they would have heard about my scholastic laziness and would hardly give me the time of day. I just wanted to be accepted. I would have lied or done any bloody thing just to have been accepted into that wonderful organisation, but now I feared my past sins would catch up with me. My name was called and I entered the room to face a man scarcely ten years older than myself. He wore the immaculate uniform to which I so badly aspired, and I really wanted to impress him despite my nerves. I stood to attention.

'What school did you go to?' was his opening question.

'Loughton Prep.' I answered, because I thought calling it a 'prep' might sound a little more impressive.

'Hmm. And after that?' he asked.

'Framlingham.' I told him.

'Really?' he said, 'What house?'

'Garret, sir.'

'Really? Me too!'

And that was it! We spent the rest of the 'interview' talking about the old school. I was far too sensible to mention my nocturnal dealings with the copied key and the bag full of beer, or the times I had been given the stick or been made to 'walk up and down'. Instead we talked about Whitty and sailing and games. I was also glad the school had polished away some of my East London slang, so that I had the right accent to be considered for the RAF. At the end of our little chat my interviewer said 'Of course you're in, you'll have no trouble old boy!'

I made my way home convinced I was going to be one of those Spitfire pilots with wings, a sports car and a glamorous girlfriend. I was going to be a Brylcreem Boy, no doubt about it.

I was now in the RAF and given the number 1333000, which proved to be a lucky one. My call-up papers arrived not long afterwards, along with the train fare to Uxbridge. I left home, saying goodbye to my parents and Janet with some emotion. My intake on 28 June was little more than documentation and another rail warrant to Paignton, No. 9 RW (Receiving Wing). Here we were kitted out with everything we could possibly need, including a 'house-if' (housewife), which was essentially a sewing kit, and a tin of blacking for our boots. We were allocated a barrack hut, where we spent time recovering from painful injections, polishing our boots, learning the complicated procedure of leaving one's bed properly made each morning, and enduring seven days of drill. This was my introduction to the bolshie world of the services. Luckily, with my experience in the Cadets the marching came easily to me, and I almost enjoyed it. Usually, being told what to do is anathema to me, but I was awake enough to realise that you had to put up with the bullshit in order to learn to fly.

Along with seventeen other airmen, on 5 July 1941 I relocated to the Initial Training Wing (ITW) in Stratford-upon-Avon, where we were put in the Shakespeare Hotel. This was a beautiful hotel, albeit with all the peacetime goodies removed, and a good place to begin the business of learning to fly – although with no aeroplanes as yet. There were lectures on the history of the RAF, the theory of flight, navigation, map reading, aircraft recognition and an outline of the various instruments we would use when flying. These lessons were interspersed with fast quick marching. I was very keen to do well, and finally found a gift for study which had so far eluded me. I researched all the lessons we had to learn, wrote down what they taught me, and learned them all off by heart. I wrote out all the instructions for the flying instruments and learned them, even though I didn't understand half of them. Every fact learned was another step towards the day when I would climb into an aircraft and take to the skies and I'm sure I've never worked so hard.

Our spare time was spent pushing a punt along the river with a pole, which was a first for me, and it was such a beautiful setting. The theatre, although not in use for plays whilst we were there, was used on at least one occasion for a general assembly of all airmen stationed in the locality.

At the end of the course, examinations were held to test our suitability, which I fortunately passed, although four failed. My new-found diligence in study had paid off. Then, very hurriedly, we had to pack our kit and board a train for West Kirkby in the Liverpool area, where our training course, along with lots of other RAF personnel, boarded a vessel bound for Iceland. We were given very little notice, and weren't allowed to tell our families where we were going. Our ultimate destination was to be Canada.

CHAPTER THREE

'MUMMY, IF YOU COULD SEE ME NOW!'

The RAF had found, through bitter experience, that the British Isles weren't an ideal location for learning to fly. The weather was lousy, with fog and low cloud often proving deadly to inexperienced pilots. Most of the aircraft produced in the country were needed for active service, and of course there was always the threat of a German fighter making a violent interjection to your training flight. Canada, on the other hand, had thousands of miles of flat, open countryside, and a far better climate for flying.

Our transport over the seas to Iceland was the *Leopoldville*, a dreadfully dirty old Polish freighter whose facilities left a lot to be desired. The lavatories consisted of a large plank with several holes in it. This was fitted up alongside the port quarter with a hand hold. It was not exactly pleasant but it was very efficient, as the effluent was easily hosed off into the sea. One of my comrades, a chap called Bishop, stood by the rail looking decidedly green. 'How about a nice pair of greasy kippers?' I asked him. The result was inevitable, and the sea washed the remains of his breakfast over the side.

We were meant to sleep in the large open accommodation area below deck. Some of us slept on tables, others on the floor, but I found a quiet bit of corridor and managed to sleep very nicely, my head filled with dreams of being a dashing Spitfire pilot. It wasn't long before the weather really deteriorated and the old tub pitched and rolled to such an extent that several portholes in the accommodation area, which had not been securely fastened, turned into very large, high-pressure hoses as the ship rolled them under water. The sea rushed in from side to side and created absolute chaos so that when I went to find where everybody was, I found a foot of water sloshing about and everyone in a very bad temper! They were all soaked through and envious that I had managed to stay perfectly dry. Eventually the portholes were secured and we had a big dry-out and general clean-up before we finally arrived at Reykjavik.

From there we were taken in open vans to a place named Helgafell and bedded down in half-finished Nissen huts with no proper sleeping or washing facilities. We had to wait for our boat to Canada, and spent at least two nights freezing in these huts which were still open to the elements at one end. In Iceland! When we lay down we were evenly dispersed along the wall of the hut, but when morning came we were all piled on top of and around each other to try to keep warm.

There was one highlight of our few days in Iceland though. The country is covered in natural hot springs, like modern jacuzzis. We all decided we had to have a go, and plunged in nude. Everything went well until a group of young local girls joined us, minus swimming costumes, meaning that none of us dare get out of the water!

Finally, after a couple of days of alternately freezing and thawing out in the hot spring, we boarded a large ship, the name of which I have long since forgotten, and left Reykjavik, joining a convoy bound for Canada. This was a time of course when German U-boats were prowling around looking for convoys like ours to attack, and we certainly would have been an easy target. But I didn't think of the dangers of being torpedoed. If you worried about it, you still couldn't stop it from happening, so I put it on a shelf and tried to forget about it. I did make sure I knew where my life jacket was though, and how to get to the lifeboats. I had all the gear, and I genuinely wasn't frightened or worried. The ship was much bigger and far more comfortable than the one which had taken us on the first leg of our journey, and was filled with many more people. We were all on our way to learn to fly, nearly all under twenty, and embarking on the biggest adventure of our lives. The excitement rose as we crossed the cold, turbulent sea.

Arriving in Canada on 20 August 1941, where the weather was sunny and warm, we boarded a train from Halifax bound for Saskatchewan, where we would arrive at the Elementary Flying Training School (EFTS) Swift Current after a five-day journey passing through some very beautiful, awe-inspiring countryside to the north of a great lake. As we passed Sault Sainte Marie the landscape gradually became the Prairies – a flat terrain without hills but having its own grandeur. The train we travelled on was enormous, perhaps a mile long. It had huge bells at the front which would clank away loudly every time we went through a town, and a very powerful horn which would sound ghostly over the empty prairie as we rolled onwards. We stopped in Toronto for a couple of hours where the local authorities had organised a dance for us with plenty of girls as well as a finger buffet, which was a very generous gesture, typical of the Canadians. At various other points along the way we stopped for fifteen-minute breaks, when we were able to have a quick look around and maybe buy some goodies.

Reaching our destination on 28 August, our course was allocated a hut with the usual set-up of beds around the sides and a large tin heater with plenty of fuel in the middle. The best pitch was always the one nearest the heater. At last we were nearer to the aeroplanes – in this case DH82Cs – known as Tiger Moths. Our flying kit was issued, and excitement was at fever pitch, with our imaginations working overtime.

Flying at last! Dressed in our new boots, helmets and goggles, we went to inspect the aircraft we would be using to take our first tentative steps towards flight. The Tiger Moth was a wonderful aircraft to learn on, very forgiving to a novice. As we walked towards it over the grass, we took in its main characteristics. It was a fabric covered biplane, about twenty-four feet long, painted yellow with two cockpits; one for our instructor, and one for us.

My first instructor, whose name I have forgotten, was a very strict type. He gave curt, clear instructions, and wasn't much liked by many of the course. I got on very well with him though, and liked the fact that he didn't mess about. For me, he was the right guy in the right place at the right time.

There were three of us in my group, and I was chosen to go up first. We walked around the aircraft, and he showed us how to check that all the various flaps and ailerons were moving properly. We then checked the pitot head. The pitot head, I learned, is the little tube which sticks out of the side of every aircraft and is used to measure how fast you are going. It has to be covered up when you are on the ground to stop dirt getting into it, and you had to check that it had been uncovered before you tried to take off.

Having completed our 'walk around', it was time to climb up onto the wing so I could take my first ever look into the cockpit of an aircraft. Mine, as a learner, was the rear one. The dashboard on the Tiger Moth was very small, with just the basic instruments which I would have to study. As we leaned in, I took my first breath of that wonderful smell of fuel, oil, leather and metal which was common to most aircraft of the time. The instructor showed me the control column or 'stick'; the needle ball, which was explained to me later; airspeed indicator; engine pressure and rev counter; throttle; altimeter and fuel gauge. We would be taking off with twenty-one gallons in the tank, which was on top of the wing. To see how much you had left, you looked at the little tube which protruded from the wing just in front of you. My instructor brusquely told me what was what, and then, at last, it was time to get in and get to grips with the controls.

Following instructions, I put my parachute onto the seat before I got in, so that I could sit on it as we flew. I just hoped I wouldn't have to call upon it in an emergency! Then I swung my leg over the leather-padded edge and took my seat. My feet naturally came into contact with the rudder pedals, my hand was on the stick, and my heart was in my mouth. After all the study, the nerves, the tests, the thousands of miles across the seas and prairies, this was finally THE MOMENT! Ken, the newsagent's son from East London, who didn't even have a driving licence, was sitting at the controls of a wonderful aircraft.

Our only way of communicating with each other was via a primitive voice tube, which was as simple as it sounds. A tube close to the instructor's mouth led behind him to my cockpit, and I would have to press my ear closely to the end of it to hear what he was saying once the engine had started and we were airborne. There was no radio contact between us.

The instructor began, in his brusque way, to run me through the final checks before we could start up the engine and take off.

'Switches OFF.'

'Petrol ON.'

'Throttle CLOSED.'

'Suck IN!'

This last command would be the signal for the ground crew to turn the propeller a couple of times, always leaving one blade pointing skywards showing that the engine was ready for its power stroke.

'Switches ON.'

'CONTACT!'

On this command, the ground crew man holding the propeller swung the blade downwards and stepped smartly away. The engine roared into life, and the propeller sprang into whirling motion. The Tiger Moth started to quiver and shake, just as I was, in anticipation of getting airborne. The chocks against the wheels were left in place as we ran through our final checks. The Tiger Moth had twin magnetos, which governed its electrical workings. Using the throttle, we ran the engine revs up, and switched from one magneto to the other while watching the readout which told us how they were performing. It was called 'checking the magneto drop'. If one reading dropped significantly, then the flight would have to be abandoned while the fault was found. Many young, green apprentice airmen had been asked to go to the stores for a packet of 'magneto drops'!

Luckily for me, all was well. The instructor waved his arm for the chocks to be removed, and we were off, taxiing along the side of the field with the wind behind us. There was a bright orange windsock which we had to take note of, to make sure we used the wind to our advantage.

'Take hold of the stick between your finger and thumb ONLY!' came my instructor's voice through the speaking tube. I could feel the movements he was making as we reached the end of the runway and turned into the wind. As it felt the extra lift, the aircraft started to vibrate more strongly, and my senses felt more alert than they ever had been in my life. My eyes were everywhere; on the control column, on the instruments which until now had just been the subjects of theoretical lessons, on the wing tips and bracing wires as they quivered, and on my instructor in the seat in front of me as he checked we were ready to take off. There was no air traffic control there, and he simply had to look above, around and behind him to see if any other aircraft were about.

The sky was clear, and with an exhilarating surge as he pushed the throttle forwards, we were bounding down the grass strip, buffeted by the wind and the bumps coming through the undercarriage. The instructor had told me to look ahead as we took off, to check that we were going straight. But with the aircraft's nose tilting up into the air, all I could see was sky so there wasn't much point, until we reached fifteen miles per hour and the back wheel lifted gently off the ground. As we levelled out I could see in front of us perfectly well, and a moment later the rumbling from the undercarriage suddenly stopped. We were in the air! Taking in every second of what was happening to me, with the wind rushing past, I strained to hear the instructor's voice down the speaking tube. We were up at about 200 feet when I was given my first chance to take some control of the aircraft.

'Make sure you are holding the stick with your thumb and forefinger. Good. Now, put your feet on the rudder pedals. Good. Keep an eye on your needle ball and airspeed. That will tell you if you are flying straight and level. And WATCH YOUR AIRSPEED!'

The needle ball and airspeed were drilled into us, as both are vital for flying straight and level in cloud. If the airspeed were to drop below a certain level, then this would result in the aircraft stalling and dropping from the sky or going into a spin. Needle and ball was an instrument which had a needle pointing upwards and a ball at the bottom of the face, which indicated side slip. It looked like a curved spirit level. In order to maintain straight and level flight, the needle and ball had to be kept in the centre, there had to be sufficient airspeed, and the altimeter had to be kept at a constant height. On this first flight the instructor showed me how to make corrections using the stick, the rudder and the throttle. If you pushed the rudder pedal to the right, the ball would fly to the left, the needle to the right, and vice versa. Provided you kept them both in the centre, you were flying a straight course.

After some wonderful minutes of just holding the aircraft straight and level, watching the world below me fly past, the instructor shouted to me again.

'Now push the stick forward. That's it, forward, forward ...'

As we pointed downwards, we got faster and faster, the noise of the buffeting wind increased and the airspeed indicator pointed to 120 miles an hour. This was FAST! And so exciting ...

'Right, now ease the stick back. That's it, back, back, back, keep going, that's it ...'

I did exactly as I was told, feeling the g-force pushing me down onto my parachute as the aircraft came out of the dive and climbed up, up, up, and finally over the top in a loop. A loop! On my first flight! I am sure that this was to give pupils confidence, and after that it was all easy and came naturally to me. From that moment, I was completely hooked and wanted to spend every waking moment in the air.

Then it was time to learn some level turns. 'Ease the stick over to the left.' he shouted through the speaking tube. 'You'll see the nose start to drop and the speed will increase, so ease the stick back until you are flying level again. If you continue you will see the horizon going past you – now ease the stick back and you are straight and level again – watch how the horizon moves relative to your wing tips.'

All too soon it was time to land. We came down into the wind, and the instructor made it look easy as we dropped neatly onto the grass. To say I was exhilarated would be a colossal understatement. As soon as I was out of the cockpit and down the wing, I ran over to the other students to tell them all about my loop, and the feeling of being up there among the clouds. 'Did you see me?' I wanted to know. I dashed off my first letter home to my family that night, breathlessly describing what I had done. I couldn't wait for my next lesson.

The next few days were spent either in the aircraft learning to take off, manoeuvre and land, or in the classroom studying navigation and the science of flying. To begin with, we learnt what to do if we flooded the engine before we had even started up! You were taught the following procedure: 'Switches OFF! Blow OUT! Throttle OPEN!' The ground crew would rotate the propeller anti clockwise. Soon we would try again: 'Switches ON! CONTACT' and most times all would be well. We learned how not to upset our instruments, how to recognise all sorts of friendly and enemy aircraft, and also had the history of the RAF stuffed down us. I wasn't so interested in that; all I wanted to learn was how to fly!

We learned how to read the P4 compass which was right in front of the stick so we could find our way around the countryside. It was a complicated piece of apparatus, which was sometimes hard to read. If you were turning towards the north, it would rotate quickly past the correct reading by about twenty degrees and you would have to allow for that. The opposite was true when you were heading south, because the compass would be more reluctant to turn away from north. We had to learn how to predict what it would read.

We also had to understand what happened if the aircraft stalled, and how to avoid going into a spin. If you did get into a spin, you had to push the stick forward and push the rudder pedal opposite the direction you were spinning in. We also had to be able to react properly if the engine failed. Once the instructor had taught me the theory, it was time to test it in the air, and his intention was always to take me by surprise. He would close the throttle, and shout, 'Right, you've lost the engine, what are you going to do?' After that, he wouldn't say anything, just watch to see how you coped. You immediately had to go into 'Emergency Landing Procedure'. That meant identifying a suitable field to land in, slipping off your height safely, and lining yourself up to land into the wind at the right angle. You would fly the approach all the way down, until at the last minute the instructor would take the stick and open up the throttle, and you could climb away once more.

We learned how to make an accurate approach to the airfield and a perfect landing, and were warned of some of the potential pitfalls. In particular, if you came down too hard and 'bounced' your landing, it was vital that you didn't pull back on the stick. If you did, the tail would go down, the nose would go up, the aircraft would stall and you would come back to earth tail-first with a crash! It was very difficult to stall a Tiger Moth though, because they had such a low stall speed. They could remain in the air at just twenty-five miles an hour if you were skilful. In fact, whenever there were strong winds around the airfield, we had to weight down the aircraft that weren't being used, because the wind over their wings could lift them off the ground! We always said they were like kites in that respect, and from that moment on I've always referred to aircraft as 'kites', even up to the present day. It was a popular description among our group of airmen.

I learned to side slip very quickly. That means losing height fast without simply putting the nose down and accelerating, to make sure you didn't overshoot the landing field. To side slip left, you would give it almost full right rudder and then put the stick over to the left. It would lean over towards its wingtips, and the height would slip away. You'd have to watch your airspeed very carefully, and control it by small movements of the stick fore and aft.

I carried out numerous 'circuits and bumps', where we would take off, fly a course, then make an approach to the airfield before opening the throttle again as we touched down. I'd take off again, and turn to fly with the wind parallel to the field.

'Don't turn cross wind yet, give yourself a longer run to the field ... yes, turn now!'

I would execute a 'rate one' turn to port, to be at 600 feet after turning ninety degrees, flying cross wind with the airfield on my left.

'OK, turn when you have the landing strip in line.'

I would make another ninety-degree descending turn to port, aiming to be at 250 feet when complete, with the landing strip straight ahead of me. Right hand on the stick, thumb and forefinger, left hand on the throttle:

'Reduce the power, that's right, watch your speed,' as I kept the indicator at about thirty-five miles an hour. The altimeter would unwind slowly as we crossed the boundary fence.

'Just hold her straight and level, close throttles, ease the stick back, good, good ...'

The aircraft would sink slowly down as the speed got lower, and if it was a good landing you would be about a foot above the ground when it sank down onto its three points, the undercarriage and tailwheel. If you were much higher then you could come down with quite a bump!

It was all leading up to the big moment: my first solo. It's the milestone in every pilot's life which means he has passed the scrutiny of his instructor, and is ready to take to the air alone. I remember the moment clearly as I still had less than four hours total flying time. I performed my final circuit of the day to my instructor's satisfaction, made a safe landing, and taxied to turn back into the wind. To my surprise, I saw him undo his straps, pull back the hood and jump out! In his usual brusque way he said something like, 'Right, you'd better have a go to see how much of a mess you can make of it,' and I was on my own.

'Just do it!' I thought, and rapidly went through all my checks. I opened the throttle, flashed across the grass, and within moments I was in the air, alone. I distinctly remember looking down at the fields, up at the clouds, and yelling at the top of my voice 'Mummy, if you could see me now!'

I performed the usual circuit, lined up for the landing perfectly, and bumped down onto the grass exactly as I had practised. I was having such a good time though, that I had no intention of returning to my instructor quite yet. 'Bugger it,' I thought, 'I'm going round again!'

I opened the taps and roared up into the sky once more. I expected my instructor to be livid, but I didn't care. I made another clean circuit and a perfect landing, flushed with youthful exuberance and exhilaration. Finally, and regretfully, wearing a suitably apologetic expression, I taxied back to where he was waiting for me on the grass. Luckily for me, he was as pleased as punch with my progress, and congratulated me on a good job well done. I was a pilot.

Not everyone did so well. On another chap's first solo, he began to taxi along the grass at about thirty miles an hour when the aircraft started to turn and drift to the left. We watched as he simply pulled himself out of the cockpit, jumped down onto the wing, then rolled off onto the grass! The aircraft went on to dig in a wing and crash onto its nose as he sat there watching it. That was the end of his flying career, and he was soon offered a different position.

None of us were allowed to become complacent, however pleased with ourselves we were feeling. During my period of initial training, there were several accidents which reminded us that flying was a dangerous profession. The worst happened to a fellow I knew named Waugh, who I remember had the most terrible teeth. He had come over from England on the boat with me and we shared the same instructor. He had also managed to pass his solo flight, but some days later he had a dreadful crash when his aircraft smashed into a frozen lake and almost completely disintegrated. A friend of ours went to see the site, and said it was so awful he had to withdraw. They found very little of Waugh's body, except a piece of his jaw with some of his teeth still in it. It was a sobering event and brought many of us quite literally down to earth. However, as our instructors said at the time, we had to put it out of our minds and carry on as though it had never happened. You couldn't afford to get jittery every time someone got lost or killed because this was war, and sooner or later we would be in the firing line where some of us would inevitably become casualties. You had to put it on a shelf and move on.

We were helped by the fact that we had tremendous morale, and that we were doing something we loved. We also made sure that we could make our own fun during off duty moments. On our course was a chap named Jimmy Edwards, who in later life was to become a famous musician and comedian. He was enormously important in keeping our spirits up. As we all waited in the classroom for the lecturer to arrive, Jimmy would entertain us by playing the part of a very strict teacher, complete with a huge handlebar moustache and a cane – this was more or less the same performance that he was later to play on stage and television, once the war was over. He also played the euphonium and the trombone, and in between lectures and flying he organised a group of service chaps into a small band which broadcast on CBC Radio every Sunday evening. He was a fine musician and a man of great talent. Later in the war he flew Dakotas in Transport Command, took part in D-Day, and was later shot down and wounded during Operation Market Garden. He won a DFC for his actions.

Getting 'off base' was always a priority for us in our time off, and we used to try to get into town to assault the local bars and maybe meet some pretty girls. Getting a taxi to go into town was always a problem, so four of us put up $2.50 each and bought a Model T Ford. I'd just applied for an operator's licence, and bingo I was a driver too, without having to pass a driving test! To this day I have still never passed one. We had lots of fun with that car – especially getting it to start when everything was frozen with temperatures well below zero. In comparison to modern cars, it was very complicated. Let me explain that there were two forward gears which worked on a belt system and it was vital that the handbrake was on when the car was stopped. To start the car and pull away, the handbrake had to be halfway forward and the gear pedal depressed. Then you kept your hand on the throttle, which was in the centre of the steering wheel, and the car would start going forward. That gave you the first of the two gears. If you pushed the handbrake fully forward and then took your foot off the pedal, you were in top gear. It was easy to stall the car when it was stopped with the engine running by taking the handbrake off.

When the weather was warm it ran reasonably well, but of course this was Canada, and the ground and our car often froze solid. That didn't stop us wanting to make various excursions however, and with some practice and advice we had a car which would run in most seasons.

In order to start the car in very cold conditions, the following had to be done:

1. Jack up either back wheel
2. Have some warm water ready
3. Switch on ignition
4. Insert starting handle and wind – it always started eventually and never failed us
5. Gently warm up with low revs
6. When certain that it is not going to stop, fill the radiator with warm water
7. The fan belt, which drives the water pump, will be off as the pump is frozen
8. Pour warm water over the pump to thaw it out and reconnect the fan belt
9. Get one of the lads to push the car off the jack
10. Put the handbrake in neutral and drive forward, apply the footbrake on and off until the belt gear system has warmed up and thawed.

It was much easier if you were able to get a pull from another vehicle, but you still had to free the belt drive and sort out the water pump. Unfortunately we often started the car running before the water pump had thawed out properly, and the radiator would boil and spray steam all over the windscreen. The sub-zero temperatures meant that the screen was soon covered with a solid white layer of frost, which the brave pilots had to remove by leaning out of the fast-moving vehicle and scraping away frantically with their sleeves. Yes, it was a lot of palaver, but it got us into town and away from base, and we all thought it was well and truly worth it.

About this time, the part of the course dealing with the study of navigation intensified, along with us being taught how to recognise pinpoints. Flying included cross-country flights from point-to-point, also instruction in what to do if the engine failed, and the basic actions to take in order to make a successful landing with the minimum of damage to yourself and your aircraft. As one flew on cross-country exercises it became obvious that Canada held more benefits than being back at home. The roads follow the points of the compass and the towns all had grain elevators which bore their name in large white letters. Also, the countryside was bare and dry, since the crops had failed for so many years; children as old as ten had never seen a good harvest. Several of my relatives, who were dirt farmers, would in later years refer to these times as 'The Hungry Thirties'.

Of course, owing to my father and grandfather's well-travelled history, I had quite an extended family in Canada, and I was itching to visit them.

The first opportunity to visit the 'Canadian Trents' came on the first Christmas I was in the country, when, along with my pal Bob Sargeant, I was given seven days' leave. Lionel Walter Trent (my father) had emigrated to Canada in 1904, Grandpa Trent followed in 1912 and over the next ten years, four sons and three daughters were to follow and live around Pathlow (the town my father was involved with naming) in Saskatchewan. They married, had children, then grandchildren, and today there are well over 200 relations who have spread all over the country. I telephoned my mum's sister, Aunty Tot, which was an experience not to be missed. About six people shared a telephone line and each person had their own distinguishing ring – one ring for one house, two rings for the next and so on, up to six rings. Auntie Tot answered (bearing in mind that most of the other lines were also my aunts and uncles).

'Who's calling?'

'Hello Auntie, its Ken!'

'I don't know any Ken.'

'It's Mabel's son, Auntie!'

With that, all the other phones came to life, which in outlying farming areas is known as 'rubbering'. A fantastic conversation followed with all six phones trying to talk at once. Eventually I got the message to Tot that we would get to the nearest bus stop in Dafoe, ninety miles south of Pathlow. With that, I rushed out to purchase presents.

Uncle Percy (Auntie Tot's husband and my father's brother) and Pete Gaetz were working in Alberta and would be driving the 400 miles home to Pathlow to spend Christmas with their families, then driving a further 180-mile round trip to Dafoe to pick us up and take us home with them. They were all fantastic.

We left the camp a few days after the phone call, and getting off the bus at Dafoe, Bob disappeared into the arms of Auntie Tot. There was a chap who looked a little like my dad, so had to be Uncle Percy. I tipped back his hat and took a look at his head. 'You're Baldy Boffin!' and he answered, 'That's right!' Amid great excitement we all piled into Pete's Model M Ford, all six of us – Percy, Tot, Pete, Bob and myself, along with Belle, Tot's eldest child, who did some of the driving. In the excitement, I managed to leave all the presents behind!

It was 4 a.m. by the time we arrived in Pathlow, where we went straight to bed. Less than two hours later we were invaded by seven more cousins with bowls of hot water, each of them washing an arm, leg or any other exposed part. It was a most unusual but wonderful awakening. We all had the best and most wonderful Christmas and it was sad to have to leave them all – but there was a war on and we had to return to duty

In early spring, the hierarchy decided that the whole station was to move to Innisfail, Alberta, about 400 miles away. We were not given permission to drive our car to Innisfail but managed to get leave for two ground crew to do the job for us – and they had a great time doing so. Alberta was still cold, but being occasionally subject to the chinook winds, it meant that literally everything could just thaw out overnight. You would go to sleep with everything covered in a blanket of white and wake up to find the earth brown once more and the frozen lakes with a few inches of water on top. That would then freeze again, leaving a perfect surface to skate on.

The Canadians were so friendly and welcoming to the airmen and staff at our base that they used to put advertisements up on the camp noticeboard inviting us to their homes for meals and a bit of civilisation.

For Bob and myself, life was to improve immensely after being invited for a meal at the house of a lady named Mrs McCall; it improved even more so after meeting her two daughters. They were such fun and the four of us did almost everything together – ice skating, dancing, kissing and the odd meal out. They looked beautiful in their fashionable clothes, trimmed with fur. The frozen lakes nearby were huge, and we used to go skating there together, with other chaps who were in the area. One of our favourite games was called 'cracking the whip', a typical piece of Air Force foolery. You would all get into a line as you skated round and round, holding hands. You'd go faster and faster, then the chap at one end would stop as hard as he could and let the rest of the line pivot around him. When you did it right, the person on the end of the line found themselves propelled at enormous speed as the tail was flicked like a whip, and they often ended up letting go completely and flying off out of control! We played that trick on one bloke in particular who wasn't very popular, having a lack of social graces which made him a rather unwelcome companion. To add to his annoying character, he had never skated before, which made him a ripe target. We set off in our line nice and fast, then the lead skater dug in to a very effective stop, the line flew round and the inevitable happened. He let go with a yell, and was still shouting his head off as he slid right over the lake to the bank on the other side, ending with a huge crash.

Our good times at Innisfail had to end though, and we said a very reluctant goodbye to Mrs McCall, and an even more reluctant goodbye to her daughters, involving a lot of lip contact.

In between all the fun we had been working hard too. There had been written and oral examinations which we had to pass before we could move on. Because I was so keen, I got stuck in and found them fairly straightforward, as did Bob, but again some fell by the wayside and were posted to train for other flying positions.

A long train journey took us from Innisfail to No. 35 Service Flying Training School (SFTS), North Battleford, where our next hurdle was the Airspeed Oxford, a small, twin-engined kite ideal for us beginners. That meant only one thing; I was destined to fly bombers. It was a big disappointment to realise that I wasn't destined to be a Spitfire pilot like the Brylcreem boys I had seen at High Beech! You can't have everything though, and after all, I had learned to fly a Tiger at no cost whatsoever to myself. The Battle of Britain was over by then, and the country wanted to take the war to the Germans instead.

My new instructor was Sergeant Driver, a highly skilled pilot but a thoroughly unpleasant individual. He was a Cockney, which should have helped me to get on with him, but he had a total lack of empathy for me and everyone else inferior to him. Both his other pupils were killed while training on solo flights, and I believe he was far more concerned that he might be blamed than he was about their loss. Driver would low-fly at just above stalling speed, which was great stuff but far too risky for us, and it was extremely unwise to encourage pupils to break one of the golden rules of aviation.

I learned steadily under him, but found it a very unhappy experience. He was the type who would always pick a fault, and never offer a word of encouragement. 'You lost too much height there!' as I made an approach, or, 'Well, at least you got us down!' after a flawless landing.

He was responsible for me needing to take eight days of sick leave. He told me we were going to do a height test to see how high the kite and I could go. We took off and began a steady climbing circuit on a lovely clear day. We got higher and higher, reaching perhaps ten or twelve thousand feet, about the maximum ceiling of that aircraft. All was going well, until he pushed the stick forward to take us down again. The nose pointed right down, and we accelerated very quickly, heading straight for terra firma. Unfortunately, because I had a slight cold, I couldn't equalise my ears against the mounting pressure. It was like diving down to the bottom of a deep swimming pool very quickly, and in no time my ears were hurting me very badly indeed. He pulled out with space to spare at about a thousand feet, but by that time the damage had been done. When we landed I was in agony and couldn't hear properly, but I didn't really know what was wrong with me. I headed to the mess hoping the pain would simply go away, but by the next morning, after a sleepless night, I had to report sick to the Medical Officer. He looked in my ears, and sent me straight to bed with some strong painkillers and special eardrops to be applied regularly. They kept me topped up with these at regular intervals, until eventually my ears started to clear. Of course I was petrified that it was the end of my flying career, and that I would be grounded after all the work and effort I had put in. Then all of a sudden after a few days, with a loud pop, my right ear cleared, carrying a piece of scabby material with it, and as if by magic I could hear again. The next day my left ear followed suit and I felt much better. A hearing test confirmed that all was well, and I was cleared to resume my duties under the unforgiving sergeant.

After a couple of weeks together he nearly cost me my wings. There was a noticeboard in the camp upon which important information was posted, but I had got out of the habit of reading it because all that mattered to me was getting into my aircraft and flying it. One evening I went out for a few beers in town with some friends. The festivities were well underway and I had drunk at least a couple of beers when another friend came into the bar and asked me what on earth I was playing at. 'You're on a washout test tonight!' he told me.

Sergeant Driver had been so unimpressed with my performance that he had asked the Chief Flying Instructor to take me up for a flight to test my skills. If I was found wanting I could be thrown off the course without a moment's delay. The details had been posted on the noticeboard which I hadn't looked at. I hightailed it back to camp and charged into the flight office, only to find that I had about ten minutes to be kitted up and ready to go!

I climbed aboard and took the left-hand seat in a very chilly atmosphere. The CFI was brusque. 'Take it up, do a circuit and landing.' I taxied out, flashed my light and got green for take-off, set the flaps to twenty degrees and took off. With the wheels up, I set the engines at climbing revolutions, then put the flaps up and adjusted the trim.

At 750 feet I made a rate one climbing turn to port. After turning ninety degrees, I was at exactly 1,000 feet and flying cross wind. Another adjustment of the trim, and I turned another ninety-degrees to port. That meant I was flying downwind, parallel to the runway and on course at exactly 1,000 feet. I flashed for permission to land, got a green light, and pushed the lever to drop the wheels. The extra drag meant I needed to increase power and re-trim. The next was a descending turn, another ninety degrees, which left me at 750 feet on half flap. When I was in line with the runway, I began another descending turn to port to leave me facing straight down the runway at about seventy miles an hour. Losing height, I added increased amounts of flap to keep the nose up. I was now at 500 feet and I as ran towards the flare path, I added more flap until it was all on, and adjusted the throttles to slow the kite, making sure that I had a safe flying speed. I approached the runway, descending all the time until I was just a few feet up. I closed the throttles, and as the aircraft slowed down, I eased the stick back until the tail came down, and she greased onto the ground with a purr. It was the perfect landing. There was not a sound from the CFI until now, when I heard, 'See if you can do that again!'.... and I did! No one was more surprised than yours truly. The atmosphere had changed so much that as we taxied in I asked if I could change my instructor. He seemed very amenable to that suggestion, because he had seen that I could fly quite competently. I breathed a huge sigh of relief. But just to keep me on my toes, his last remarks to me were 'You can fly all right – but you drink too much!'

The course proceeded with teaching us how to fly and land on one engine. We also had to learn to fly using instruments alone, which we practiced on a contraption called a link trainer. That was an early sort of flight simulator, where you sat at the controls of a little wooden aircraft in the hangar, surrounded by maps and the usual flying instruments to show you where you should be. Instructors would tell you where you should be aiming for, and you had to 'navigate' there accurately without actually being able to see where you were going.

On one occasion I was on a navigation examination, which consisted of a long distance cross-country flight about five hours long. I was the navigator, with another pupil flying and we got hopelessly lost. I told the pilot (who was a pal of mine) to descend and read the town name on the grain elevator. It read 'Humbolt Sask' – which was where Auntie Dorothy lived. We were saved! We made up the chart and log, including drift winds, all a figment of my imagination but fixed as near as possible with the wind conditions which were prevailing at the time on the route we should have taken. I crossed my fingers and put the charts and log in and just hoped for the best. It was indeed 'the best' – I passed!

When it came to the final flying assessments I was confident that I had done a good job. The last hurdle was the Wings Exam, which asked the familiar questions about navigation, theory of flight and RAF history. I had no problem with any of it, because for the first time in my life I was actually working bloody hard at something I enjoyed and felt passionate about.

The course ended with the Wings Parade on 5 June 1942. We all marched proudly with our best uniforms on, and stood to attention when we were at last presented with the coveted decoration. As soon as we were dismissed I rushed inside to find my trusty 'housewife', and sewed them onto my tunic. Now I understood why pilots all walked around with their chests out; they wanted everyone to see those wonderful wings! In England I'm sure there would have been a stuffy, formal celebration, but instead the wonderful Canadians took us into town and myself, Bob and Bish had a great time with a lot of beer!

About 150 of us passed out at the same time, and they listed us all in order of our achievements. I came in at number 22, which should have meant that I was given an automatic commission to Pilot Officer. The top 40 candidates were usually favoured in this way. Unfortunately, and typically for me, they decided I didn't deserve such lofty notice because I had been caught too many times trying to jump over the fence returning after a late night from the evil but pleasant clutches of the North Battleford bars the worse for wear. Although I frequently managed to get away with it, the duty guards were far more alert than my old House Masters at Framlingham, and all too often I had been marched in front of the Station Commander minus hat and belt to be put on a charge. That all goes on your record, and they decided I wasn't 'officer material'. I wasn't too unhappy though. I didn't want to be an officer, with all the responsibilities that brought; I just wanted to get up in the sky and attack the damned Germans. The money wasn't an object either. I was already earning ten bob a day in danger money.

Jimmy Edwards got a commission, being 'officer material' ...

CHAPTER FOUR

WAITING FOR
THE GREEN LIGHT

So life went ahead for me in the wrong direction and I was posted to a gunnery station in training command at Mont-Joli, Quebec on 1stJuly. In those days it was a small base on the south bank of the St Lawrence River. While I hadn't made the dizzying ranks of the officers, I was now elevated from the lowly rank of AC2 to the heights of sergeant, and found going into the mess like joining a friendly club. Here it was that I met up with Doug Wiltshire, a bridge player. My parents had been keen kitchen players, introducing Janet and myself to the cards at a very young age. However we had been taught Auction Bridge since Contract was not invented until the early thirties. It was a good pocket money earner, especially when we played a French flying officer whose name sounded uncannily like Monsieur Croissant. He invited us to his house to play but cheated outrageously by using secret signals to his partner and taking us for thirty dollars each, which was quite a lot of money then, so Doug and I plotted revenge. We worked out our own system of signalling, holding our cards in a particular way to show our intentions. It worked, and I got all my money back, plus a fair bit extra too. Served him right! After that we used to practice our methods of cheating in friendly games when there was no money at stake. The hardest part was trying to look innocent and not catch Douggie's eye!

Remembering my dodgy schemes at Framlingham, I made extra money by buying bottles of Coca-Cola from the mess. I'd store them in my locker in the crew room then sell them on to the other chaps when they felt thirsty, as they weren't allowed to go back to the mess while on duty. It was all completely above board, unusually for me, and made me a nice few quid.

One night there was a big party in our mess, possibly in preparation for a move. The organisers had arranged for plenty of ladies to be there too, so there was a real buzz about it. We spruced ourselves up in anticipation and prepared the place with food, drinks and decorations. The evening began well, with the gramophone playing great music for us to dance to. The highlight for me, and possibly the beginning of my downfall, were the huge trays of fresh oysters which were piled up on tables around the edge of the room. I'd always loved oysters since my childhood holidays on the beach, when I'd pinch them from fishermen's baskets on the shore. I went from table to table opening and eating them just as fast as I could. I was pretty good at it after years of practice, so I ended up eating far more than most people. In fact, by the end of the evening I had managed to get 134 of them down me! I didn't eat every one that I opened though. I had managed to pick up a pretty brunette, who seemed just as keen as I was to eat oysters, drink beer, and have some fun. Before long the oysters began to have their inevitable effect, and we thought it might be a nice idea to find somewhere quiet so we could become better acquainted. Now there weren't many places which were private on an RAF base, so we had to use a bit of imagination. Usually there weren't any women on the site, so there were two toilets available for us to use: one in our accommodation area, and one next to the mess bar. But since there were plenty of women that night, the toilet by the bar had been given over to their convenience. We thought it might make an ideal spot for our tryst, and managed to sneak in and lock ourselves in the cubicle. Things began to get pretty heated when suddenly there was a *BANG, BANG BANG!* on the door and we were rumbled. Someone had spotted us going in, and had told the mess officers. As I came out feeling very sheepish, the officer suggested to me politely that I might wish to vacate the premises. The young lady made a hasty exit, never to be seen in the mess again. The following day, a friendly French Canadian sergeant took me aside. 'You know the lady you were getting cosy with last night?'

'Yes ...'

'You didn't know she was the Station Commander's daughter did you?'

No, I didn't! But once again luck was on my side. Because of his position, the Groupie (Group Captain) didn't want any fuss made, and I never heard any more about it.

It was just as well I had these entertainments to divert me, because my time at Mont-Joli was terribly dull, until two incidents happened which made life a little more hair-raising.

Our duties consisted of flying untrained gunners in Fairey Battles with a machine gun in the rear cockpit. Battles were quite slow and steady, looking like an overgrown Hurricane with a long canopy which extended from the pilot, over a central space where bombs or other things could be stored, then over the navigator/gunner. The gunners at Mont-Joli were firing at drogues being towed by another kite. It was dead boring but I did love flying and was the first in the flight office every morning and the last one to leave. It meant I would get the first and last flights every day, and many in between. I gained hundreds of flying hours, which proved valuable to me later in the war as I learned to react instinctively, and to handle the kite in all conditions. Most of all, I learned to make a decision quickly. Despite all that, I was still short of common sense, which got me into some serious trouble.

The countryside around Mont-Joli was very different from the Prairies. The St Lawrence River ran about half a mile north of us; its hills, valleys and gorges were all very beautiful and provided some exciting illegal flying, which primarily meant LOW. Once I went up a valley as close as possible to the ground, when suddenly the valley ended and a very high bank appeared which was much too high for the kite to climb over. The valley was too narrow to turn around completely, so we gained a little height to increase the turning space and from as close to the valley side as possible we did the tightest of steep turns, managing just to miss the bank and the other side.

The next piece of stupidity involved the CFI and the Station Commander, and landed me in some hot water. I was low flying again, this time over a frozen lake, and daring myself to get as low as I possibly could. This was completely against regulations. You had to keep her absolutely level, one eye on the instruments and your hands constantly ready on the stick and throttle. It was moments like that which really tested you as a pilot. The lake flew past so close I felt as though I could reach out and touch it, and it seemed to rush by faster because we were so near to the ground.

Suddenly, there was a *bang, bang, bang,* and the aircraft started to shake as the whirling propeller hit the ice. Trying not to overreact, I eased the stick back – to pull back violently would have caused the tail to hit the ground which would have been curtains. The kite vibrated because the propeller was damaged and unbalanced, so I climbed to about 3,000 feet and stayed near the airfield, fully expecting the engine to pack up with the shaking – and then to have to do a belly landing. The Merlin engine was too good though, and ran long enough to run down what was left in the fuel tank. I didn't want the officers to realise what I had done by flying so low against the rules, so I came up with a plan to make it look as though I had crashed on landing. I came down onto the runway and put on full brake with the stick right forward, expecting the kite to stand up on its nose – but this it refused to do. I did, however, burn out the brakes. I taxied in and eventually had to cut the motor as I lost control and – Sod's law – the kite came to rest right outside the CFI's office window, whereupon he was out like a shot. I clambered out of my damaged aircraft and told him that I had run into a snowdrift on the runway which was covering a patch of ice. Amazingly, he swallowed my story. The Station Commander was wiser to the antics of the young though, and with more experience knew just what I had been up to. He drove me out to the 'scene', asking me to show him the marks on the ice – there were none, of course! He told me that if I just told him the truth, he wouldn't take any action. I stuck to my story because I didn't want to show any weakness, and that was that – well for the time being anyway, as there was to be a big problem a few months later.

Soon I was flying and towing a drogue for other pupils to practise on, and after the exercise it was usual to fly over the dropping area and let the drogue go. A drogue was a long tube, a bit like an overgrown windsock, which was towed on a long length of wire. It represented enemy aircraft. The ammunition in the other plane's machine guns would be dipped in some sort of dye, so that any hits would leave coloured marks and they could see who had managed to score.

It could be a risky business though, and I had more problems which threatened to end my war prematurely. On one occasion I had been up on a routine exercise and had lined up to come in for landing. I put the wheels down as usual, and checked that the undercarriage lights were green to show that they were indeed ready for the runway. All was well as I approached, and I eased the stick back gently to touch down beautifully. But as I cut the engine and rumbled across the ground losing speed, the starboard wing dropped inexplicably lower and lower, tilting the kite until the wingtip dug into the ground. As soon as it did so it acted like a strong brake, and the whole kite swung hard around to the right, pivoting on the wingtip. The obvious cause was that the starboard undercarriage had collapsed, or perhaps not even deployed in the first place. The airfield span anticlockwise past my cockpit as we turned, eventually coming to a stop when we completed a full circle. Breathing a sigh of relief and trying to sit up straight against the lean of the aircraft, I double-checked the landing gear lights. Both were still green, which showed that it was a malfunction and not my fault: another sigh of relief. My next mishap was far more serious, however, and could easily have cost my life.

Before dropping the drogue after another exercise, I thought it would be fun to watch it passing me in the opposite direction, so I flew into several very steep 180-degree turns and bingo, the drogue passed me as intended. On the third occasion, as I came out of the turn, the stick was stuck slightly forward, so I pushed it further forward, intending to pull it back and so clear whatever it was that was causing the problem. To my horror the stick jammed, and with sickening speed we were plunging headfirst towards the ground like an out of control lift. We were at about 3,000 feet (not much time left), and I wasn't going to linger for a certain violent end. Abandoning the rigid stick I shouted at the top of my voice to the crewman to jump out, opened the canopy above my head and was standing in the cockpit, buffeted and deafened by the rushing slipstream, ready to jump, when I realised he hadn't appeared. I knew I couldn't leave the aircraft with him stuck inside, so I sat back down and made some very quick calculations and decisions. As the altimeter showed our height dropping ever faster, I worked out that if I wound the elevator trim full tail heavy it would lift the front of the aircraft. It was that or nothing, so with shaking fingers I reached for the little wheel by my left shoulder and wound like hell. At about 400 feet, just moments from disaster, the stick suddenly loosened itself and came back to where it should have been. The nose came up, and we were immediately heading straight up into the air again like a roller coaster. The g-force of the sudden climb was very strong, crushing me into my seat, and if I had left the controls as they were we would have looped hard and crashed straight into the ground. Just before blacking out I managed to wind the trim forward again to flatten us out. The next thing I knew, we were at 2,000 feet and still climbing, although not as fast. My breath was coming in ragged heaves, and I was shaking and sweating profusely with the fright of what had nearly happened to us. Frightened to use the elevators, I skidded the kite round with the rudder and dropped the drogue, headed back to the runway and managed a safe landing. My crewman had a big bruise on his head and reported sick. On unsteady legs I went straight in to report what had happened, and explained how the stick had become jammed in the forward position. The Flight Maintenance Sergeant was a friendly, older man who lived close to the base with his family. I used to play with his kids and chat to his wife, so luckily we had a good relationship. He had a good look at the aircraft, couldn't find any faults, and we agreed that we would take it out for a test flight the next day.

The following morning he met me on the airstrip and sat in the navigator's position. 'If it happens again and you don't get out, it's your fault!' he said. We left the canopy off just in case. I went through all the pre-flight checks, had a normal take-off and climbed up high in case there were any problems. I threw the aircraft all over the sky and couldn't detect any sign of the difficulty I'd had the previous day. That didn't mean that all was well though, if fact far from it.

Due to my previous 'accident', the CFI decided to investigate, and concluded that I had been flying dangerously, causing injury to my crew. I was put under 'open arrest', which meant being confined to station and reporting to the guard house twice daily. This was not for me – I had joined the RAF to fight the Germans! I was also quite shaken up by what had happened, and it affected me for many years afterwards. I would often wake up in the middle of the night and lash out shouting, dreaming that I was trapped in that out of control aircraft. Even more than the close encounters with flak and fighters, this narrow escape made me realise the danger I could be in.

I wasn't going to hang around under arrest when I needed to be doing something positive and active, so I decided to go AWOL for a while to sort myself out. I think it was a symptom of the boredom and frustration I felt, being held up in Canada while over in England men less experienced than me were taking an active part in the war. I wanted to be a part of that, to hit back at the Germans as hard as I could; after all, that was why I had signed up in the first place. Disillusioned, I left camp on 11 April and headed to the hills to go skiing, having told Doug Wiltshire what I was doing. I made arrangements to stay in touch with Doug, who would be ready at the mess telephone at regular times so that I knew what was going on. On the second evening I called him, and he said, 'Ken, you'd better come back to camp quickly. There's been an accident.'

The kite I had been flying had crashed, killing both pilot and crew. Apparently three planes were practising formation flying, and the kite that we had experienced the problem with was the leading plane in the centre of the group. When you are formation flying you don't look at anything except your leader; if you take your eyes off him for even a moment you risk a mid-air collision.

It seemed that after completing a 180-degree turn, the pilot of my former aircraft had also experienced the stick jamming, and the kite starting to dive. The other planes in the formation had no idea anything was wrong, and followed him down until it became clear by his actions that he was in trouble. They could see the pilot wrestling with the controls, and peeled off sharply as they watched him dive headfirst into the ground. I was shaken by the phone call, and knew that I had to go back. On 13 April 1943 I returned to camp, where I was put on a charge for breaking open arrest and being absent without leave. I was marched into the Station Commander's office by two guys from the guard house. I pleaded guilty to going absent but I wanted them to understand why I had been so desperate to get away. I told them that they hadn't believed my explanations of either of my flying incidents, and that the result had been that two men had died in an unsafe aircraft. They realised I had a very strong case, but also that they couldn't simply let me get away with it and stay on station.

The result was that I lost two days' pay and was given a reprimand which didn't bother me at all, and was posted back to Britain, which I was delighted about. At last I might have the chance of using my training and experience to get back at the Germans! My thirst to get on with the job was stoked by a news story which went around our base and the neighbouring town like wildfire. On 16 May, Lancaster bombers from a special new squadron, 617, attacked a series of dams across Germany. With incredible skill and bravery, the newspapers said, they had destroyed the Möhne and Eder dams, flooding the industrial valleys beneath with millions of tons of water and causing huge disruption to the German war effort. Their leader, Wing Commander Guy Gibson, was to be given the Victoria Cross, and the other surviving crews were feted as heroes. While I had been cooling my heels towing drogues in Canada, they had done something extraordinary, lifting the spirits of the nation and hitting the enemy where it hurt. That's what I wanted to do, and the sooner the better!

My posting was to Moncton Reception Centre, whilst waiting for a ship back home. Before going on board, I purchased three Crown and

Anchor boards. Crown and Anchor is a traditional gambling game, which you play with dice. Instead of numbers on their faces, the dice have diamonds, spades, hearts and clubs, as well as a crown and an anchor. The board had the same. To make a bet you would put money on the board according to how you thought the dice would land. I left myself with just enough cash to start playing. On 11 September 1943 I set sail on the Queen Elizabeth with some UK servicemen and thousands of Americans, who fortunately for me had never seen Crown and Anchor. It started in a small way with a maximum stake of two dollars, which was necessary since my capital was very limited, and also in order to get equal amounts of bets on each of the six squares. I had grown up among the market traders of the East End, and had quite a good gift of the gab. I can remember selling home-made fizzy drinks for my dad, 'Lemonade, in the shade, peanuts, popcorn, candy, come on dear, how much have you got, come and see!' so I was pretty good at drumming up some trade and reeling in some players. After starting with small amounts of cash it proved a real money maker, and I had to enrol some extra help. I enlisted a couple of blokes to run the boards and after a few hours there were three managed games, two in the stern and one forward. I just walked around pocketing cash, with my mates also getting a share of the winnings. Of course there was always the risk of getting torpedoed, but I never had time to think about that because I was so busy collecting money. When the ship landed in Greenock, Scotland, I had won more than £3,000 in all kinds of currency. The only problem was that as soon as I earned it at Crown and Anchor, I had lost it again in one of the many games of Craps which were also going on. Down in the depths of the ship, dozens of men at a time were gathered in a shouting, swearing, uniformed mass, all concentrating on whichever one of them was throwing the dice. Men were lying on the floor, perched on chairs or hanging out of bunks, craning their necks to get a view of the action. I would collect a wad of notes from my Crown and Anchor tables and make my way down to join them, waiting impatiently to stake my winnings at huge odds to see if I could get 'over the hump' as they say, and multiply my fortune. We were all possessed by a feeling of recklessness and exhilaration, born perhaps of an awareness that we were all sailing towards the war and an uncertain future. So many men wanted to play that it could take two hours before your turn came around, by which time I was ready to risk everything on getting a seven or eleven – potential winners. Hordes of breathless, eager faces would watch as you rattled the dice in your hand then threw them against a bulkhead to see how they landed; you weren't allowed to just roll them on a table because it could be too easy to cheat. Depending on your throw, there would be cheers, jeers, profanities or laughter, and the next man in line would snatch the dice up with eager hands.

The gambling went on night and day, and I slept very little due to the constant ebb and flow of my luck. I remember very little else of the five-day crossing except that the weather was calm.

By the time we docked, I found I had lost far more than I had won. My £3,000 of ill-gotten gains from Crown and Anchor had been whittled down to £500 by the Craps games, plus a great big bag full of change of all nationalities and denominations which was just too heavy for me to cart about the place. I separated out the sterling and dollars and gave the rest away. Shouldering my kitbag, I fell in facing the train which would take me closer to the war.

CHAPTER FIVE

FINAL APPROACH

O nce again I found myself back in West Kirkby Reception Centre, by which time I had noticed a rather unpleasant itching under my arms. Closer inspection revealed that I, and many of my travelling companions, had become infested with lice. While I had no bad bites, some of the others were terribly affected and scratching like mad. We had to hand in our clothes and kit for decontamination and get ourselves cleaned up. This delayed us for several days, and when we finally got our decontaminated kits back, all the boots and shoes were ruined, since the leather uppers had shrunk and separated from the soles. We spent an uncomfortable few days at West Kirkby getting de-loused and organised, which was quite a rude awakening for us after the relatively free and easy regime in Canada. We weren't allowed to leave camp, and had to wait until news came of our postings. Eventually, the welcome news came that I was on the move. Travelling by rail, I was posted to Number 11 PAFU (Pilots Advanced Training Unit) Shawbury on 9 November 1943. After the large Canadian trains, our railway looked like something out of a Hornby train set. The clickety-click as we went over the rail joints was the same, but missing were the very loud bells and ghostly siren – all the English trains had to offer was a shrill whistle.

There were many other contrasts to the pampered life we had been living in Canada. Over there there was food aplenty to eat, and you could supplement your diet with a choice of delicacies from the shops, which were still open and stocking the same variety they had been offering before the war began. Everything there was bright, clean and plentiful, and even the addicts among us could keep well supplied with tobacco at no inconvenience. The skies were usually clear, and offered excellent visibility for a pilot. England, however, was a stark reminder that there was indeed a war on. It was the beginning of winter and all was grey, overcast and dismal. The days were often almost as dim as the nights, when the strictly enforced blackout meant that finding your way on the ground, let alone in the air, became a real challenge. Visiting shops, after three years of wartime austerity, meant carrying coupons which gave you the right to choose from a pitifully small range of goods on spartan shelves. It was a painful reminder to me of what I had left behind when I had left to become a flyboy.

Before taking up duties at Shawbury, I was allowed a short period of leave. It had been two years since I had been called up, and I was very much looking forward to seeing my parents again. They were still running their little shop, but by then they had been hit by the chronic lack of luxuries too. They had a little allowance of sweets and tobacco which they were allowed to sell each week, but once that was gone they had to rely on the post office to supplement their income. Luckily for my father, before the war he had invested in a huge box of sugared almonds, his personal favourites. He managed to eke them out for the whole five years of the war, delighting in having a supply of sweeties when other commodities had run out. In fact, I believe he still had some left when the war ended, which he managed to sell on at a good profit! It was wonderful to see them again, and I was very relieved to see that the bombing had left them and the shop intact.

After all too short a time, it was back to Shawbury and duty. The difference this time though, was that I knew I was getting close to going into action, which I found very satisfying and exciting. I had spent far too long marooned in Canada, away from where things were really happening, and I had kicked my heels in frustration at being unable to get at the Germans. At last, I thought, my chance was approaching to get really stuck in and do my bit against the enemy who had attacked my country, destroyed so much of my home city, and caused the death of so many of my friends. There were just a few hurdles to get through before I could take to the air as an operational bomber pilot.

Airspeed Oxfords were the aircraft chosen to familiarise us with the local flying conditions, and also to help us to learn the complexities of flying with more than one engine. The Oxford has two engines, one on each wing, and a fuselage which has a bomb aimer's position in the nose. I was familiar with them from my time in Canada, and knew that they were ideal preparation for the bombers I would come to grips with soon after. The countryside was so different here: rolling landscapes, small, odd-shaped fields and not a straight road to be found – so very unlike the square fields and regimented roads of Canada which had made navigation there so easy.

After a few days of learning the locality, I was ordered to take an Oxford out for a familiarisation flight. The object was to learn the area in darkness a little, and in particular to spot any helpful landmarks which could point me back towards base in an emergency. The skies were clear, the forecast was good, and I took off full of confidence. I headed south towards Shrewsbury, a few miles distant, looking for a large hill known as the Wrekin. It was an ideal landmark for a pilot wanting to get a bearing towards home. I found it fairly easily, and by using the natural light of the moon and stars was able to spot other, smaller landmarks around it. Pleased with the evening's work, I turned back north, ready for an easy landing, some food in the mess and maybe a pint or two to settle myself in to my new base. As I made my way back, however, I suddenly became aware that despite the weather forecast, conditions were deteriorating. Fog and clouds were rolling over the ground in front of me, boiling and billowing upwards until they completely obscured the ground, and with it any useful landmarks. Before I became completely disorientated, I turned immediately back on myself and headed back the way I had come. Sure enough, the fog thinned and I found the Wrekin again. I then took a course which would take me back towards the airfield. I knew how long it had taken me to get there, so I could guess how long it might take to get back again.

I turned once more towards the fog, completed my timed run, and descended to about 500 feet. No sign of the ground, so I started to call on my TR9 radio. That was kept for times like these, and gave you a ten-mile range to get a QDM – which is a bearing to follow to get you lined up towards your base. The only problem was that I was far from being the only unfortunate who had been caught out by the change in the weather, and the line was jammed with other callers. By this time I was in the murk in the hope of spotting the ground, flying blind and very worried I could collide with one of the Welsh hills. After several attempts at contact I was getting very worried about my future wellbeing, so I switched to the emergency frequency of 500kc. This time I was answered at once and was told to 'stand by'. While I waited I made several ninety-degree turns, so that I was effectively flying in a square. After what seemed like a lifetime, but was probably only two or three minutes, a calm voice advised me to steer a course of 272 degrees, proving that I was east of the Welsh hills and likely to be flying over relatively flat country, which was quite a relief. Getting onto the course was easy to do, but it didn't actually help me to see what was below or ahead of me. I turned onto course, and decided to descend until I either saw ground or crashed. I put on full flap, tightened the harness, reduced the speed to just over stalling and went down to about 100 feet. Everything was impenetrably dark all around me, and I felt curiously cut-off from the world. I may as well have been at 10,000 feet, staring into the gloom and praying that I wouldn't hit anything. The night rushed by me in a sightless haze, while somewhere below me in farmhouses and fields, the people of Shawbury ate their tea or snored in their beds oblivious to the drama overhead. At least I was going in the right direction, but I couldn't land if I couldn't see the ground! I did know that if I could avoid running into anything solid like a hill, building or tree, there was a chance I could land it and stay alive.

After an age there was a light to my right – then another light – and then more to my left, diffused and off-white in the ghostly gloom. Ahead of me, more lights were converging on each other from either side. By fluke I had found myself in a landing 'funnel', leading to a runway. I gave it some throttle to bring me well above stalling speed, and put the wheels down. Breathing more quickly, I realised that this could be my chance of salvation. I was concentrating on lining up between the converging lights, when out of the mist another kite appeared. He had also found the funnel so I kept him safely to my right in loose formation, and soon the runway loomed up ahead. I flashed my recognition sign, which was 'W', and signalled my intention to land. By coincidence the other kite had the same ID as me, and started flashing at the same time, which evidently confused the flying controllers. From the flight control hut at the end of the runway a red flare arced up into the night, which meant 'danger, don't land.' They must have been concerned as two kites were trying to land at the same time. To hell with that I thought, so I took no notice and kept formation with the other fellow, looking across to keep him ahead of my right wing. I made a good landing on the grass to the left of the runway. Breathing a sigh of relief I looked over my shoulder across the wing to see the other plane making a good landing on the tarmac, only then to obey the red flare and open the taps to take off and go soaring into the foggy darkness again. Why he did it I do not know, but by the time I had taxied onto the runway he was dead. I had called out for a vehicle to guide me, and just a few seconds later there was the scream of an engine and a sudden massive explosion not very far from us which lit up the sky through the fog. Strangely, I felt no remorse over his demise, thinking only that he had been a bloody idiot to have taken off again when he had just landed safely. I didn't know him; he was just another guy to get the chop in an accident, just like those I'd known in Canada. This was war, and you couldn't allow sentiments about that sort of thing to cloud your judgement.

Relieved simply to be alive, on the ground, and in one piece, I switched off my engine, opened the door and jumped down onto terra firma. 'Where am I?' I asked the ground crew in the truck. As he drove me to the mess, he explained that I had landed in a neighbouring airfield to Shawbury, but would have to stay the night because there wasn't any transport available to take me back there.

Any regrets I may have felt at that inconvenience were immediately relieved when the first people I bumped into in the mess were Doug, my bridge playing friend from Mont-Joli, and Cyril, another flying friend. Over several drinks I regaled them with my tale of close escape. The following day the fog had cleared, and I was able to return to base.

The next couple of months were spent on increasingly taxing training flights, and I paid particular attention to the weather forecast! I am convinced though that the hundreds of hours experience I had gathered while twiddling my thumbs in Canada had given me the vital edge that night. A less experienced pilot might have lost his way and crashed far sooner, or tried to make a second landing like the unfortunate soul who was killed so close to the airfield. I was now a model student, having escaped the monotony of Mont-Joli, and I wanted nothing more than to prove my worth and get operational.

My next step along that path was being promoted to Flight Sergeant and being posted to 30 Operational Training Unit (OTU) on 14 March 1944. This was almost the final step before finally getting to carry bombs in anger. The aim now was to get familiar with the Wellington, a very successful twin-engine bomber, and the main war horse before the Halifax and the world-famous Lancaster. This was more like it; the Wellington was a working war machine, one which had a proven record of taking the fight to the Germans. It was the biggest aircraft I had flown at that point, and I relished the challenge. Before I could sit in the cockpit though, I needed to assemble a crew. Six people were needed to take the Wellington into enemy territory. A pilot, evidently, but also a navigator, wireless operator, bomb aimer, flight engineer and rear gunner. The process began in a big room at the base, where all kinds of crewmen were gathered together. The C/O gave us a short pep talk about how we were the future of Bomber Command, then invited us to mingle for half an hour or so to see if we could form ourselves into six-man crews. I knew that this was a critical moment; if I was going to fly into danger I wanted to do it with men who were competent at their jobs, but also easy to get on with. I had no time for show-offs or anyone who might panic when things got tough. I would have to rely on them to do their job to perfection if I was going to do my job well and get us home after every operation. Luckily for me, nearly all the chaps I ended up with were first-class.

The first I hooked up with was Brinley Reynolds, known as Brin, a navigator who was quiet and businesslike. He told me that his father was a miner who still lived in a little mining cottage. Brin had been determined to make something of himself, and had studied his way away from a life down a pit, matriculating from school after a lot of hard work. He was always stylish, kept himself well, and seemed calmly intelligent. He seemed to fit the bill, so I played my hand by telling him about my experience and flying hours. He liked what he heard, and that was it – we were a pair. He proved to be an invaluable member of the crew, always concentrating on the job in hand. I never heard him talk about birds or boozing, he took his job seriously and could tell me at a moment's notice where we were and where we needed to go.

Before long we had cottoned on to Noel Wadsworth, a lovely chap from Manchester. He, like me, was an ordinary working-class bloke who had joined up and learned the arcane art of bomb aiming. He had a lovely wife waiting at home. He wasn't particularly ambitious, and was happy to remain a bomb aimer, but he was determined to be the best bomb aimer he could possibly be. When he was guiding us in on our bombing runs over Germany his voice never got loud or panicked, he simply sounded businesslike and matter-of-fact, as though we were on exercise. I spotted a natural pilot's ability in him, and taught him the rudiments of flying. He flew many hours and became a proficient and safe pair of hands in the cockpit. My reasoning was that if I was hurt, someone would have to fly us home, and he seemed to be the one with the most aptitude. I even let him land the kite once. We were all frightened stiff, but he managed very well.

With Noel came his friend Clarence Dalby, always known as Clarrie. He was a little man, perfectly suited to his role as a rear gunner. The turrets of aircraft at the time were small, and shorter blokes were often assigned this role. He was very young, certainly still a teenager, and looked as though he needed mothering. Noel sort of took him under his wing and looked after him. Before the war he had an unskilled job in a mill, but he turned into a very good gunner with sharp eyes.

Our crew was coming together, but we still needed a wireless operator and flight engineer. Mingling among the chatting airmen, I heard an unmistakeable Australian accent, one which had clearly been refined through expensive schooling. Les Skelton, nicknamed 'Red' after a famous comedian, was a clean-cut bloke with a slightly pointed face who came from a wealthy family. Despite his life of privilege, he was a very diligent wireless operator who was always on the ball and had fantastic radio discipline. If the navigator ever needed a bearing, or if we needed to get in touch with base, he was always right on the ball.

So far so good: just a flight engineer to find. Shortly before the half-hour was up and we were expected to be complete, we met a chap whose name I have since forgotten, but which might have been Johnson. The reason I forget is that we only had him for about a week. All of a sudden, one day he failed to show up for a training flight. Word came through that he'd been marked down as 'LMF', the worst possible fate to befall an airman in training. LMF stood for Lack of Moral Fibre; in other words he was a coward. He had been so scared that he had gone AWOL, and had been disciplined. Luckily for us, he was replaced by someone far more capable. Bill Dunsford was a smiling, fair-haired, good-looking fellow who was quietly confident and showed his mettle when I was injured by flak over Germany – but more of that later.

Thus it was that my crew came together. To them I was 'Skip', and to me they were Brin, Noel, Clarrie, Red and Bill. Together, they were terrific. A machine can only be as good as the smallest of its working parts, and if one component fails the rest can follow. Through all of our operations there was never a raised voice nor a moment of panic unless in exceptional circumstances. Nothing was forgotten, we were never lost, and we could rely on each other completely. That said, I was careful to keep a professional distance from them. I never went out to get drunk or socialise with them, because I needed them to have the understanding that I was their boss, and that I should be the one they deferred to when we were in the air. That approach seemed to work very well, and there was never any attempt to contradict or disobey me. When you are in life-or-death situations, it needs to be clear who is in charge, and I couldn't risk any compromise to that arrangement.

So far we had all learned a lot about flying, navigating, bombing and all the skills we would need to get our aircraft to its target and carry out our mission. A sign of how close we were to actually flying on operations for real came when we were asked to face some rather unpleasant possibilities. Firstly we might get shot down by anti-aircraft guns or fighters and have to get out of our aircraft in a hurry. Secondly, if we did manage to get our parachutes open and land in one piece in enemy territory, we would have to be able to look after ourselves.

Up until then I had never really entertained the notion that I might have to get out of my kite in a hurry, but our instructors made it abundantly clear that we would have to be prepared for anything. If we were so badly hit that we had to get out, the plan was simple. I explained it to my crew.

'If I shout "EMERGENCY, EMERGENCY, JUMP, JUMP!" then get the hell out as fast as you can. And if you get out faster than me you'll be doing bloody well!'

There was an old bomber fuselage on the airfield which we used to practice on, and I made sure we got down there often. We would all get into our positions, complete with parachutes and other paraphernalia, and then I would give the emergency signal.

My escape hatch was just above me, and it was very narrow. I had to release the catch, stand on my seat, then try to wriggle out with my chute under my bum. I often got caught up as I did it, and I dreaded to think what would happen if I was trying it in a burning, plummeting aircraft. The other crew had different exits in the nose, fuselage and tail. Clarrie had what we considered the easiest option. He just had to grab his chute then rotate his turret ninety degrees, open the turret doors and fall out of the back. To make it more realistic, I had someone on standby with a stopwatch. 'GO!' and there would be a mad scramble, a lot of swearing and jostling, and finally there we would be, breathless heaps on the grass beneath the aircraft. With practice we got the time down, but any small thing could still hold you up: an unhelpful buckle, a strap caught on a protruding piece of machinery, or just getting your bum caught in the narrow hatch. When we were all getting pretty confident at it, I threw an extra complication into the challenge. I knew that if we were actually hit by flak or a fighter's cannon shells we would be dazed, confused, and not ready to react as quickly as we should. Getting out of a stationary fuselage on a calm day would be a piece of cake in comparison. So we went to the pub.

A couple of pints later, and we went back to the practice aircraft and tried again. Sure enough, the booze had dulled our reactions and speed, and we were far slower in getting out. Minor problems became magnified, new snags presented themselves, and we found whole new ways of swearing. The process was invaluable, and we became even more adept at our evacuation procedure.

The strange thing is that even though we practised day in and day out, I never once thought I would need to use our new jumping skills. I had confidence in my flying and confidence in my crew, and I thought we would always come back in one piece.

Of course, jumping out of a burning aircraft was only the first difficulty we would face if we were hit. Once we landed, we would be alone in enemy territory, and would have to either try to evade capture, or resist interrogation if we were caught. Some crew carried escape kits, and even wore clothing which would make them look like farmers or labourers. I was having none of that though. If you were caught in uniform you could expect to be taken prisoner and then to a POW camp. If you were caught out of uniform, you could be shot as a spy. No thank you! My one concession to escape was a fine sliver of metal, the shape of a small nail with no head, which had been magnetised. It sat, wrapped in cotton thread, beneath the wings of my battledress jacket. If I needed to navigate I could suspend the blade with the thread, and it would point my way north. Once captured though, I'm sure I would have made every effort to escape again; I had that kind of foolhardiness which comes from a misspent youth! A succession of experts gave us lectures on how to get out of difficult situations, and one was from a chap who had escaped from the prison camp Stalag Luft III in the famous Wooden Horse, making his way home via Sweden. He was making a tour of all the bomber airfields, to explain to crews what to expect if the Germans got hold of them. By all accounts, my upbringing as a boarder in a public school would have been ideal preparation for life as a POW, and my nocturnal exploits to fetch beer and fags would have stood me in good stead for all kinds of escape attempts! Luckily I never had to put this theory to the test! He told us how we could expect to be treated by the Germans, who we could approach for help if we were on the run, and how to handle ourselves under interrogation. We also heard propaganda about Allied bomber crews being strung up from lamp posts if they were caught near a city they had just bombed. But I always tried to push the thought of being shot down or captured to the back of my mind. If you dwelt on it, you could get the frights, which led to dangerous mistakes and perhaps the very thing you were hoping to avoid.

As we trained, I remember keeping an eye on the group ahead of us, who were even closer to passing on to an operational squadron. Many times I would watch them take off in the evening, go for a pint, eat some food and have a good sleep, then watch them arrive back at base as I was getting ready for breakfast. 'Bloody hell,' I thought, 'Will I have to do that?' Before long I found out that yes, I would!

We started to spend hours on the bombing ranges, trying to knit ourselves together as an efficient, accurate, working bomber crew. We were given ten-pound practice bombs to drop from various heights, and always tried hard to get them on target. Round and round we would go, struggling against the combined forces of airspeed, height, wind and direction to get it right. Once we were over target, I was no longer in charge of the plane; Noel, the bomb aimer, would take over, as it was his job to spot the target and talk me onto it. He would be in the nose, staring fixedly into his bombsight, his hand hovering over the release switch while

I did my best to follow his orders. Noel's early instructions were anything but relaxed. 'No, go right! RIGHT! Oops, no left a bit, SLOW DOWN! You've gone too far! Shit! Sorry, missed it, can we go round again?'

As we progressed, the simple flights became more complicated. Instead of just flying to the bombing range, dropping a few ten-pounders and then heading home for a beer, we began to fly every day as a simulated operation. We were given orders for take-off, instructions for our Time Over Target, and bearings to head home again. Daylight flights to start with, consisting of six-hour or more cross-country runs, progressed to night flights organised as an operation; dropping the ten-pounder over the target at the range, then altering course for the three-hour cross-country back to base. Little by little we stretched our abilities further and further, until the time came when we were the ones taking off in the evening and returning in time for breakfast. A typical route might be to take off and head for the ranges at St Tudwal's Island off the Welsh coast. A new bearing would take us to another target, before we headed back over blacked-out Britain to base. The Wellington was a pleasure to fly, and stood us in good stead on these trips. We were getting pretty good at our various jobs, and knitting together very nicely as a team. Noel's target instructions had become calm, measured and accurate. 'Right a little ... steady ... lovely, bombs gone, thanks Skip.' I could tell by the tone of his voice just how far left or right he needed me to go.

We'd been warned about what sort of defences we might have to face when we were over Germany, and on one of these exercises I got a good taste of them. We were due to make a mock attack on the northern town of Goole, and had set our course accordingly. The anti-aircraft defences around the town were on full alert to expect us, and were there to make life hard. Sure enough, we arrived exactly on our Time Over Target, thanks to the usual fine navigation from Brin. Unfortunately the Army Anti-Aircraft Command chaps were very awake. Noel started his careful 'Right a bit, left a bit' from the nose, then all of a sudden 'Bloody hell!' Night had turned into day, and I was dazzled by an all-enveloping light which made it impossible to see where we were going. I lost the stars, I lost the ground; everything was lost. All around us was white, and my eyes, which had become accustomed to the dark, were painful, blinking and almost useless. I knew what had happened; we had been warned about it. We had been 'coned' by searchlights. That meant that two, three, or even more, had locked onto us and were following us across the sky, blinding me and giving a much easier shot for gunners below. The feeling was shattering, and for a moment I had a flash of panic. 'Christ, they think I'm a Kraut! What if the gunners haven't been warned about us and they think we're the the enemy? What if we lose our bearings and crash? What if…?' But all the while we were flying onwards, and suddenly we went past the edge of the cone and plunged into darkness once again. No one had shot at us. Of course we had missed our target, but it had been a very good lesson to learn. It was after this experience that I asked Brin to make sure we were always a minute late over our target, with the intention of letting the enemy catch sight of someone else first.

The training was good and when the time came, the feeling of achievement was very satisfying.

The next stage was conversion onto the Halifax, with four engines and the addition of a mid-upper gunner - Flying Officer Riccomini. He was a good-looking, well-educated bloke with a permanent commission as an officer. I don't know why he wasn't flying, but he enjoyed the fact that he outranked us all on the plane. We all played along with it, feeding his weakness if you like, because he was actually very good at his job and never tried to pull rank or disagree with me when we were in the air. In theory I was meant to salute him, but I never did unless there was someone important observing us! I called him 'Sir' on the ground, but in the air, where I was known as 'Skip', I would just call him Ricky. It was an arrangement which suited us all well, and didn't upset the relationship we had built up among the crew.

All the training in the world, however, would be of no use to us if we were unable to think straight because of the effects of altitude. We would be expected to operate regularly at heights of 20,000 feet and above, where the air is thin and oxygen is in short supply. Our trainers wanted to assess how we would react to being starved of oxygen, both to test our personal thresholds and to give us a clear reminder of the consequences of forgetting to use our oxygen supplies. Together with Brin and a small group of other pilots and navigators, I was taken by bus to the building which housed what was known as 'The Chamber'. This was all quite new technology to us, and we were all understandably quite nervous about what might happen, and what effect the test might have. The officer in charge was quite aware of this though, and took care to explain the whole procedure for us. His confident manner helped somewhat to allay my fears, and I took my place at a little desk in the chamber with the others. It was a long, thin, tube-shaped room filled with dials and pipes, and when you were inside they sealed the small door from the outside. It was not a place for someone who suffered from claustrophobia, especially when they started to pump air out of the chamber to simulate a loss of air pressure. The higher you go in an aircraft, the lower the pressure becomes, and the less oxygen there is to breathe.

On the little desk in front of me there was a set of papers with simple questions on them, easy maths problems and suchlike. They lowered the pressure to the equivalent of 5,000 feet, and asked us through a loudspeaker to answer the first question. Easy, we thought, and grinned at each other as we filled out the answers.

They then sucked more air out of the chamber, lowering the pressure at thousand-foot intervals, and for every thousand feet we were asked to complete a question. Our thought processes gradually became a lot slower. When we were at 12,000 feet I was finding it very hard to concentrate or to write a coherent answer to anything, as my brain was struggling to work properly without the right amount of oxygen. By the time we reached 16,000 feet I dimly realised that several of the other chaps were passing out or falling asleep, nodding over their desks with the questions forgotten.

It was a very important lesson for us, a reminder of how fragile we are without the oxygen we need to fuel our bodies and brains. If our supply failed, or if we forgot to switch it on, we could expect to have the same loss of consciousness in the air – with potentially catastrophic results.

It wasn't long until we had become accustomed to each other, and indeed to the complexities of flying a four-engined aircraft. I needed to rely on the others far more, as with four engines to keep an eye on with all their various dials, switches and knobs, the cockpit got very busy. Bill and I in particular became a team; he provided a welcome second pair of hands during take-off and landing. Training became more and more intensive, and we spent hours in the air on mocked-up operations. I got used to parking my bum on a tightly packed parachute for hours on end, so that when the time came to do it for real I wouldn't notice it. Bombing practice, lectures, bombing practice, lectures, lectures, bombing practice; the days ran by quickly. The time when I could finally strike back at the Germans was fast approaching, and I felt keen and confident that I could do my bit and not let the side down. First, though, I had to make myself acquainted with the aircraft which would become my second home for the next year of my life and define my time in the RAF; the hero of the Dambusters raid and the best heavy bomber of the war. All of my training over the prairies of Canada and through the fog of England, from the Tiger Moth through to the Halifax, had led me to the Avro Lancaster. And what a kite she was.

Enormous, but sleek and graceful looking, she sat on the tarmac at RAF Hemswell on two big fat wheels beneath her wings, and another under the tail. This was the aircraft which had broken the dams; this was the aircraft which had taken the fight to the enemy and was destroying the factories and marshalling yards in daring raids every night. I couldn't wait to get inside and take her up in the air.

Together with an instructor I climbed the short, steep ladder at the starboard rear of the fuselage and found myself in a low, cramped, dark green tunnel festooned with protruding cables, pipes and struts. If I turned left, a crawl would take me over the Elsan toilet down to the rear gunner's position, accessed through a revolving doorway. Grateful that I wouldn't have to squeeze my six-foot frame that way, I ducked my head and made my way forward. The Lanc smelled like any other kite of that period: a mixture of oil and rubber, leather and hot metal. In many places the dull green paint had been rubbed away by the passage of crewmen, leaving the shine of raw aluminium. In a couple of steps I found myself next to the fold down seat of the mid-upper gunner. Looking up, I could see the perspex dome where Ricky would spend operations, scanning the night sky for any sign of fighters, with hands ready on the triggers of his twin machine guns. While we were flying, his feet would be about level with where my head was. The next obstacle was the huge, very scuffed main spar, which ran across the width of the fuselage at about waist height, giving about three feet of clearance to the ceiling. It was about two feet deep and I had to clamber over it carefully to avoid banging my head or catching myself on any of the other bits of machinery poking out all over the place. On the left was the rest bed, a small platform where we would be able to lay any casualties. Dropping down on to the other side of the spar, there were the cramped positions of the navigator and wireless operator. The w/op faced forward in front of his bank of dials and switches, some large and brightly coloured red and yellow. He also had control of the heating unit, which brought hot air from the engines into the aircraft. I found out later that the hot air blew very effectively into his position and kept him nice and warm; he often complained during daylight raids about being too hot while the rest of us shivered. We also discovered that the Lancaster had a very strange way of circulating air. If anyone farted, and we always blamed Clarrie in his rear turret, everyone could very soon smell it through their oxygen masks!

Just ahead of the w/op, with a table facing the left side, was the space reserved for the navigator, with a small chart table for all his maps and instruments. It would be curtained off during night raids so that he could use a light to see his maps without affecting our night vision. He was close enough to reach forward and touch me on the shoulder if necessary.

Beneath my feet was the very heart of the Lancaster. The bomb bay was thirty-three feet long, stretching down the length of the fuselage and perfectly made for carrying a substantial load of explosives. It also housed a camera which would take photos of the bombs as they fell, to show the intelligence experts whether we had dropped on target.

Ahead, daylight was pouring in through the huge canopy of the cockpit, and also up through the perspex blister of the bomb aimer's position in the nose. To get down to his position, Noel would have to lower himself down a hatch before either lying down to aim the bombs or climbing up onto the seat to man the forward-facing machine guns. Just above that hatch was the fold down 'second dickie' seat, which was where the flight engineer would sit. Next to him were all the dials and indicators of the various fuel tanks and pumps. Getting up into the pilot's seat proved to be a test which I hadn't encountered in any aircraft before. It was above me on the left, and to get into it I had to mount a step with my right leg, grab a handhold set above the windscreen, heave myself up and swing my left leg across so I could sit down and take my place. I'd have to sit on my parachute, and the instructor suggested that I put that in place first, before dragging myself up. Once seated, I had a fabulous all-round view thanks to the large canopy. I could see below the wings, above my head and behind me – invaluable when searching for landmarks or enemy fighters. In front of me was the most complex dashboard I had ever seen, covered in instruments, switches and lights. I would have to become completely adept at using them all if we were to deliver our bombs effectively and, more to the point, find our way home again safely. I had learned most of it at lectures beforehand, so I was reasonably familiar with everything, but the instructor ran over it all again just to be sure, paying particular attention to the engine feathering controls to my right which would be used to stop an engine slowly ready for shutdown, or in the event of a fire. With two Rolls Royce Merlins on each wing, each with their own controls, there was a lot to watch out for.

I'd heard that the Lancaster was a joy to fly, and my first flight happily proved that to be the case. When taking off you had to be careful not to let the torque from the props swing you to the left on the ground, but once you were moving forward at speed and the tail came up, it was a completely different aircraft to any bomber I had flown before. The controls were light and responsive, and it was very manoeuvrable. In the

Halifax, if an engine stopped you were advised not to turn in the direction of that engine for fear you could lose control and start to spin. But the Lanc was so beautifully balanced that you could turn into a dead engine with no problem at all. The crew all agreed that we were on to a winner. Several weeks of intensive bombing practice, and we were at last ready to go. As a crew, we were as tight as we could be, and all had confidence in each other. We were ready for war.

Before finally becoming operational, on 18 May 1944 I was commissioned as a Pilot Officer, complete with new service number, which made me very proud even though it wasn't something I had ever particularly aspired to. My motivation had always been to get at the Hun, rather than get rank, but the extra cash would certainly help. Fortunately for me the RAF was happy to overlook my previous foibles, and in recommending me for my commission my commanding officer said my one offence (of going skiing for two days in Canada!) was of 'a slight character'.

For the first time, RAF Pilot Officer Ken Trent 176283 was to get his uniform from a tailor instead of the standard RAF issue gear from stores. I had a week's leave in which to sort myself out, and of course headed to London to see my parents. I turned up in my usual sergeant's battledress, but then took myself off to All Kits in Cambridge Circus where I ordered the whole lot: shirts, trousers, greatcoat, mess kit … and when I came home in it all, with the officers braid sewn onto my sleeve, my parents were absolutely delighted. I had been a pain in the arse to them most of my life, failing at school and costing them a fortune in a wasted education, yet here I was, an officer! My mother couldn't wait to start telling her friends 'My son's an officer, you know!' I was pleased that at last they were getting a return on all the time and money they had invested in me, and glad to make them proud. On a more practical level, it certainly didn't hurt that the new uniform was far softer, better fitting and more comfortable than the one I had left behind!

All too soon, the time came for me to leave. I think they both knew where I was going and the danger I was likely to be in, but we all hid our emotions, as you did in wartime. I can't remember saying goodbye to them.

We were posted to Elsham Wolds on 13 July, where two squadrons were based – 103 and 576 – we were to join the latter. I had a rail warrant to Lincoln, and then I caught a bus as far as Barnetby le Wold, which was the closest stop to the base. As I was classified earlier in my RAF career as 'not officer material' it never occurred to me that as an officer I could just drop into the local pub and ring up for transport. Instead, I shouldered my kitbag and started the long walk to the airfield. This would be it, my first operational squadron. Not just a training unit. When I walked through the gates I would almost be a fully-fledged Bomber Pilot.

CHAPTER SIX

TO WAR

It was a beautiful English summer day, warm and with few clouds. The base which was to be my first operational posting was three miles away across the fields. With nothing to do but walk and think, my mind started wandering and suddenly I was gripped with a feeling which until now had never troubled me.

Fear.

It came down on me like a black curtain. How does one cope with it? In a few days I would be flying high above enemy Germany, hundreds of miles away, amid guns and searchlights in the dark, with the lives of six other men depending on me. The terror of what could happen was suddenly very real, there in that English summer lane. The heavy kitbag weighed me down, my feet began to drag, and the confidence which had buoyed me up until now seemed to drain away into the dust. I forced my feet to continue – left, right, left, right, left, right – but as I walked the fear walked with me. The kitbag got heavier, I was hot, shaking and had now completely lost my nerve. 'Will I ever walk back down this lane again, or is this a one way journey? For God's sake, pull yourself together. You have a good crew; you can't just let them down, and yourself down. What's wrong with you? JUST DO IT!'

But it was no good. I stopped and turned. All around me was typically quaint, English beauty. The enormity of what I was about to do was terrifying.

This is what I had striven for, worked and trained for, for years. This is what I so badly wanted. Or was it?

I knew I had come too far to back out. Hitching my kitbag higher on my shoulder, I gritted my teeth and forced my feet onwards. The gates of the base finally appeared and, after a final look back down the lane, I presented myself at the Guard House. I was in, and there was to be no turning back.

I was shown my quarters, unpacked my new uniform and tried to get a grip on myself. I still had the frights, but being back in the system helped a little. Perhaps being at home had softened me too much. Unpacking done, I found myself in my room wondering what to do, finding it hard to be alone with my thoughts. Steeling myself against the fear, I resolved to escape from my solitude by heading to the mess for a pint, although even this posed a challenge. Until now I had been used to the non-commissioned sergeant's mess, usually a fairly rough and ready place where lowly types like myself could get boisterous and beery without too much fear of the consequences. However, my recent promotion meant that I would be heading to the officer's mess, where elevated creatures such as the Station Commander may be enjoying a relaxing glass of wine. Fortunately for me, when I walked through the door in some trepidation it was quiet. As I made my way to buy a drink, a slim officer propping up the bar with a pint in his hand heard me and turned around. His gentle northern accent was welcoming. 'Hello, are you a new chap? This your first op? What are you drinking?' The calmness of Flight Lieutenant John Stevens DFM, known as Steve, was just what I needed at that moment, and he went on to become a lifetime friend and a profound influence on me. He was a skilled pilot, about seven years my senior, and had already completed one tour of 30 operations. We started to chat, and quickly established a warm friendship, which was most welcome. He became my regular drinking partner, and we would spend many nights out in the pubs around Lincoln, or chatting up the chorus girls in the Theatre Royal. He had thinning dark hair which he combed long over the top of his head, and was one of the few men I know who became better looking with a hat on. Sharing a couple of pints with him on that first meeting did wonders to banish the anxiety with which I had been struggling, and by the time I headed off to bed I felt far better about my prospects.

After a few short weeks of familiarisation, the day finally dawned for my indoctrination: my first operation. I proudly noted it in my logbook, 15 August 1944. I was to fly as flight engineer with an already experienced crew under F/O Wearmouth – it was known as a 'second dicky' trip, and the idea was that I would stay in the skipper's shadow and learn the drill.

The base was a hive of activity, with the full crew being transported to the kite during the day, the gunners cleaning all windscreens, including the screen round the cockpit area, and packing the nose with strips of 'Window' foil to fool German radar (for ease of distribution over the route later). I'd never had to use Window before, but I had learned all about the theory of how it worked. Once we were over the enemy coast, the bomb aimer would shovel armfuls of the shiny aluminium strips out of his front hatch while all over the sky, other bombers would be doing the same. German radar would latch onto this load of shimmering metal in the air, and would become terribly confused about what it was; the resulting interference would turn the radar operator's screen to fuzzy snow, and we could fly on unmolested by fighters. That, we were told, was the theory, and it actually appeared to work to a large extent. I was told that on this trip we wouldn't need too much of it because we weren't going too far into enemy territory. By now my nerve had returned, thanks in part to Steve and also to just getting back into a routine, and I was glad to be a part of the bustle and organisation.

After the traditional bacon and eggs, we followed the skipper into the briefing room to discover that the target was an airfield near the Belgian town of Le Culot. I was quite heartened when I overheard another pilot say 'Oh, that's nothing!'

There were lots of raids going on at the same time, with more than a thousand bombers taking off to attack airfields across Belgium and Holland. Nineteen kites from our squadron were ready for the off, but the operation was to be in daylight. That meant a higher danger of being attacked by fighters, although the Luftwaffe was so badly outnumbered by then that we felt quite confident, especially as we were promised an escorting fighter squadron. I listened as carefully as I could, trying to take in all the advice that the briefing officers gave us. Where to cross the coast, where the worst flak was, the location of enemy fighter stations, time on target, the weather situation; the pilots were making notes on all of it and I tried to do the same, struggling to keep up with the flow of information while concentrating on the map on the wall in front of us with coloured wool marking out our route.

Once aboard the aircraft I sat in the unfamiliar engineer's seat, and concentrated hard to make sure I did the right things in the right order. Keeping an eye on the skipper all the time, I backed up the throttles on take-off and kept a lid on any feelings of fear or tension. As we passed over the enemy coast, easily visible in clear skies, I felt a tightening in my body, an acceleration of feeling which meant I was on high alert. This was the real thing, no longer an exercise, and the bombs loaded in our belly were armed and ready to do their destructive work. I believe my sense of adventure, fondness for taking risks and sheer bloody-mindedness which had been bred into me at school was finally standing me in good stead.

After confirmation from the navigator, the bomb aimer started to shovel Window out through the front hatch, from where it streamed out behind us in a flashing trail in the sunshine. We were already close to our target, and soon the bomb doors were open. Over the radio we could hear the Mosquito pilots of the Pathfinder squadron, who had gone in to drop flares to mark the target. 'Bomb on the green flares,' and sure enough, there in front of us were green markers hanging in the sky showing where we were to aim. I watched with a pilot's eye as the skipper reacted to the instructions coming from the bomb aimer on the run-in to the target, comparing them to my own crew. I was relieved to find their calm approach similar to ours. Although there had been no flak or fighters hitherto, I must confess to being relieved when I heard 'bombs gone!' and felt the kite lift as the weight was lost. 'Standby for the camera flash.' We had to fly on the same course for several seconds as the bombs fell before the camera mounted at the edge of our bomb bay took a picture of where they had fallen relative to the target. I was glad the bloody things had gone, and we could turn for home.

On the way back I had my first taste of flak, as we flew between Brussels and Antwerp. In the bright daylight, we could see the black puffs of shells exploding all around the nearby Lancasters. Every now and then we would fly through one of the bursts ourselves, and the kite would shake in their blast. They made dirty black smudges in the sky, but I knew from conversations with more experienced pilots that they could destroy us with one shell in the right place. Luckily our navigator had done his job well, and we managed to steer between the worst concentrations of fire. Back over the coast, and I helped to put the kite into the right state for landing, before an easy and anti-climactic end to my first raid. After all these months of training, I had finally started to get my own back on the enemy who had bombed my country, and it felt good. One down, twenty-nine to go until I finished my tour.

At first I was rather too full of my success. I went immediately to my crew and told them all about what we had done, how little resistance there had been, and other little tips I had picked up from the skipper. I felt proud, confident, and very satisfied that I had passed my first test without giving way to nerves. They took it all in avidly, knowing that anything I had learnt would stand us all in good stead later.

Luckily, I had the wiser ear of Steve to share it all with too, and he was very helpful in bringing me back to earth a little with some sage words of wisdom. I remember being in his car one evening soon after that first raid, heading for the pub. I told him about the raid, and he started to drip-feed me little nuggets of advice, each of which was a potential life saver. As he drove, I told him that we had been one of the first over the target, and he said, 'Yeah, you want to watch that. You don't want to be first there, because the defences will be concentrating on you. You've got far more chance of getting coned, or hit. Best thing is to be just a few seconds after the first kite, hiding in its shadow. And if any poor bugger does get coned, follow him. All the flak will be aimed in front at him, so by the time you get there it will be gone and you will be safe.' He made me realise that you had to look after number one, that if someone else got hit it wasn't your problem and that you should be grateful it wasn't you. At first it sounded very cold and slightly ruthless, but this was war and you had to fight for your survival.

Our chat was interrupted by a minor crisis. We had been bowling along in his Morris 12, doing about seventy, which was quite fast for the time. We were driving to Nottingham along Watling Street, the old Roman road, and heading towards the only humpbacked bridge. Suddenly a horse-drawn wagon, loaded up with bales of hay, pulled out of a field ahead of us and headed in our direction. The wagon blocked our view of the bridge. Steve tried to slow down, but the brakes had suddenly failed. He pumped the pedal, but he was just pumping fluid out of the system until his foot went to the floor with no discernible effect on our speed. What if something else was coming the other way on the other side of the bridge? There was no way of stopping, and I remember him saying 'Well, Nelson took a chance …' as we flew past the cart, over the bridge and through to the other side. Luckily, there wasn't anything coming, or that would have been the end of us. It was typical of his confident, aggressive style of flying too.

Another piece of advice he gave me was about being attacked by fighters. Several chaps had told me that the best defence was to try to ignore them, to blend in with the sky or head for a cloud and hope they would lose you and give up. But Steve was having none of that. 'Let them bloody have it!' he said. 'Imagine you are a fighter pilot. There are hundreds of bombers all over the sky. Would you chase one which is showing its teeth and firing all its guns at you, or would you choose one which isn't fighting back? Show them you aren't afraid, and they'll pick on some other bugger.' Again, it was cold and ruthless, but he was absolutely right. I passed all these tips on to my crew before we got to our first operation.

That day finally came on 26 August. Kiel was to be the target of the first bombs my crew ever dropped in anger, and it would be a night-time raid.

After the nosh, we headed down to the briefing room, trying to look as though we were confident and not at all overwhelmed by our task.

We took notes furiously, and I tried to remember all the extra advice Steve had given me. Soon enough we were airborne in clear skies, just one bomber among more than 370, bringing death and destruction to a distant German town. Riccomini and Clarry were looking for any trouble from fighters, Les Skelton was listening in on the wireless for any information, and we were all doing our own specialised job. The clear skies gave way to a low cover as we crossed the North Sea, but Noel was doing his job well. In due course - Kiel! We knew we were there, as the flak became very active, and several kites suffered damage around us. I hadn't seen flak at night before, and it was deceptively beautiful. Red streaks came arcing up towards us like fireworks, and sometimes seemed to burst with an orange flash. The problem was that between every red streak of tracer there were other rounds which would really do the damage. The skies were clear of cloud as we ran in to the target, but there was plenty of smoke from the bombs which had already been dropped, which impaired visibility. The Germans had also put up a smokescreen which made things harder. The others in the crew had never been fired at before, and I tried to be fairly nonchalant about it to allay their fears. The Pathfinders had dropped green TIs (target indicators) over the target but they proved to be a little too far south, so were corrected with red TIs for us to aim at. TIs were like enormous flaming chandeliers hanging in the sky, and were visible for miles around. Noel was down in the nose with the bombsight and saw the red TIs, so sent me in the right direction. When they were in line with the cross on the bombsight, he pressed the tit, and called with relief, 'Bombs gone!' The reports later confirmed that the area had been hit with a well concentrated attack. We, of course, immediately headed for home once our camera had fired. I had developed the idea of a very slight nose-down position, which gave me a little more speed, meaning that I would be one of the first back – although it did mean we had to keep a close watch out for our own aircraft in the dark. German fighters tried to attack us on the way, but we managed to shake them off with an evasive corkscrew. We also had to avoid some heavy flak before managing to get across the Channel. We landed at five to two, de-briefed, had a good slug of rum, and then headed off to bed – we had done it, and I had managed to survive the baptism of fire which had caused me such fear a few short days before. One of our Lancs didn't come back, which was the first time I knew someone had gone missing because of enemy action.

There was little time to dwell on things however, as the squadron was very much in the front line of operations and our next trip was to prove an epic of endurance.

On the night of 29 August, we and sixteen other Lancs from our squadron took off into five-tenths cloud, headed to Stettin in Poland. To get there we had to cross hundreds of miles of occupied Europe, and our powers of navigation and flying were tested to their limits. Our Lancaster LM227 was tested to the limit also, as Stettin was one of the furthest trips made by Bomber Command during the war. Our tanks were filled with their full load of 1,254 gallons of aviation fuel to make sure we had enough to get back. Part of our route took us close to neutral Sweden, where there was no blackout and we could see the towns and cities lit up. It was a wonderful sight after flying over blacked-out countries for so long. After flying numerous 'dog legs' to avoid major flak concentrations, we finally got to the target at 14,000 feet as instructed. There was complete cloud cover over the city though, and we were instructed to go down to 12,000 feet to run in beneath the cloud and drop our bombs. As we approached we could see the red and green flares dropped by the Pathfinders, among some heavy bright orange bursts of flak. The flares were well placed though, and we dropped our bombs right on the button, despite the streams of shells coming up at us from the beleaguered city. Making a pretty sharp exit from the immediate danger area, our nav found us the best way home. With all the dog-legging and the sheer distance we had to cover, we were still over enemy territory after five hours of flying. Our combat adrenaline was starting to ebb away, and tiredness began to take its insidious hold on us all. As we passed over the coast, I called up on the radio, 'Hey Red, Brin, how are things?' only to get no response. They were asleep, exhaustion having overtaken them at last.

'RED! BRIN! WAKE UP!'

'What? Oh, bloody hell, sorry Skip, I must have nodded off ...'

The rest of them were little better, and all admitted they were straining every sinew just to stay awake. My own eyelids were drooping. We had taken off at twenty past nine at night, and it was now around two o'clock in the morning. There were still hours of flying left before we got back to base, and I was close to dropping off myself, despite the noise and cold. It was becoming dangerous, over the sea at more than 10,000 feet and dog tired. If we all succumbed, we could find ourselves flying on until the fuel ran out, God knows where. I made a plan, to which they all agreed. 'Right, all of you, go to sleep. You have fifteen minutes. Then I'll wake you all up to check everything is all right. If it's all OK, Noel can take over from me so I can get some shut-eye, and we'll get another fifteen minutes – then I'll take over again, and we'll take it in turns to be awake until we're over the English coast. All right?' Gratefully they dropped off again, and I tensed all my muscles in an attempt to stay awake. The fifteen minutes of lonely vigil crawled by as slowly as the silver-tipped sea below us, until at last it was my turn. 'OK everybody, wake up. All right? I'm going to switch on George, but you need to stand by to take over quickly if anything happens.'

'Righto, Skip.'

I reached forward to the little lever on the left of the cockpit and pushed it forward. George, the automatic pilot, would keep us on the correct course and altitude while I dozed. With relief, I just slumped in my seat, my chin on my chest over my folded arms. After what seemed like seconds, Noel was waking me up to take over again, and the crew to make checks on our position and the guns. We all trusted each other, and there was never any question that the man on duty would succumb to temptation and fall asleep themselves. Fortunately there were no fighters following us, and once we had crossed the English coast with just a few miles to go we all stayed awake. We finally landed at twenty to seven in the morning. Once we were safely down, we got through the debriefing as fast as we could, got to our beds and simply crashed out. I know crews were often offered Benzedrine tablets to help them stay alert on long operations like this, but I never took them because they might stop me from sleeping later.

Twenty-three Lancasters were lost that night, and we had so nearly been the twenty-fourth. It's just as well we weren't, because LM-227 became one of only thirty-five Lancasters to survive 100 trips during the course of the war. That was no mean achievement when you consider how many were either shot down or returned damaged beyond repair. They became known as 'Ton-Up Lancs', and in fact I flew two others on my tours, LM-594 and ME-801.

Just two days later, on 31 August, we were detailed to attack bunkers housing stores of V-2 rockets near a place called Agenville. It's close to Amiens, in the heart of the battlefields of the First World War. V-2s were huge missiles which would climb up to the edge of space before falling back to earth at supersonic speeds to crash down on London, a really terrifying weapon as Hitler had intended. The Allied armies were taking too long to overrun the rocket launch sites, so we had to try to destroy them ourselves. Knowing that the rockets were aimed at my mum and dad made it a very welcome operation.

It wasn't a long trip, not like Stettin, which meant we had an escort of Spitfires flying with us. They gave us a great feeling of protection from marauding fighters, and indeed they managed to keep them off us altogether. We took off into five-tenths cloud just after one o'clock in the afternoon along with fifteen other kites from our squadron, and headed towards the Channel. Ahead of us, we could see the distinctive horseshoe shapes of unpleasant cumulonimbus clouds, which we did our best to avoid. They often carry severe up and down draughts which could throw even a heavy aircraft like ours about like a toy. When we reached the target after a reasonably uneventful flight, we could see the green and yellow target indicators scattered about the sky among heavy cloud, and our bombing instructions were scrambled and confused. The orders were to bomb from 8,000 feet, which was bloody low, and gave the gunners a far better chance of hitting you. In fact several of our kites were hit and some of the crews injured by flak, which came up at us thick and fast.

Once the bombs were gone, we couldn't wait to turn around and get out of there, and we had a fast return to base, arriving in daylight at five past five.

After a few short days of rest we were called to work again on 3 September. It was just two weeks before the launch of Operation Market Garden, the attack on the bridges leading into Germany along the road which ran from Eindhoven through to Arnhem. I don't know if it was in preparation for that attack, but we were detailed to bomb an airfield near Eindhoven. As it was another short trip, we had an escort of Spitfires to look after us, although by then the Luftwaffe was practically a spent force, especially in daylight, when our fighters outnumbered them everywhere except in the furthest reaches of the Reich which were out of their range. Fifteen kites from our squadron took off to join with those of other squadrons. It was cloudy until we got over the Channel, then we had an easy run into Holland under clear skies. We could see the enemy coast clearly ahead of us, and gritted our teeth as we attempted to thread our way between the flak outbursts. The bombing run went well, and we turned for home with the usual mixture of relief and apprehension that the defences might still have something unpleasant up their sleeves. This time however, it wasn't the enemy we had to worry about, but the weather. Shortly after getting back over the sea, the cloud came right down, and we were quickly flying blind. I dropped steadily, trying to get a sight of the sea, but nothing materialised. I remembered some advice Steve had given me, which was to go low early, to find the base of the cloud. So we continued to drop … all the way down to 200 feet, when we suddenly spotted the welcome waves of the Channel. Soon enough we could see land, and managed to find our way back to the airfield without too much trouble. One of our other kites was forced to divert though, which led to no end of ribbing in the mess later.

These were the first of many more trips to spoil the Germans' day, and we very quickly became the veterans we had all aspired to be. Even today, decades later, I can remember clearly the routine of a day on ops: the concentration, the sudden bursts of activity and fear, and the hours of monotony over the sea and non-hostile territory…

CHAPTER SEVEN

A DAY IN THE LIFE
OF A BOMBER PILOT

'So what are the chances of us getting to Lincoln tonight then?' Steve is hopeful that we might be able to get into town and head to the Theatre Royal. That's one of our favourite places when we are lucky enough to be off duty, usually the first night of the week. We would head for the front row of the stalls, making sure we had the best view in the house of all the crumpet on stage. There was a bar on the right-hand side of the stage where we met them during the interval to make arrangements to examine their talents further. He's probably been looking at our copy of *The Stage* magazine to find out where the best skirt would be performing tonight.

'Doubt it,' I say. 'Weather's looking clear. I reckon we could be off on one.'

He grunts into his tea. The chatter around the mess at breakfast always centres around the same subjects. The weather, and if there will be an operation tonight. Last night we'd been off, and had enjoyed quite a good session at The Castle Hotel in Westgate. I'd still managed to be up at seven though, and after a wash and a shave I was ready to face the day.

Breakfast over, we join the trickle of airmen heading down to the Crew Room to find out what the day might have in store for us. If there is no op, and we're to head off to Wainfleet Sands for bombing practice, then there would be no rush and we could feel a little more relaxed. The leaders of the various positions would have been to a briefing already on what was to happen; the bombing leader, nav leader, w/op leader, and senior pilot would have met the operation planners while we were eating our breakfast. They are all experienced aircrew, often decorated and with at least one complete tour behind them. It's their job to make sure that the highest standards were kept up in every aspect of our performance. The findings of their meeting would be posted up on the noticeboard, and we'd find out from there what the future had in store.

As we walk in through the door I hear the shout going up, 'Ah, bloody hell, we're on tonight!' Another peeved voice comes through the groans, 'No! I've got a sure-fire date waiting for me!'

There it is, pinned up on the noticeboard.

'The Squadron will be on operations tonight. The following captains with their crews are to be ready for duty ...'

Sure enough, my name appears on the long list of others ready for tonight's raid. Briefing at 1500 hours. So that's it; tonight will be a busy night and the dancing girls will have to wait. I gather my crew together, some of them still looking a little the worse for wear after last night, and let them know the good news. All thoughts of debauchery quickly vanish in the serious atmosphere of getting ready for war.

Preparation begins right away. We all pile on to the bus which will take us on the trip around the air field to our Lancaster. As we bump our way across the grass and tarmac, each of us is running over the duties which we will have to go through when we arrive. Our kite is one of many, lined up along the airfield squatting black on their wheels, tails down. Ground crew are fussing all over her as we arrive and jump out. The first thing to do is a quick check around the outside, to make sure that all is shipshape and nothing has fallen off or been forgotten.

'Come on then, Bill, let's get the engines started!' I say to our flight engineer. A quick climb up the ladder into the fuselage, and the friendly, warm smell of oil and metal greets us as we enter. A clumsy clamber across the spar, and I pull myself up into the pilot's seat from where the bank of controls, instruments and indicators looks up at me expectantly.

While Ricky and Clarrie shine the glass of the cockpit and gun positions, Bill and I have to check our engines. We go through the now familiar routine of starting up. Looking out through the cockpit windows, I can see ground crew waiting by the starboard outer engine, looking my way expectantly. Now it's time to concentrate, to make sure this wonderful aircraft isn't going to let us down tonight when we are far away, over enemy territory.

I run through the pre-start checklist, my hands moving instinctively to the controls. Throttles half open. Air intake cold. Radiator override to automatic. Tank selector to number two tank, master cock on. Fine pitch on the propeller control, check the super charge control. Air heat control to cold, radiator shutter override switches to cold. Switch on the booster pump. Ignition and booster coil ON.

Again I look out of the window. A ground crew man is getting a bunk up onto the huge landing wheel, with the lead from the trolley accumulator going into the aircraft's electrical supply to save draining our own batteries. Without this, we risk using all our electrical power to start her up. He reaches into the engine to get to the primer pump.

'CONTACT!' I hear from him. 'OK, contact!' I signal back. Bill presses the starter, and the engine coughs slowly into life before settling into that beautiful Merlin roar. We repeat the sequence twice more, each engine warming up at 1,200 revs. But when the signal comes to start the port outer engine, it just splutters and refuses to fire. 'I think it's flooded, Skipper!' shouts the crewman. He means that too much fuel has got into the cylinders to allow them to fire, and we have to cycle the engine to push some of it out again.

'OK, switches off, petrol off, full throttle, BLOW OUT!' I shout. He gives me the thumbs up to show we are going through the correct procedure for clearing the cylinders and starting again. 'OK, pressing the starter now!' The great three-bladed propeller turns slowly as the power from the trolley turns the motor over. After half a dozen revolutions, he shouts up, 'Righto, try again'

'OK, switches on, petrol on, throttle closed, CONTACT!' Immediately the engine coughs and growls, and is soon purring happily like the others.

Bill and I have to make sure each one is working correctly, by keeping an eye on the temperature gauges and pressures.

'Better test the hydraulics!' Bill shouts. It's very noisy with four Merlins all racing away close by. We lower and raise the wing flaps, and since we have no bombs on board we open and close the bomb doors. Finally we leave them open, so that the armaments crews can load us up with whatever bombs we will be carrying. All is well.

Once the engines are warm, we run them up to 1,500 revs to check the magneto drop. They are all reassuringly fine. Bill then puts them up to plus four boost, making sure the two-speed supercharger is working. The red light winks on, as it should. I move each propeller into coarse pitch in turn, open the throttles to take off power and check the boost and rpm dials. The kite strains against the chocks, shaking. Another magneto drop test shows me the engines are all singing for us the way they should be. As always, the ground crew have done a wonderful job in maintaining our kite. Some flak holes which were left from our last operation have been patched, moving parts have been checked and oiled, and she is ready to go.

We shut down each engine in turn, enjoying the sudden silence as the last falls still.

Our gunners are still wrestling with boxes of Window, the strips of aluminium foil we will drop that night to confuse the German radar. Noel, our bomb aimer, is responsible for shovelling it out of the aircraft, so he's making sure it's packed carefully to begin with.

'There's a lot of it today, Skip.' he says, 'Must be going a long way in.' It was our only way to guess where we might be going; the more Window we were issued, the deeper into Germany we would be heading.

'Right, nosh time!' shouts Bill, as we finally get everything stowed to Noel's satisfaction. We can leave our aircraft to the ground crew now. The armourers will wheel out the twenty-foot trailers of bombs and fix them in our bomb bay, as well as making sure there is plenty of ammunition for our defensive guns. We though, have a little spare time. The bus takes us back to the mess, where we have some lunch and try not to think too much about what might befall us tonight. The food, and the remaining effects of last night, slows us all down a bit and most of us head back to our quarters for a rest. It's sure to be a long night. My head hits the pillow and I' m out, for all too short a time …

'Bacon and eggs?'

It's a traditional treat for us airmen before an operation. While the rest of the country has to live on powdered eggs and a limited meat ration, we are lucky enough to enjoy fresh eggs every time we are off to deliver bombs to the enemy. We sit together as a crew and wolf it down. We might not get anything else to eat for many hours, so it's good to fill up. We don't drink much though. The toilet facilities on board are pretty much non-existent, so none of us want to be inconvenienced any more than necessary. Shortly before 1500 hours, we join the throng of chattering airmen heading to the crew room. The same question is on everybody's lips; where will we be going tonight? We cram together at the table, one crew among many. Bill and I, Brin the Navigator carrying his bag full of maps, charts, instruments and pencils, our two gunners, and 'Red', our Wireless Operator. All eyes are on the curtain across the wall in front of us. It hides a board showing a large-scale map of the Continent, and details of our mission.

'Thank you gentlemen.'

The Station Commander enters, and there's a scrape of chairs as we all stand up, the chatter instantly hushed.

The first to speak is the Intelligence Officer. He knows what we all want to know, and wastes no time in pulling back the curtain which hides the map. Our eyes follow the lines of black wool which have been stretched and pinned across it, marking our route and target for tonight. Noel had been right; we are going a long way in.

'All right gentlemen, some of you have been here before, and you know it's a tough one. For those of you that haven't, make sure you remember to stay to the east here, to avoid this large concentration of flak.' With a stick, he points out highlighted areas, where German defences are at their strongest. Some of our friends have already been lost there; we know it well. 'This place is well lit with searchlight batteries here,' he points, 'and here.' Try to get your run-in straight, and endeavour to drop on target. We want to knock out these factories and the railway lines which serve them. The target will be marked by Pathfinders with flares. Let's hope you get some good photos. Any questions?'

A gentle murmur goes around the room, but no one raises their hand.

The Armaments Officer gives details of the weapons we are to carry tonight. Mainly high explosives, with incendiaries added to make sure there is a proper conflagration. Noel is busy writing down all this information in a notebook, because it's his job to make sure they are all correctly fused before we drop our dangerous load into the German night.

Then it's Les's turn to make notes, as the Radio Leader gives details of the frequencies we will be using. They are changed regularly to keep the Germans guessing.

The weather forecast is vital for us. We need clear conditions if possible for take-off, so that we can climb quickly and be on our way without wasting fuel. The conditions over the target are even more important. If cloud comes over and the target is obscured, it will be impossible to make an accurate attack and we could find that we have flown all that way for no reason. The weather man presents us with a series of charts showing the fronts affecting us and Europe. Thankfully, it's too warm for ice to be a problem. We all know how frightening it is to be at altitude and feel the kite becoming more and more sluggish as ice forms along the wings and propellers. A ton of ice could form very quickly across the wings, weighing the aircraft down while simultaneously changing the wings' shape, reducing the lift factor. In extreme cases you could even crash. But he is reassuring.

'Fine tonight chaps. A few clumps of high cloud, but mainly clear with a slight headwind on the way out. Luckily there's no real moon, but for all that you will need to keep an eye out for fighters. There may be a little fog by the time you return, but not enough to be concerned about.'

There are no questions; we are all too busy taking in what they have already told us. Looking across the table I can see Brin drawing on his charts; I have already sketched out our route in my notebook, making sure I know where the flak concentrations are.

The Station Commander comes to the front again. 'Thank you. Your order of take-off, gentlemen ...'

This was carefully arranged. When you have a squadron of fully-laden bombers all wanting to get to the runway and take off as closely as possible, you can't have confusion. We all make notes of our correct places in the queue which would stretch along the taxiway to the runway.

'Now the Air Officer Commanding would like to say a few words ...'

The boss gives us his usual pep talk about how we are to strike at the heart of the enemy, and do our bit to shorten the war. I only half listen; my mind is racing with everything I have to remember, and the urge to make sure I complete the operation and bring us all home safely.

'Thank you, gentlemen. Good luck.'

Each crew immediately begins to talk among themselves, comparing notes and sharing concerns.

'I told you were were going there!'

'You'd better not forget that flak!'

'Make sure you've got that bit marked out properly!'

'Looks like a tough one, Skip ...'

Leaving them to check over their own duties, I see the engineers responsible for our kite and sign their Form 700. That means I accept it's in good order, and ready to fly. It gives me details of the work which has been done on it, and confirms that it has been signed off by the officer in charge. Air Frame – checked. Electricals – checked. Engine Maintenance – checked. Armaments – checked. I sign, confident that our crew have done their usual fine job.

Briefing over, and it's off to the locker room. After the tension of the last hour, it's a time to let off a bit of steam. There's a lot of noise, with everyone talking and shouting at once, putting on a brave face in front of each other. It's nervous humour; we aren't truly frightened just busy and trying not to think of what might happen. It's like the changing room of a team before a vital match, only with far more clothes. I'm already wearing my long johns, warm knitted and soft next to my skin. Over that I have my battledress. The next layer is my quilted flying overalls, dark red and an inch thick. They've got a flap at the front for all the necessary calls of nature which may need to be made during a ten-hour operation. Finally, the dark overalls covered in pockets into which I stuff my notes and pencils. Just getting it all on is enough to make me hot and bothered, but I know I'll be grateful for it all when we're at 20,000 feet and everything is freezing to the touch.

'Damn!' I hear from Steve. He's pulled his quilted overalls and flying overalls on, but has forgotten to put on his long johns. As everyone laughs uproariously, he tries pulling them on over the top of everything else, failing of course and looking very silly. Perhaps he meant to do it, to keep up the spirits of his crew.

I'll carry my helmet and gloves to the plane. The gloves are thick and warm, and I've trained myself to operate all the controls while I'm wearing them, but I'd rather go without so they can stay off for now.

I'm struggling into my heavy flying boots, nearly ready, when Noel yells, 'Oi, Skip, got the kettle?'

'Of course I have!' I yell back, as my foot slides into place. As if I could forget the kettle. Where other pilots have teddies, pieces of ladies' underwear or photographs as their mascot, mine is a big, iron kettle with a handle on the top; the sort of thing cowboys might hang above their camp fire. It comes with us on every trip, usually in the cockpit, and we would feel lost without it. It reassures us that all is well, because when we land we will take it on our first night off to the nearest pub. Everyone will order a drink for the kettle, and it will be filled with booze to be dispensed among us after the pubs have shut. When it runs out, one or other of us will make a quick trip around neighbouring tables and nick half-finished pints from unsuspecting airmen to top it up. So far my lucky mascot hasn't let us down and is gradually becoming covered with painted crosses, each indicating another operation completed.

A final scramble to make sure have all our gear, parachutes, Mae Wests and flasks, and we are out on time, waddling to the buses waiting outside in the dusk. Once again we are driven out to our aircraft, now fully fuelled and full of deadly bombs. We all relax a little as we jump clumsily from the tailgate of the bus and walk over to it. It feels like an old friend, comforting and reassuring, almost like a big brother welcoming us and ready to protect us through the dark, unfriendly night.

While Bill and I do our final walk around the aircraft and check the pitot head cover has been removed, the others begin the time-honoured tradition of pissing on the tailwheel. We all do it; every crew does it, despite a recent King's Regulation which outlaws the practice claiming that it rots the tyres. For us, it's a statement of intent; it says that we will come back, and it's something we won't miss, despite the inconvenience of having to reach through three thick layers of clothing to get to one's tackle. It also makes it less likely we will have to go while we are in the air. The Elsan toilet can be a place of unspeakable horrors after a long flight or if we have had to take evasive manoeuvres. A corkscrew could see its foul contents slopping out over the sides and I always try not to have to use it.

Bill and I take our turn at the tailwheel, before lugging our parachutes up the steep ladder and into the belly of the aircraft which will be our home for the next ten hours. That special Lancaster smell envelops me again as I lurch over the main spar, ducking my head automatically, past the navigator and wireless operator positions, and finally to the cockpit. It's much harder this time, burdened as we are by the bulky suits, hefty boots and other accoutrements. At last I can get rid of my heavy parachute when I get to the cockpit, and I heave it up onto the seat above me. Reaching up, I grab the handle over the windscreen and pull myself up after it, plonking myself down with a groan at the effort. I probably won't leave the seat again until we touch down back at base.

Bill helps me to clip the parachute in place and then I pull my seat harness tight across my shoulders. I need to be held tight in case we have to pull any evasive manoeuvres. Finally I put on my flying helmet and plug in the oxygen tube and intercom leads.

'Hello Clarrie, you OK?'

'OK, Skip!'

'Ricky? Red?'

'All OK'

'Where's my bloody protractor?'

The last comes from Brin, as he sorts out all his maps, charts and bits and pieces on the chart table he has just behind me. We all laugh, and it helps to break the tension a little.

After the usual checks it's time to start up, and I can make out the ground crew gathering around the engines. Looking out to the right I see the kite next to us start up, flames and smoke coughing out of the exhaust pipes. It's our turn, so I signal to the crew on the ground.

'OK, start up!'

'Contact!'

Soon the starboard outer engine is ticking over nicely, and we move to the inner one before switching to the port side. Our earlier checks had been worthwhile, and all four engines sound happy. We run through our final checks, glad to have jobs to do to keep our minds occupied.

Navigation lights ON. Set the pressure on the altimeter. Check the vacuum on the pumps for the instrument flying panel. Radiator switches open. Check brake pressure. Read the heading on the P4 compass, and set the non-magnetic gyroscopic compass so it shows the same magnetic heading. Check the other gyroscopic instruments are working.

'OK Skip, we're off!' Bill has been watching the lines of other aircraft while I've been at the instruments.

Sure enough, the kite next to us has started moving. I wave the chocks away, shouting, 'Clear port!' to Bill, as I see the engineers pull the wedge from under the left wheel. He's seen the chock go from the right, and he shouts 'Clear starboard!' and we increase power slightly to follow the neighbouring kite and join the queue of Lancasters lining up for the runway. There are still final checks to do even as we roll across the tarmac. Check the mag drop when the queue stops. Pitot head heater on – this would make sure our airspeed indicator would still work if things got icy. Trim check, elevator slightly forward, rudder and aileron neutral. Master engine cocks ON. Prop controls to fine pitch. Fuel checks, booster pumps ON. Air intake cold, radiator switches automatic, fifteen degrees of flap, check the gyro instruments.

I have done this many times before, and run through the little checklist in my head. TMPFFSS; Trim, Mixture, Pitch, Fuel, Flaps, Switches and Sperry.

'OK Skip, don't forget, take off, climb to 1,000 feet then heading 110 degrees.' Brin's voice comes through, reminding me of the instructions he had noted down during the flight briefing.

We can see the steady stream of aircraft taking off from the runway, sluggish under the weight of their bombs, straining to climb up and join the others overhead. Soon enough, we turn the corner and it is us next. A small gaggle of well-wishers have gathered there to see us off. Some are WAAFs who are waving their hankies and we wave back at them. The runway stretches away in front of us, and in the distance I see the little green light winking to tell us that we are clear to take off. 'OK, stand by!' and I open to full throttle against the brakes. I give a push with my foot to give us full starboard rudder, ready to counteract the swing of the aircraft to the left due to the torque produced by the rotation of the propellers. The kite starts to shake as the engines roar, and there's no stopping us now. 'Brakes OFF!' We pick up speed rapidly, and I have to ease off the starboard outer throttle because there's still a slight drift to the left. Quickly I feel the tail rise and the Lanc becomes horizontal and under full control as we rumble on.

'I've got them Skip.' says Bill, as he takes the throttle controls from me and locks them in position by tightening the locking nut. The airspeed indicator tells me we are at 100 miles an hour as we flash past the hut with the green light. A moment later I flick the elevator trim wheel by my right knee a few degrees, and the rumbling from the ground suddenly stops. We are up. Thank God for that.

Up, up into the black night, 3,000 revs at full throttle, 160 miles an hour and climbing steadily. Wheels UP, ten degrees off the flap, re-trim. At 750 feet reduce to 2,650 revs, throttle back to plus four boost, and we're gaining height at about 500 feet a minute. It will take more than half an hour to get to our cruising height of 20,000 feet. I check the instruments in front of me. All the needles and figures are easy to read because they have some kind of phosphorescent coating so I don't need to switch on the hooded cockpit lights. That helps me to keep my night vision clear until we get to the target, when it will be dazzled by the glow of searchlights, explosions and flames.

Keeping an eye on the sky all around us, I turn onto the course my navigator has noted. I know we are going the right way, as with hundreds of bombers in the sky at once we can see some silhouettes and exhaust flames. If we time the operation correctly, up to a thousand bombers could pass over our target in just a few minutes, so our navigation has to be absolutely spot on. If we get it wrong … well, with this many of us doing 200 miles an hour with no lights, it would be easy to collide with a friend. All of us keep a very close eye on our neighbours. There is no strict 'formation'. We have all been given an exact time when we have to be over our target, and we know how to get there. It's up to us to get there at the right moment, and that is why Brin is so important. He knows that if we get there just a few seconds too early, before everyone else, we will be the target of every enemy gunner. Likewise if we are late. Ideally, we will follow somebody else in, get the bombs gone, and be gone as soon as we can.

'Bloody hell, I could have reached out and touched him!' cries our rear gunner, as another Lanc slides beneath us just a few feet away in the darkness.

We concentrate hard on keeping an accurate course and avoiding other aircraft, and the time goes very quickly. After a period of quiet, Brin's voice comes through.

'OK Skip, enemy coast ahead. We are on course and on time.'

We are heading over the northern edge of France, which is well-defended by the Germans, but hoping to squeeze between two known areas of flak. Looking ahead, I can see where the jagged silver pattern of the sea gives way to the threatening black stain of the land. There are no friends down there. There are just are empty-eyed searchlights waiting to blind us, guns waiting to dismember our plane and send it howling downwards out of control, airfields with fighters waiting to shoot us down before we even know it. The target is still hundreds of miles away.

Ignore the drawbacks. Just do it.

We all sit up slightly in our seats, the gunners grip the triggers a little more firmly, and I make sure we are on course to avoid the flak concentrations we were warned about this morning at the briefing. Brin has us dead on track. All of us are wondering how long it will be before we can turn around and come back towards the sea.

Noel is on the ball. 'Right,' he says, 'I'll start to sort out Window.' We've been told to start dropping the aluminium strips soon after crossing into enemy territory. If it does its job properly, it will confuse German radar and make it hard for fighters to follow us. He's already undone most of the bundles as we have been flying. He climbs down into his aiming compartment, opens the hatch, and starts to throw out handfuls of the shiny strips which flash behind us in the night, turning enemy radar screens to snow.

Things start to get nervous now. Everything tightens, our movements become faster and more efficient as adrenaline pumps through us. Flak starts to appear in a concentration away to our right, beautiful snakes of light hunting out any aircraft unfortunate enough to get caught. The pencil thin beams of searchlights wave blindly looking for us, but we are too far away. Soon they are left behind. All of us though remember the weather officer's warning about fighters.

The miles mount up as we look down on the blacked-out continent below. Won't be long now. 'Twenty minutes to target, Skip.' Brin sounds alert, sharp, and I'm guessing the tension is affecting him just as much as me. He has plotted us a very careful course. We didn't want to be the first over the target, which would expose us terribly to all the defences, but neither did we want to be the last, and have everything concentrated on us. Noel starts to work on his switchboard, flicking the switches to activate the fuses on the bombs which are clipped so perilously beneath us.

Looking ahead, I can start to see the target. It is already lit up – the Pathfinders' flares have illuminated it clearly and some bombers have already delivered their loads. The city is on fire. All around us there are hundreds more men in hundreds more bombers, all clenching their jaws like me and getting ready for the most important few minutes of the operation.

'Ten minutes, Skip.'

'OK, bomb doors open.'

Suddenly the flak opens up much closer, and more searchlights finger the sky. This is the moment. No turning back. Just do it. Remember Steve's advice, don't be the first. All hell is going on ahead of us, and we are flying towards a wall of flak. We must go through it to get to our target. If we get it wrong, we will have to go round again. The enemy knows where we are going, and puts as much shit into the area as he can. Noel, lying on his belly in the perspex of his bomb aimer's compartment, fixes his sights on the target and starts to talk us in. Somehow he manages to ignore all the fire coming up at him.

'That's it Skip, straight, straight, a little to the left …'

Ahead of us the sky is on fire, glowing with the orange flares of the Pathfinders, the violent bursts of bombs and the arcs of flak and tracer. I see one unfortunate Lancaster get coned by searchlights; three of them lock onto it at once, followed by many more, and I know that in the cockpit the pilot will be blinded by the dazzling light. The flak gunners lock onto it, and soon it seems every gun is aiming at that one aircraft, which starts to roll all over the sky and dive in an attempt to get away. The men inside could have been eating bacon and eggs with me a few hours ago, now they are trapped in their heaving plane as the shells burst all around it. Away to the right, another has been coned too, and explosions are making colourful but deadly patterns on every side. But it's them, not us, and every moment the guns are concentrating on them, we are getting closer to our target in the darkness. Their peril means our salvation.

'Left, steady, that's it Skip, nearly there …'

'Oh no, can you see that?'

There's a spouting flame in the air off to the right, which lights up the silhouette of a stricken Lancaster. It's taken a hit to its fuel tank on the port wing, which is soon burning out of control as the aircraft spirals downwards towards its death. The fire is far too big for any hope of salvation, and within moments the explosion comes. It's fierce white in the middle, and dirty orange on the outside, with huge pieces of debris flying out in all directions. We all know what that means. The burning fuel has started explosions inside the aircraft, and the bombs have gone up with them. The aircraft will have been blown to atoms in a white hot moment, along with the men inside. We feel our kite shake from the blast wave. They may have been from my squadron.

'Right a bit Skip.'

I tear my eyes away and concentrate on the job in hand. Suddenly it sounds as if someone has thrown a handful of stones at the outside of our kite. A near miss.

'Right, right, steady, looking good. Left a bit, OK Skip, good, keep her steady ... BOMBS GONE!'

The plane leaps in the air as the weight of the bombs leaves us, and I re-trim quickly.

'Bomb doors CLOSED!'

'There's the photo flash.'

'OK let's get the hell out of here! Course please, Nav!'

I put the nose down just a fraction as I pull the stick over, to give us an extra few miles an hour. At about 265 degrees we complete our turn and are soon heading as fast as we can for home, leaving the chaos, flashes, bombs and burning behind us. Brin is an expert at plotting the shortest route away from a city and its defences. Soon it is just a glow on the horizon, and the fingers of the searchlights claw uselessly at the sky. We all start to breathe a little more easily as Brin counts down the time to base. We've done the hard part, let's just get back in one piece. Looking out of the canopy ahead and to my right, I see the reassuring sight of the North Star. It means we're heading home.

'We'll be over the coast in twenty minutes.'

The adrenaline is leaving us, and we start to feel tired, looking forward to the tot of rum at the debrief. Despite the cold, we try to make ourselves comfortable for the all-too-long return. My shoulder straps suddenly feel very tight. I start to wonder if we will be able to fill our kettle later, and what girls may be at the pub.

'CORKSCREW PORT, SKIP! CORKSCREW PORT!'

Clarrie's shout, loaded with fear, cuts through my reverie and calls for an instant response as my insides tense. I push the stick forward and to the left, boot the left rudder and we are falling through the sky. He has spotted an enemy fighter, and has signalled for the only manoeuvre which can both throw it off our tail and give Clarrie a shot at him. I hear the guns distantly above the noise of the engines, feel the extra vibration through the aircraft, and I know he and Ricky will be letting fly for all they are worth. I've told them not to hold back, but to show all our teeth to any fighter which comes after us. If he sees we are ready to fight back, then maybe he will go after easier prey. I'm going to make it as hard as I can for him. The speed picks up and soon the kite is shaking with the buffeting it's getting, while I'm glad of the Lancaster's light controls as I try to hold it on course. Tracer bullets fly past my wing into the night.

As we reach the bottom of the corkscrew I reverse the controls, pulling back and to the right on the stick and kicking the right rudder. As we begin the climb which continues our corkscrew shape, I feel myself being pushed down by G-Force onto the parachute beneath me. If we are hit, will I be able to bail out? I push that thought from my mind as I pull at the stick. If I pull too hard, I risk toppling the sensitive gyros which would render the artificial horizon and non-magnetic gyro compass useless.

'I can't see him, I can't see him … where's he gone?'

Our eyes stare into the darkness, looking for a glimpse of our attacker, but there's no sign. Has he gone, or is he lining up for another attack? In the nose, Noel is looking to see if he is coming up beneath us – a deadly place because we have no guns pointing downwards.

Coming off the top, I reverse the controls again to continue our spiral, feeling the negative force squashing my stomach towards my throat. I dread to think of what is happening to the contents of the Elsan toilet behind me. As we go down, I call out, 'Where is he, boys?' I'm scanning the sky looking for any tell-tale exhaust flames or tracer marks which would give us an indication of where he was. No sign. Tense moments as the kite starts to shake again before I pull up. An eternity later I hear Clarrie again.

'OK Skip, action over, I think he's buggered off. Can't see him. We might be OK.'

Thank God for that. I finish the manoeuvre just in case, pulling back up to our cruising height warily. As the others rearrange themselves and Brin searches for various bits of navigation equipment which have slid off his table, I'm glad my straps were done up tightly after all. I only wish the lid on the Elsan had been that tightly fastened, as the stench of a spilled pan wafts through the aircraft.

'We're coming up to the coast, Skip.'

Away to the right some predictive flak goes up. Nasty stuff, it is able to calculate where you will be, at what height and in which direction you are heading. It must be aimed at someone else, I think gratefully, and press on towards home. We all breathe a sigh of relief as we leave the enemy coast behind. Now, unless we are unlucky, there should be no more flak or fighters. As long as we aren't damaged, have enough fuel, and can see the runway, all should be well. I know there have been instances of fighters following bombers home, waiting until they have put on their navigation lights, then shooting them down and making a run back to Holland or Germany, but that's pretty unusual and we can afford to be optimistic. Somewhere in the skies around us there are hundreds of other kites like ours, full of men with jangling nerves who can't wait to get their wheels on the ground again.

Noel comes up out of the nose to take up position near me. He has a tight smile of relief on his face.

'Steer two seven zero degrees, estimate twenty minutes to base.'

They are twenty very long minutes, but we have plenty to do to prepare for landing. As we lose height, I begin our checks.

Navigation lights ON. Auto Pilot cock to SPIN. Air intake COLD. Check brake pressure. Is the kettle OK? Reduce speed to 170 miles per hour. Steer a course to bring us downwind of the airfield. 'Wheels DOWN.' There's a clunk, and the aircraft slows with the extra drag. There's the airfield, what a wonderful sight, with a welcoming pathway of lights to take us home. 'Not long till rum, boys!' Check propeller is in fine pitch. Turn cross wind, down to 750 feet, half flap. Turn into wind, line up with runway. Speed down to 110. Full flap. Safety beckons as the altimeter unwinds.

Down, down, down … We are flying very close to the ground now, tense as we get over the runway, ease the stick back as the speed drops off to keep the nose up, and the ground of home is rushing under my wings until with a gentle thud we touch down, all wheels together in a flukey textbook landing. I squeeze the brakes on, and we roll to taxiing speed. With gentle dabs on the brakes, I steer us around the taxiway and towards our hard standing. Finally, we come to a stop. We have made it.

I close the throttles gradually, leaving us at about 800 rpm for a couple of minutes then turn off the master cocks to cut the engines off slowly. When the last one coughs to a stop, I switch off the ignition and run through the final checks. Pressure head heater OFF, undercarriage indicator and fuel gauge OFF. I've opened the bomb doors so the armourers can fill us up with bombs for the next trip. That's it. Peace and silence. Our beautiful Lancaster has taken us hundreds of miles into danger and brought us back in one piece. Through flak, searchlights, fighters and fear, she has looked after us again. I breathe out and want to sink back into my seat and fall immediately asleep, but unfortunately duty calls and we must attend the debriefing. After all the hours of sitting in the cockpit, my muscles are clenched and tired, protesting as I lower myself down into the fuselage and climb once more over the main spar, down the ladder, and into the waiting bus already crammed with crew from other aircraft. Amid the relief of getting back is the uncertainty of who might be missing, but we won't find that out until later. 'I think I saw a Lanc get it …' 'Did you see that factory go up? …' 'Anyone seen John yet? …'

As we get to the busy crew room, most of us are thinking of just two things: rum and bed, in that order. The ration goes around, and as usual I'm lucky enough to get two slugs because Ricky doesn't drink and always lets me have his. Still clutching our clutter of bags, notebooks and instruments, we head to the nearest free table and I plonk my kettle down with a clang. The rum is already going to my head.

'Glad to see you back,' says the debriefing officer. 'Right, let's get this done quickly. How was it?'

We give him as much as we can about the enemy defences, conditions above the target and whether or not we dropped in the right place.

'Was the target clear enough to see, or was there a lot of cloud cover?'

'No, it was fine, Sir,' says Noel, 'Wasn't too bad over target and I'm pretty sure we dropped right onto the factories you told us about.'

'Very good. Any problems?'

'A fighter came and touched us up a bit, but we scared him off. He might have come from one of the new airfields you mentioned.'

A few more questions, and he seems satisfied. 'Well done. All right, I'm sure you've had enough now, off to bed with you.'

I look around to see if Steve has come back. Neither of us will leave the crew room without making sure that the other is all right. To my relief I see him at the other end of the room, finishing off his own debriefing.

I push back the wooden chair and come slowly to my feet. 'Well done chaps,' I manage to say. 'See you in the morning.' I make it back to my room, and pull off one of my flying boots before my head hits the pillow. Another operation done. It's five o'clock in the morning, and starting to get light.

CHAPTER EIGHT

OLD HANDS

I suppose one of the advantages we RAF boys had over the soldiers and sailors was that we were based on home soil, in comfy beds instead of mud-filled trenches or uncomfortable hammocks; and they never let us forget it! It also meant that when we had a night off we could enjoy ourselves in whichever pubs were close by. Inevitably, that led to all kinds of adventures, as crews would head out in search of women and drink. Apart from Steve, my regular drinking partner, I would head out with other skippers from the squadron, and of course my kettle. My crew would join up with others to head for other establishments, and we rarely saw each other on nights out.

There were several pubs which became regulars for us, and thanks to Steve's car we were able to get around them quite easily. In Nottingham we had what was known as 'The Circuit'. That meant a start at the Trip to Jerusalem, known as 'The Trip'. Then to The Black Boy, which was actually the bar of a posh hotel, then the one we all called the 'Airborne Nag', The Flying Horse. From there it was a quick dodge up an adjacent alley to our favourite, The Barley Mow. We were always made very welcome there, and sometimes stayed over if we got too pissed. We became so welcome, in fact, that Steve wooed the landlord's daughter and eventually married her, producing five wonderful children.

As you can imagine though, as this was wartime, people's emotions were often running high and once lubricated by alcohol they were apt to allow those feelings to spill over. At one pub, The Lifeboat in Cleethorpes, that's exactly what happened. We went there quite a bit because it was right on the front, a holidaymakers' bar like the ones on the front in Southend. It was usually reasonably well behaved and welcoming to us, and we were treated as regulars. On this particular night, four of us had crammed into Steve's car to get there, to have a warm up drink before going on to a dance where we hoped to find some pretty girls. As well as Steve and myself, there was Harry Sutton and Sandy Lane. Harry was a lovely chap, but a little lah-de-dah; the product of a posh education. Sandy on the other hand was a tall, fit, athletic type who was always ready for some action.

When we arrived we could hardly get inside for the crush of soldiers, or 'Brown Jobs' as we called them. I don't know why there were so many of them out and about in Cleethorpes of all places, but they were all having a high old time. Usually you would be able to listen to music, either from a gramophone or the piano, but if there was music that night we couldn't hear it over the hullabaloo of soldiers drinking, swearing, laughing and fighting.

We were the only RAF there, but we managed to keep ourselves to ourselves, and the Brown Jobs left us alone … until I went to the toilet to release some of the beer I had drunk. As I stood there peeing, three pissed soldiers came in and stood, in a close huddle, to pee together. As they did so, they sang, although for the life of me I couldn't tell you what tuneless dirge they had chosen. Feeling fairly full of myself, I said, 'Ha, the Andrews Sisters!' Perhaps it wasn't the cleverest thing to say in a pub full of Brown Jobs, and one of the charming trio abruptly stopped his crooning, fixed his eyes on me and growled, 'Not so much of the effing 'sisters'!' I think it would have ended there, had it not been for Harry coming through the door and hearing this last comment. As soon as he opened his mouth I knew there would be trouble. 'I suppose you know you're talking to an officer and a gentleman?' he drawled, in a peeved, upper-class voice. I'm sure you can imagine how well that went down. A moment later he was clutching his face, which had been on the receiving end of a punch in the eye. I made a grab for the door, only to find Sandy coming in. He saw the situation in a moment, and, never one to miss a fracas, I knew he'd relish the chance to use his fists. Immediately behind him was Steve. As the first punches were thrown, he and I both took off through the door and back into the bar. Pushing our way through the melee of khaki, we nodded cheerfully to the rough-looking squaddies all around us … 'Hello boys, enjoying your evening …' As I grabbed the kettle, they knew something was going on; some kind of telepathy was passing between them, but we managed to push through until we fell through the doors and were disgorged onto the pavement. Running like hell towards the car, we kept turning back to see if we'd been followed but so far so good. Steve pulled off, and headed back to the pub to see if we could pick up our braver comrades, keeping the engine running in case any Brown Jobs decided to come out and try to turn it over with us inside.

Moments later the doors of the pub burst open, and Harry and Sandy came out amid a roar of drunken soldiery. Sandy had a split lip and not too much other damage, but poor old Harry looked a real mess. His eye was closed and there was blood and bruising all over his usually immaculate officer's face. They jumped in, and Steve roared off.

'Wait a minute!' cried Harry, 'Where are you going? This isn't the way back to camp!'

'Too right,' said Steve from the driver's seat, 'We're off to a dance, remember?!'

And to protestations from our injured friends, he took us to the dance where there were indeed lots of pretty girls. Steve and I spent the night chatting them up, with some degree of success, while Sandy sat in a corner prodding at his bleeding lip with his tongue and Harry simply looked grotesque and could hardly see what was going on. We plied them both with drink until the pain subsided, and I'd like to think that they had a good time!

In between the good times the offensive against the Germans had to be sustained. September 1944 continued with a raid on fortifications around Le Havre, on the 6th. There had been a bit of rush to get ready, and three of our kites hadn't been bombed up. Five-tenths cloud over our base thinned out as we flew and we had a clear run to our target, which wasn't too far away. We bombed in three phases of four aircraft each, into heavy flak because it was a naval base and consequently well-defended. Thank goodness there were no fighters. The green and red target indicators were clear, and the bombs seemed to go into a well concentrated area.

Three days later we were sent back to have another go at the same place, but there was a lot more cloud over the target, which gave us cover. We came down to 3,000 feet, below the cloud base, and dropped right on target before scurrying back into the welcoming cloud and heading for home.

Our next raid was much further, and potentially even more dangerous; Frankfurt, on the night of 12 September. At the briefing we were told about the importance of this city to the German war effort, with its factories, railway junctions and industrial complexes. That would of course mean that it would be very well-defended, and so it proved. Nineteen kites from our squadron took off, and we bombed from 17,000 feet onto the red and green flares which the Pathfinders had dropped. The flak was intense, and it took all our nerve to stay straight and level on target while Noel talked us in. We could all hear bits and pieces rattling off the fuselage as our Lancasters took a pounding, especially when fighters came in to attack those which the flak had missed. Frankfurt isn't far north of the old town of Darmstadt, which had been targeted the night before by Five Group. From our cockpit we could see the glow of the flames where its medieval centre was still alight. The gunners and fighter pilots were particularly vengeful that night, and we lost a lot of friends. Seventeen Lancs were shot down, including Flying Officer Aldridge from our squadron. It was to be the last major raid on that battered city.

We had quickly developed a coldness about losing people. The inevitability of death became a constant companion to us, which meant we had to inure ourselves to it, or go under. You had to bloody well ignore it. At the end of a mission, as the debriefing room emptied, you'd know who was missing and what their likely fate had been. They might have been sharing a pint with you the evening before, but now you couldn't even afford yourself the time to wonder if they had been taken prisoner, since the odds were strongly against it. 'Charlie's got the chop' would be about as far as we allowed ourselves to go. You would put it on a shelf, close it off from your mind, and get to bed. It couldn't stop you from sleeping, or you wouldn't have the nerve to go up the next time you were called for an operation. For me it was a constant battle never to return to the state of fear I was in when I first arrived on the squadron.

One friend I lost, later in the war, was Robert Cunliffe, whom we called 'Joe'. He was always part of the crowd with Steve and I, and we had a lot of fun together. He was tall and fair, with a Midlands accent and a ready laugh. On one particular night when the pub closed we managed to purloin some chairs and tables and a load of fish and chips, and set ourselves up for a picnic right in the middle of the road outside. The kettle, which we had taken care to fill, provided us with ample refreshment as we caroused and tried to forget the stress of the last mission. We told jokes, recounted our heroic flying exploits, and of course talked about girls, just like any young men out for a night of fun. I had partaken too much of the kettle's intoxicating contents, and gradually the horizon started to tilt; unfortunately and inevitably I began to tilt with it. Gravity took its hold, and before I knew it I was on my back in the gutter, with Joe and everyone else laughing uproariously. 'Get up tha darrft bugger!' Steve shouted, as they watched me struggle with the effects of the kettle. It was a wonderful night of youthful fun, which I will always remember.

A few days later, Joe didn't come back from an operation. His belongings simply disappeared. The people who ran the squadron seemed to have developed a canny knack of removing all evidence of someone's existence without anyone noticing them do it. One moment he was there; the next it was as though he had never been. It helped us to get over the loss quickly, and Steve and I became accustomed to having a regular stream of new drinking partners.

By now we had started to consider ourselves as old hands, with a few missions under our belts. Steve's advice was paying dividends, and we were learning our own techniques all the time.

The fifteenth of September saw us sent to drop mines on routes which could be used by German shipping, and we had a fairly uneventful trip to the Kattegat.

The next day, the sixteenth, saw us on a daylight raid on an airfield on the north coast of Holland called Leeuwarden, in support of Operation Market Garden. It was a relatively short trip, thank goodness, and the weather wasn't too bad. We saw the red target indicators clearly, and got a good concentrated drop on target. There wasn't much flak, and no fighters, so all in all quite an easy operation, and another one to tick off the list, which was creeping up steadily because we were being kept so busy.

We had a week off operations after that, possibly because the weather wasn't really playing ball. Finally, on the twenty-third, we were sent to Neuss, just outside Düsseldorf on the Rhine. Nineteen kites from 576 Squadron took off to join more than 500 others in six-tenths cloud, which got worse the closer we got to the target. Luckily the Pathfinders had been there and marked it clearly for us in red. Their colour bled brightly through the clouds and we managed to drop in the right spot. There was a lot of flak though, because Neuss had a very busy industrial area with factories and railway junctions right next to the Rhine docks. Fighters came after us too, but they caused us less trouble than the weather; I remember that raid as being really bloody cold! Another of our squadron's crews didn't come back that night.

There was no rest for us the following day, because the order was to attack Calais. The Canadians had the Germans bottled up in the city, but there were still lots of guns and strongpoints holding up their advance, and they thought perhaps a visit from us might soften them up sufficiently for the attacks to be successful.

Still tired after our long trip to Neuss the previous day, we clambered into our Lancaster in horrible conditions. It was raining heavily and the sky was completely clouded over, ten-tenths and very gloomy. We were expected to find the target and attack from 2,000 feet, a low bombing height which left very little room for error and would be sure to have us at the mercy of anti-aircraft fire. We had already learned the different kinds of flak we could expect. If we were high up, the gunners would fire heavy calibre bursting shells, usually the famous 88mm, which could bring down an aircraft immediately with a direct hit. They threw red hot shrapnel in all directions, which could easily puncture a fuel tank or fatally damage a wing. Worse still was predictive flak, where the guns were centrally controlled by people who would analyse which way you were going and throw up a barrage right in front of you. However if you were making your attack at a lower level you were within range of faster firing guns, such as cannon and machine guns. They would fire tracer rounds, fizzing red as they came towards you to show the gunners how to correct their aim. Because of the target's location, close behind Calais, this particular bombing run would take us right over the port's defences. The Met Officer promised us better conditions over the target, but as I climbed soggily into my seat and looked out through my streaming canopy I couldn't see any signs of improvement. Gritting our teeth, we took off for the relatively short flight, resolving to get the job done quickly. We were agreeably surprised then, when half way over the Channel the miserable cloud suddenly parted as promised and gave us a beautiful view of the sunshine glinting off the rooftops of Calais. Unfortunately it also gave the enemy gunners a clear view of the sunshine glinting off our canopies, and they were more than ready for us. As we started our run-in, making our approach over the Channel, they started firing, and because Calais was such an important site they had a load of guns which all seemed to be aimed at us.

'That doesn't look good, Skip!' came the call from Bill, and I have to say I agreed with him.

It was like going to see the dentist to have a tooth removed; you know it's going to be deeply unpleasant, but 'just do it'... and we did. At 2,000 feet you are sitting ducks for flak gunners, and we had to go right through the curtain of fire flashing up from the port. At night, machine gun and cannon fire is almost beautiful; pretty red tracers arc lazily up from the ground and as long as they don't come near you they make a spectacle like fireworks night. During the day they are far less attractive, but you can still see the red glow of the tracer bullets. What we could never forget, though, was that between each of the vivid red streaks were at least three regular bullets or shells, which could rip us apart if we flew into them. As we approached Calais, we could see red streaks coming up from so many points that it was impossible to count them. Black puffballs stained the sky from the bigger guns. At the back of our minds was also the unsettling thought that if we were unlucky the blast from our own bombs could knock us out of the sky.

We were getting used to it by now though, and Noel was as calm as ever. 'Left a bit, left, steady, lovely ...' as the kite shook from near misses and we again heard the pitter-patter of shrapnel against the fuselage. After an intense few moments, suddenly we were through it. We flashed over the town, and into the countryside beyond, where the target was hidden in some woodland which had been clearly marked on our maps. 'Right, steady, right ... Bombs gone!' Noel was able to watch the fall of the bombs, and said we'd really smashed them up. Good! We were able to route ourselves away from most of the Calais defences on the way back, and were relieved finally to bury ourselves in the all-pervasive cloud on the way home. When we got back, in the rain again, the poor ground crew were left shaking their heads at the number of holes we all had in our kites. Crowther came back on three engines, but Flight Lieutenant Bennett didn't come back at all. None of us had seen what happened to him.

While several of our squadron went back to bomb Calais again over the next few days, it appeared that the enemy was on the verge of defeat; indeed by the end of the month the smoking ruins of the harbourside and town had been taken by the ground troops. My crew and I were rested until orders came once more to head to Germany.

This time we were off to Saarbrucken with more than 500 kites, once more in support of ground operations. Instead of bombing industrial targets, we were to soften up German defences for a push by the Americans on the ground in that area. By smashing up the railway lines and main roads they hoped that we could stop the enemy from bringing supplies and reinforcements through what was an important communications hub.

It must have been an important mission because they asked us to take off in filthy conditions once more, with the lowering clouds closing in on us almost the whole way to the target. We had to bomb low on red and green target flares because of the weather, and we were fortunate that the flak wasn't too intense or accurate. Their searchlights, usually so active and dangerous, seemed to be asleep, and we managed to get to our target of railway yards uninterrupted. Later debriefings showed that we had done a good job, and really 'smashed them up' to help the advance of the US Third Army.

There was more strategic bombing for us two days later. Operation Market Garden, the attempt to push quickly into Germany through Arnhem, had recently reached its tragic conclusion and High Command was worried that the Germans could still mount a counter-attack on our troops. We were sent to a town called Emmerich, which could have been used as a staging post for any enemy operations, not far down the River Waal from Nijmegen. We joined an armada of 340 Lancasters, while at the same time a similar number headed to the nearby town of Kleve. We had been loaded with incendiary bombs, and also carried a huge 'cookie'. That was a cylinder two and a half metres long the shape of a massive oil drum, which carried 3,000 pounds of explosive. It was designed to take out whole factories or streets, and was also known as The Blockbuster.

Take-off was in horrible weather once more, with all of us grumbling about the visibility. We should have known to trust the Met man though, for as we approached the Dutch coast the clouds cleared away again to give us a pretty clear run to our target. It also gave us a clear view of the squadrons of Spitfires and Mustangs which had come along as escorts, giving us a warm sense of protection against marauding fighters. Pathfinders dropped the usual coloured flares, and Red was getting regular updates from the Master Bomb Aimer. 'Go for the red flares away to starboard Skipper. Got them Noel?'

'Got them. Right, Skipper, right. Keep going. That's it. Steady now ...'

'My God, look at the flak!'

There were heavy bursts of it all around us, and it was predictive gunfire, the kind which tracks you across the sky. We flew through several ugly black blots, feeling the turbulence of the explosions shaking our loaded kite, but thankfully our luck held and we got the bombs away without serious incident. The enemy fighters were either on the ground beneath us or deeper in Germany, because we never saw one of them; perhaps our wonderful escort had scared them away. I don't think our squadron lost a single aircraft that day, although four were lost from other units.

On the way back, as we dropped down to about 6,000 feet over the North Sea, I unclipped one side of my mask. 'OK, off oxygen.'

To the inexperienced, that meant that we were below the height where we needed to breathe extra oxygen through our masks and they could be unclipped. To the crewman who had done a few ops though, those few words meant something entirely different; what they actually meant was 'It's time for a fag.'

I kept one side of the mask clipped on so that I could use the intercom easily, took my hands off the steering column, reached for a packet and some matches and prepared for a moment of bliss after the stress of the operation. Of course smoking was forbidden on the aircraft, but we all thought that there were so many other things which could kill us that smoking was in fact a relatively low risk. I settled the cigarette between my lips, struck the match and held it to the tip. Inhaling deeply, I felt the wonderful effects of the smoke calming my frayed nerves. That is until I saw the glow at the end of the fag leap higher and higher in a surge of flame six inches high, singeing my eyebrows.

'Christ, don't light up, the bloody oxygen's still on! Noel, switch the damn thing off will you?!'

'Sorry Skip, just doing it now ...'

A moment later the danger had passed, and we could indulge in relative safety. What a disaster that would have been, to survive flak, fighters, ice and cloud only to be killed by your own cigarette!

While the attacks on Calais, Saarbrucken and Emmerich had clear military objectives, our next attack was to be simply a show of strength to the Germans. It would be my first thousand-bomber raid, the first of three operations by the Allies on the Ruhr on 14 October. Our target was Duisburg, which lies towards the northern end of the Ruhr above

127

Dusseldorf and Cologne. The attack upon it was to be called Operation Hurricane. That name proved well-deserved, as wave upon wave of us flew over and dropped 5,000 tons of bombs during our part of the operation. A second RAF raid later dropped a similar amount. The Americans went to Cologne with their Fortresses too, and raised the total for that day to more than 10,000 tons; a record amount which the authorities say was never surpassed in the war.

The operation passed reasonably well for us. Taking off at first light, we were relieved to find the full cloud cover give way to five-tenths over the target. Our escort of prowling fighters kept the marauding Germans away, and we were delighted to follow their progress as they circled protectively around us. We'd simply been told to bomb the built-up area of the town, which was very easy to spot, being immediately next to the river and a clear intersection with other waterways. It was also on fire, caught as it was in the middle of such an enormous raid. As we approached I could see the first pinpricks of bright orange fires burning, which became more cohesive and widespread as we got closer. Noel in his bomb aiming compartment below me had a clear view of the devastation which we were wreaking, as fearsome explosions decimated the town and sent columns of flame and dust leaping into the sky. Predictive flak came streaking up to meet us, but as usual Brin had done his work well and we were slightly behind most of the main force. With so many targets for the enemy gunners to aim at we were unlikely to be hit, and so it proved. Dropping our bombs on the inferno below, we managed to avoid any collisions with friendly aircraft and headed north away from trouble. Behind us, Duisburg boiled.

As we returned, we could see that other aircraft from the squadron were being bombed up with high explosives and incendiaries. As we debriefed, they were being prepared to go to the same target to complete the work of destruction. They took off at last light, towards the flak and the darkness and the flames, while we roused ourselves from a well deserved rest and headed into town to meet pretty girls at the theatre. It was to be my last operation with 576 Squadron.

CHAPTER NINE

MILES FROM THE PUB

6 25 Squadron, based at Kelstern, had been operational with two flights of Lancasters for a year already, but the powers that be decided that it should be expanded to three flights. Fifteen crews from 576 were to form its backbone. I duly waved my farewells to the comforts of Elsham Wolds, and travelled the few miles across Lincolnshire to my new home. Luckily Steve had been transferred with me, because the sight which greeted us was not designed to raise our morale. Kelstern was virtually the highest point in the county, exposed to wind, rain and fog; and of course we were moving there as the cold hand of autumn reached out across the country. Our accommodation was to be draughty Nissen huts, and worst of all Kelstern had the deservedly miserable reputation of being the RAF base furthest away from any pub.

Steve and I headed for our sleeping quarters, which were essentially a dormitory in a hut with a stove heater in the middle. Fortunately for us we arrived before the other crews, so we were able to bag the beds closest to the stove! We stowed our gear with some chagrin at our straitened circumstances, the only enhancement to the spartan surroundings being our faithful kettle which we conspired to keep topped up with booze.

As we had only just arrived though, the only source of a much-needed drink was the mess. Just a short distance from our hut it stood: another larger Nissen hut, grey and squat with all the allure of a rainy day. Determined to make the best of it, we trudged over to find that you had to climb a few concrete steps to get in through a door, which was usually kept closed to keep the wind out.

Inside, though, things were a little more jolly. On your right was the bar, which was kept well stocked. In the centre of the hut was the most unusual fireplace I have ever seen. The barman told us it had been constructed following the careful instructions of Station Commander Group Captain Donkin who had very particular ideas of what a good fireplace should be like. Four brick-built arches formed a square around a large open space upon which a pile of logs was already burning strongly. Smoke was pouring out of them, and because the door was kept closed the smog was pervading the whole hut. We were assured that 'within an hour or so' of the blaze being first lit, the chimney in the ceiling above would start to draw properly, and the fug would disappear. In the meantime we would have to grin and bear it if we wanted to enjoy a quiet pint. The fire was never allowed to burn down, as 'erks' (aircraftmen) on punishment duties, known as 'jankers', kept it supplied with freshly cut logs. For the first half an hour we found it insufferable, but then after the fire heated up and logs were added one at a time over the evening, the smoke dispersed and we became acclimatised. Our clothes bore a perpetual waft of woodsmoke while we stayed with the squadron.

After a few days Kelstern became less dreary, and we began to regard it as our home. We found the quickest route to the nearest pub, but also found we had transferred to a squadron which liked its 'high jinks'. Young men who risk their lives in desperate bombing raids tend to be all too ready to let off steam, and Kelstern saw some wonderful pranks. I managed to acquire an old motorbike and side car combination, which I kept on the station to get about on. Wing Commander Barker had made me the Flight Adjutant for 'C' flight, even though I was completely hopeless at office work, so it wasn't long before I was given a deputy who took the more complicated duties off me. The motorbike had been one of the perks of the job, and I loved it. The sidecar was a big, old-fashioned affair which took two people sitting side by side and had a bar which swung up and over to hold you inside.

As a challenge, I managed to fit my entire crew on board, all seven of us, in our bulky flying clothing, plus maps, equipment and kettle. It was a dangerous contraption at the best of times, noisy and smelly and very hard to steer properly. But with Clarrie and Bill crammed into the sidecar with Ricky balanced on top, Brin and Noel piled behind me on the seat and Red hanging on God knows where, we arrived at our kite for a training operation in one piece, laughing our heads off.

I was outdone in my motoring endeavours, though, by a pilot who owned an old Austin Seven car. I was outside on my motorbike, and he was ahead of me on the roadway heading towards the mess. As I watched, dumbfounded, he drove straight towards the building without slowing down. Fearing an accident was imminent, I followed closely only to see him drive right up the steps, crash rudely through the door and roll to a stop by the bar. As if nothing had happened, he opened his door.

'Afternoon. Pint, please.'

Not to be outdone, I decided to follow his grand entrance. Turning the motorbike around to get a bit of a run-up, I revved the engine and gave it full throttle for the steps. As I passed the point of no return, there came a sudden dawning realisation that the little Austin Seven was considerably narrower than my motorbike and side car ... sure enough, after clattering up the steps, with an awful splintering sound the machine stopped dead, wedged firmly in the doorway. I followed my inevitable trajectory, and flew head over heels to land on the floor of the bar on my backside looking up at an appreciative audience.

It was incidents like these which helped to make our lives bearable. When you know you might die in just a few hours, life has to be for the living.

Another way to raise your morale, of course, was women. One of our number in the pilot's hut balefully reported to us one day, 'I think I've got mechanised dandruff.' He meant crabs. We ushered him to the medics, who gave him a tube of special ointment. 'This will sort them out,' he was told, 'Squirt a small amount, the size of a sixpence, into your hand, then rub it all over your privates. That will kill 'em off.' Well, we didn't see him for a while after that, and wondered what had become of him. Three days later, Steve and I finally found him in the bar. 'What happened?' we asked. It turned out that instead of using the recommended dose, in his enthusiasm to be rid of the crawling pests he had used most of tube in one go on his nethers. 'The pain, the PAIN,' he said 'It nearly scalded me to death!' As we laughed he explained that he'd been told to repeat the procedure the following day to be sure of killing any newly hatched crabs, and he'd been more careful with his application. The repeated pain in his goolies had almost made him pass out, and he'd been forced to take to his bed. As I wiped away tears of laughter, Steve ribbed him mercilessly. 'You're complaining?! What about the poor bloody crabs?!'

Fifteen of us pilots came to Kelstern from Elsham Wolds. Only five would survive the war, which soon beckoned us once more.

My first mission with the new squadron was on 25 October, and our target was Essen, right in the middle of the German manufacturing heartland. When the briefing officer pulled back the curtain on the operations map, we knew we could expect strong defences, especially around the Krupps steelworks, which were to be a primary target. It was a daylight raid, which meant we couldn't hide from fighters in the darkness, and we would have to rely on a good covering of cloud for disguise. In the event, the attack went fairly smoothly. The defences couldn't see us clearly because of the conditions, and we dropped our loads of high explosives and incendiaries on flares showing through the clouds. Putting the nose down slightly, we headed for home and got back unscathed. It had been another one to tick off, but the next operation was to be anything but routine. It would eventually lead me to Buckingham Palace and an audience with the King.

CHAPTER TEN

THREE ENGINES
AND A LIFE RAFT

2 8 October 1944 dawned unremarkably. The squadron records say the weather was fair with average visibility. We knew it was to be a daylight raid, and we trooped down to the briefing hut after breakfast to hear the worst.

'Right gentlemen, target for today is ...' and the briefing officer removed the curtain over the map board: 'Cologne.'

We all shifted uncomfortably in our seats. Cologne was a well defended industrial city in the southern area of the Rhine, known to us all as 'Happy Valley', which had already taken a battering from Bomber Command over years of war. Its approaches were sown with anti-aircraft batteries and fighter stations. This was to be a two-phase operation we were told, with more than 700 aircraft joining the attack. There were two aiming points: one to the north of the area and one to the south.

'The harbour installations here on the Rhine are a prime target, as are the railway yards here and here, and these power stations. Good luck.'

The Met man told us to expect a fair bit of cloud, which could mean we would have to search for our aiming point, but that was nothing we hadn't experienced before. The most dangerous element was a front of cumulonimbus clouds between us and the target. We were told to climb hard from take-off to get over the top of them, as it is most unwise – in fact downright dangerous – to fly through the violent up-and-down draughts produced by this type of cloud. Clarrie looked a little off-colour, but he assured me that he simply had a mild tummy problem.

We scrambled into the bus after a light lunch, and jumped down next to our Lancaster. After the usual rituals, take off in 'F-Freddie' went smoothly and Brin set us a good course for Cologne through the clouds, hoping to arrive as usual a minute after our expected time. As we crossed the coast aiming for the continent, climbing steadily, Bill spotted the unmistakable anvil-headed shape of the cumulonimbus cloud straight ahead, while we still had a few thousand feet to climb. Entering the cloud the storm began. Violent gusts began to shake the aircraft, rain pelted the cockpit and I had to take violent action to counteract the up-and-down draughts and keep her steady. We climbed hard, the whole kite throbbing with the effort of the engines to haul us out of danger. We were over the worst of it and would soon be breaking through the top when Clarrie's voice came through my earphones.

'Hello Skip, sorry, but I need the bog.' To ask this early in the mission was no doubt due to a) his tummy problem and b) the pressure reduction at 22,000 feet turning an urgent call of nature into a need for immediate action.

'Oh all right. Ricky, keep an eye out will you?'

'OK Skip.'

To get to the Elsan, Clarrie had to point his power-operated turret perfectly backwards, release a catch to open the doors behind him, then slide backwards between them before he could turn and make his way forward. Moments later, an unearthly shriek burst into my earphones.

'Help me! HELP ME!'

'What the hell's going on? Clarrie?'

'Help me! My legs! Help me!'

He sounded like a stuck pig, screaming full blast into our ears in a dreadful sound which was utterly disconcerting. The sound of it terrified me, and I froze for a few moments in confusion. What on earth had happened to him? My first reaction was to get him to be quiet.

'Clarrie, shut up. If you don't turn your bloody intercom off, we won't help you. Ricky can you help him? Noel's on his way.'

134

The two of them had always been good friends, and Noel was as shocked as I was by Clarrie's screams. The lad was only eighteen years old, a child in a dangerous world, and it was very upsetting to hear the terror in his voice. We were nearly through the cloud, but all my attention was needed to counteract the continued shaking. Noel had taken his clip-on oxygen bottle with him as he clambered clumsily past Red and Brin, and over the main spar. It wasn't long before I found out what was wrong.

'Oh no. OK Skip, we've got a problem. The turret wasn't locked open properly, and it's rotated and trapped his legs. He's caught half way out of the turret and screaming his head off. I think his legs are broken. We've got to centralise the turret!' I could hear the emotion in his voice as he tried to free his friend, whose screams still sounded dreadfully in my ears. We were now over enemy territory, miles from both our target and from home, in dangerous cloud and without a rear gunner. I couldn't simply leave Clarrie trapped in the jaws of the rotating turret. It was a moment where I had to think as clearly and coldly as I ever have in my life, and a solution occurred to me which might solve our problems. It would, however, leave us without any defence from our rear gun for a while. It wasn't a difficult decision.

'Right, Bill, I'm going to feather and stop our port outer engine. That's the one which drives power to the rear turret. If we can stop that, the turret will stop trying to turn, and Noel might be able to push it round and free Clarrie's legs. We'll have to do it fast because the coolant might freeze at this height and we'd lose it when we restart. That could start a fire. All right?'

'OK Skip.' His voice was strained.

We had by now reached the top of the storm cloud, nearly at the limits of the Lancaster's operating height. It stretched out for miles in front of us, its bubbling white surface betraying the angry currents of air within. Now was not a time to be losing power, but there wasn't much of a choice.

The throttles for the four engines were grouped together in a cluster by my right hand. I reached for the furthest on the left, and pulled it steadily backwards. As the propeller slowed, we could hear the engine note change compared to the others. The loss in power meant that we couldn't keep climbing, but would start to lose height slowly. I levelled the kite out and adjusted the trim, making it easier to stay on course. It took only a few moments before the engine slowed down and Bill pushed the button to feather the propeller. That rotated the blades along their axis until they faced the direction we were flying and consequently stopped turning. One blade remained pointing upwards like a warning sign. Luckily for us, the Lancaster was a fabulous aircraft which could fly well on three engines.

That complicated procedure over, I realised that the screaming from Clarrie had stopped.

'Noel? What's happening? I've stopped the engine. See if you can rotate the turret by hand. Is he all right?'

'Hello Skip, it's Ricky. Clarrie's passed out because he's lost his oxygen. I think he pulled the tube out of his mask when he got trapped. Noel's trying to turn the turret now.' Nervous moments passed.

'OK Skip, the power's off and I've managed to rotate the turret and free Clarrie. He's not looking good. I'm going to drag him out of here. Ricky, give me a hand.'

Imagining the scenes behind me, I concentrated on keeping the course which Brin had set for us. With only three engines and a full bomb load, we had already started to lose height and were heading slowly but inexorably down towards the storm clouds again. Ricky and Noel, clumsy in their thick suits, struggled to pull the unconscious Clarrie out of his turret at the back of the unsteady aircraft. I tried to hold the kite as steady as I could for them.

'Got him Skip. I'm going to put him on the rest bed and get him back onto oxygen quick.'

'OK.'

We sank lower, and started to feel the stronger shaking of the storm cloud as we brushed the top of it. We would have to get the engine started very soon.

'All right Skip, he's down and on oxygen. I'll make sure he's secure and get back to you.'

'OK Bill,' I said, 'let's get it started again.'

'Unfeathering the prop.' The blades rotated, caught the wind, and the propeller began to turn.

'Throttle up.'

At last we had power again from the engine, which was very welcome, and we began to climb out of the cloud once more.

Above, below, in front of and behind us, all was white.

'Skip, look!'

Noel had come back towards the nose to shovel out some Window, and was pointing out of the cockpit at the newly restarted engine which was emitting volumes of filthy blue smoke. Were we on fire?

'Hell. Throttle OFF!' I closed the throttle fast and stared fixedly at the engine as Bill feathered the prop again. Slowly the stream of smoke tailed off to a thin smear, sucked behind the wing into the great white cloud. I waited a few endless moments.

'All right, let's try again. Throttle UP, unfeather!' I pushed the lever forwards, slowly this time, still watching the propeller, praying for it to catch and spin as the engine fired instead of just whirling in the wind. Gradually it turned faster, the rev counter went up and I could feel the power return. It was working, but then suddenly a plume of smoke erupted from the engine cowling, worse than before and leaving a dirty black ribbon trailing behind us into the all-enveloping cloud. Worse were the flames which started to lick out from under the exhaust stubs.

'Damn, throttle OFF! Bill, standby to use the Graviner, I think we're on fire again.'

The Graviner was a pressurised fire extinguisher built into every engine. When activated it would very quickly smother the engine in foam, and hopefully put out whatever blaze was affecting it. It was a measure of last resort, because the instructions were never to try to restart an engine after using its Graviner. The thinking was that if the engine caught fire again there would be no way to put it out.

The smoke became thicker and the flames continued unabated, and our situation was becoming increasingly threatening. We were losing height through a storm cloud, with a useless burning engine, no rear turret, and no rear gunner. Just do it.

'All right, operate the Graviner.'

Bill pressed the tit, we watched the engine and held our breath. The flow of smoke began to trail off again until finally it stopped. Black oily stains covered the cowling and wing, but at least the fire appeared to be out. I assessed our situation. The buffeting was easing, as we were passing through the cloud to the east of the front. We were still on the right heading but had lost a little time.

'Brin, how are we looking?'

'We're still on course, Skip. If we are to get there, estimate over target in forty-five minutes if we can maintain normal cruising speed.'

I had a decision to make. Did we go to the target – or go home? We had passed over the storm front and would be unable to climb over it to return the way we came on three engines. We could dump the bombs, lose height and return at low level, safely under the cloud. The last option was to carry on. I chose the last option.

'OK everyone. We're going ahead to bomb as planned. Brin, keep us on track. Red, listen out for any change of plan, and Ricky, keep an eye out for fighters.'

'OK, Skip.'

Not one of them expressed any sign of doubt or disagreement. The hours of shared operations had built up such a strong bond of trust and respect between us that they were ready to carry on to our target, crippled as we were, without a murmur of discontent.

'Noel, you can get back into the nose.'

It is a testament to Brin's navigation that we arrived just at the right time over Cologne. Although we had less power because of our missing engine, we were steadily losing height, which gave us a little more speed to compensate. As we arrived over the target we were at 15,000 feet, far lower than the rest of the main force. Flak was shooting up past us and pockmarking the sky with violent black streaks, while bombs were dropping down around us from the aircraft above, although I trusted we would be very unlucky to be hit by one. Getting lined up was a tricky job, because there was a fair bit of cloud around the southern edge of the target.

'Skip, we're getting instructions from the Master Bomber.' Red had been listening in carefully. Forget the southern targets, they're clouded over. Go for the markers to the north.'

'Understood.' said Noel, back in his position in the nose. To the north we could see the plumes of dust, smoke and flame left by previous raiders through breaks in the cloud. 'Left a little, Skip.'

At this lower altitude we were maintaining our height, and I concentrated hard on Noel's voice talking me onto the target. 'OK, OK, steady, steady, BOMBS GONE!' At 160 miles an hour, at one minute past four, we were just two minutes late.

The weary Lancaster leapt as the tons of explosives fell away.

As Brin gave me instructions for getting away as rapidly as possible, Noel checked everything had fallen and the bomb doors were closed properly. We had made it this far, but now we had to get back over occupied Europe, whose defences would be on full alert. It was still broad daylight.

'Right,' I called into the intercom, 'I'm putting the nose down to get low and fast. We want to be under 1,000 feet by the time we reach the cloud, maybe lower if we go over a defended area. Ricky, keep your eyes peeled, and Brin, do your best to keep us out of danger.'

'All right Skip. Don't worry. I'm already planning the safest route to the coast.'

He sounded confident that we could do it, but our return journey was to be every bit as eventful as the journey out.

Thanks to Brin's skill with maps and compass, we managed to avoid not only the enemy defences but also the worst of the storm clouds. Losing height steadily, we headed north below the clouds towards the coast. Villages, woods, railways and roads flashed by beneath our wings, but no fighters or flak threatened us, alone as we were.

'Coast approaching, Skipper.'

Sure enough, there was the tell-tale streak of grey ahead of us on the horizon. I would have seen it earlier if we hadn't been so low, but now we were down to a few hundred feet. Putting the nose down had given us the speed to avoid any defences wanting to fire at a single aircraft, but very little altitude to make any evasive manoeuvres. Still losing height, we streaked for the sea over the green fields of Belgium as fast as our three engines could carry us. Being so low, it would be very difficult for ground defences to spot us and fire before we were over them and away.

My plan was to stay low across the North Sea to make us hard to spot for any marauding fighters looking to take revenge for what had happened in Cologne.

'Looks like we made it, Skip!' Noel called, as we finally flew over a pebble-strewn beach. 'Let's get home and get Clarrie to hospital!'

I needed no second bidding, and I followed Brin's course, which would leave the continent behind and take us directly back to Kelstern. I think we all allowed ourselves a sigh of relief after what had been a very tough few hours. The sea came up to meet us. It wasn't far now, and as dusk began to fall we could see the dark smudge of England in the distance. The tot of rum at the debriefing would be very welcome, and I allowed myself to daydream about it as we settled into our seats, prepared for the last straight leg of our trip. I hoped Clarrie was comfortable.

'Skip, what's that?' It was Noel, down in the nose after checking once more on Clarrie.

'What? What can you see?'

'Down there. On the sea, about two o'clock. Something's floating. Can you see it?'

I peered ahead. The nose of the Lanc came out a long way ahead of my cockpit, and whatever it was could already have disappeared from my view not far ahead.

'About two miles away Skip. There's a bloody life raft with a load of bods in it, look!'

Sure enough, ahead and to my right, I could see a dark grey blob on the lighter grey sea. As we got closer it was plain that it was a life raft, used by aircrew who had ditched from a shot-down aircraft. This one was adrift in the North Sea not far from the Humber Estuary in a choppy swell, and darkness would soon be falling. My guess was that it was a British crew, since few German aircraft made it this close to our shores any more.

'Lets see if they're all right,' I called. I banked steeply to starboard over the life raft, and could see seven men waving at us. Noel saw them too.

'Bloody hell, Skip, what a place to be … can we do anything to help them?'

Well we certainly couldn't pick them up, but I wondered what we could do which might be of some use. Looking around, I spotted a collier about a mile away to the north.

'Right chaps, I think there's a boat north of us. Noel, can you see it?'

'Hang on … yes, I've got it.'

'Right. Noel, you keep an eye on that boat. The rest of you, don't take your eyes off the life raft. I want to be able to go back to it in a moment, all right?'

'Understood, Skip.'

We headed towards the distant boat. It soon took shape; a small collier with a trail of smoke coming from its funnel was steaming north. I guessed it was going to fill up with coal for Battersea Power Station.

'Make sure you can still see that life raft chaps. Red, can you signal this boat to help?'

Red grabbed his Aldis lamp, which was used to flash messages in Morse when we couldn't use the radio. As I circled low over the boat, he flashed the message 'Life raft in water, one mile, bearing 200 degrees'. After a moment the collier began to slow down, the wash from her propellers slackened and the bow wave dropped away. We assumed she would turn and steam to the aid of the dinghy, but suddenly the water churned and she picked up speed again in the direction she had been heading before.

'What are they doing? Don't they understand?'

I guessed they didn't want to stop because they could be very vulnerable without any real armaments to defend themselves with.

'Can you still see the raft?'

'Almost due south, Skip'

'OK, Noel, take us back there.'

'Round you go then, Skip'

I made a sweeping turn, pointing back the way we had come, and thanks to the others' careful observations we were over the life raft of downed airmen again very soon. 'All right. Red, get on the radio. Tell base where we are, and what we can see. I've had an idea. I'm going to fly over them again and switch off our IFF so we show up on the radar as an enemy. It will help them to pinpoint us and find the life raft.'

'I've got it Skip. Sending now.'

He got on air, tapping out the call sign of our aircraft PB536 and explained what was happening as we circled the raft. As soon as he finished, we switched off our IFF. Identification Friend or Foe sent out a signal which would be picked up by our radar operators, telling them that we were a friendly aircraft and not to be attacked. With it off, we would show up as the only enemy plane around, easy to spot and pinpoint on a chart.

We had now been standing by the life raft for half an hour.

'Keep an eye on the fuel, Bill.' He had been watching our gauges ever since we lost the engine, and was keeping a log of the engine revs and boost pressure we were using. From that he could calculate how much longer we could keep flying. 'I know we're only running on three, but we have to get back yet.'

'We're all right for a little longer, Skip.'

We circled the raft again and again, scanning the unfriendly sea for a glimmer of hope for the stranded airmen.

'There, Skip!' shouted Noel, 'Nine o'clock! Lights! They must be ours because they're coming from the coast!' Sure enough, I could see the lights of three boats in the growing murk of the evening.

'Right! Same as before. Noel, get us to those boats, the rest of you keep an eye on the life raft.'

I turned as he told me, and soon we recognised what looked like three

Motor Torpedo Boats, or MTBs. They were ours. 'Red, tell them what's happening.' As he flashed his Aldis light, I circled over them, waggling the wings up and down to make sure I had their attention. Once I was satisfied they had noticed us and got the message, I turned back towards the raft.

'Noel, once we're close, fire a Verey Pistol out of the hatch to mark their position.' It seemed to work. Noel opened his escape hatch and fired a flare, which fizzed out over the sea with a burning red glow. We circled as the boats altered course and headed in the right direction.

'Great! I think they've got it! Well done everyone.'

'Time to go, Skip,' said Bill, as he ran his eyes over the gauges once more.

As the three boats churned their way through the waves behind us, Brin decided to make doubly sure they would find the life raft. He back-plotted the course and distance of the raft from a point he fixed on the coast, passing it to Red to send to Bomber Command HQ before giving me a course to steer for home. My enthusiasm for a tot of rum was now stronger than ever, and I was determined to get us back to enjoy it. Staying low, we headed straight for Kelstern and finally landed at exactly seven o'clock, half an hour later than anyone else. They took Clarrie out carefully, nursing his injured legs as Bill and I went through our post-flight shutdown drill in silence. We had been in the air for five and a half hours.

The rum tasted even better than I'd imagined, and as I took a seat opposite the debriefing officer, I could finally exhale and start to relax. Across the room I could see Steve waiting for me, giving me the thumbs up.

'Welcome back, Skipper. Much to report?'

'Well ...'

A couple of days later I was at the flight office for the morning meeting. The wing commander approached me with his hand outstretched. 'Congratulations, Ken,' he said, handing me an envelope. 'You've been awarded the Distinguished Flying Cross.'

I was amazed. As I opened the envelope, which was addressed to Ken Trent DFC, to find the purple-and-silver-striped ribbon inside, the wing commander filled me in on what had happened. It transpired that the ditched crew had been from a Halifax bomber belonging to 10 Squadron which had been part of another raid on the day we had gone to bomb Cologne.

To their misfortune their port outer engine had failed as they crossed the enemy coast, and I wondered if they had been caught up in the same cumulonimbus as us. The aircraft had started to lose height, so they'd turned back and jettisoned their bombs in the sea, only to find their port inner engine coughing to a standstill too.

With severely restricted power, they'd been lucky enough to ditch the doomed plane into the sea and get into the life raft, which all bombers carried but rarely used. Following our fortunate intervention, HMS *Middleton* had come to their rescue after they had spent more than four hours at sea. The whole crew had been saved.

'Incidentally,' said the wing commander, 'You got some excellent bombing results too. Your photographs showed you absolutely spot on the aiming point. Well done.'

Naturally I couldn't wait to get the DFC ribbon sewn onto my tunic, and as soon as I had a moment to myself I dug out my faithful housewife and did the job as carefully as I could. Later I would receive an invitation to be presented with the cross itself by the King at Buckingham Palace.

I was also very aware that the award was something I shared with my crew. Without their dedication, bravery and skill, 28 October 1944 could have ended very differently.

An East End Boy.... aged about
six months.

My sister Janet and I, left to our
own devices at St Osyth.

Making myself useful with Dad.

Left: Off duty fun in rolled up-trousers, Canada.

Right: Bob Sargeant, myself, Derek Boyer doing the totem pole impression, and unknown friend, Canada.

Our transport into many adventures - the Model T Ford we shared. I am second from left in both pictures.

Mummy, if you could see me now! Sgt Pilot Ken Trent,
complete with newly attached wings. A very proud moment.

My first crew at OTU.
Noel is at the back, in front of him are Brin and Clarrie. I'm in the middle at the front, with Red front right. On the far left is our first flight engineer, who didn't make it to our first operation.

Above: My regular crew.
Left to right: Bill Dunsford, myself, Noel Wadsworth, 'Ricky' Riccomini, Clarrie Dalby, 'Red' Skelton, Brin Reynolds.

Fancy a pint? My great friend and mentor Fl/Lt Jack Stevens DFC DFM, known to all as 'Steve'. This was our favourite pub in Nottingham with the landlord and landlady outside. He liked the place so much he married their daughter!

Steve and his crew.
He is in the middle with his hat on and his hands in his pockets.

Snowed in at Kelstern.

Above: Bomb doors open! We carried various combinations of 'cookies' and smaller bombs on our operations. © *IWM CH 17458*.

Below: Steve and his crew sitting on a cookie.

Above: 'Have you got the lucky kettle?'
A crew bus like this would take us to our kite. © *IWM CH 8781*.

Below: The view over the starboard wing from my position in the cockpit
on a clear day. © *IWM TR 1156*.

We flew this close together at night too sometimes! © *IWM TR 198*.

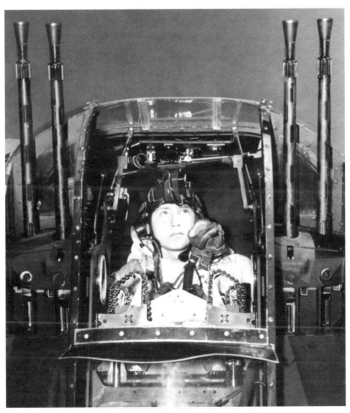

The rear gunner. This was Clarrie & Gremlin's position; cold, lonely and vulnerable. © *IWM CH 12776*.

Gremlin, just as I remember him.

Ricky's position - the mid-upper turret. © *IWM CH 8795*.

Some of the navigator's array of complex machines - Brin was an expert at keeping us on track. © *IWM E(MOS)1436*.

A flight engineer checks his dials and switches - this was Bill's job, from his fold-down seat in front of the hatch to the nose. © *IWM CH 12289*.

The bomb aimer's office in the nose, where Noel would press the button to drop the bombs on our targets. © *IWM CH 12283*.

We could never have flown without our ground crew. Maintenance, fuel, transport, armaments; we needed this many people to service one Lancaster. To them, it was *their* kite. © *IWM CH 15362*.

The big raids on Germany continue. British war plants share with the R.A.F. credit for these giant operations.

THE ATTACK
BEGINS IN THE FACTORY

'Just Do It'. This war time poster shows it just as it was. We had to ignore the flak and searchlights to hit our target as the flames spread beneath us. © IWM PST 14359.

Working on the wonderful
Merlin engines. © *IWM TR 17*.

The cockpit glass was always clean and the guns always
ready to fire. © *IWM TR 188*.

Ready for take off. Here is one of the Lancs I flew, LM227 which survived more than 100 operations. Of the 7,377 Lancs built, only thirty five reached 100 operations or more and I flew three of them!

A Lancaster dropping Window during our attack on Duisburg on October 14th 1944.
© IWM CL 1405.

This wonderful picture was specially commissioned for this book by the Military Gallery.
© The Military Gallery. www.militarygallery.com

drawing by Richard Taylor

Their artist Richard Taylor captured my Lancaster PD116 as it was being prepared for our
raid on the Farge U-Boat base (on 27th March 1945).

The damage caused by our bombs to the Farge submarine pen. Its roof was up to 7 metres thick.
© *IWM CL 2607*.

Bielefeld viaduct after 617 Squadron bombs finally brought it down on 14th March 1945
© *IWM C 5086*.

A Grand Slam dropped by a 617 Lancaster on the Arnsberg Viaduct, 19th March 1945. I was also on this raid and dropped a Tallboy which hit one end of the target. One of the explosions you see in the picture below could be ours! Above: © *IWM CH 15375.*   Below: © *IWM CH 15378.*

A Tallboy ready for loading, similar to the ones I dropped on raids with 617 Squadron and the one that got 'hung up' over Berchtesgaden. © *IWM CH 15363*.

Our raid on Hitler's hideaway at Berchtesgaden. © *IWM C5247*.

How I would have looked in the cockpit flying my Lanc at high altitude.

© IWM CH 8971.

A picture from the same angle showing me at the controls again over 70 years on.

This was in NX 611, 'Just Jane', at the Lincolnshire Aviation Heritage Centre in May 2016.

I can still remember takeoff procedure as if it were yesterday!

Memories....

A visit to Bomber Command Memorial. It was an emotional moment as I remembered my friend Joe Cunliffe, and all the other boys who didn't come home.

Above: The Dambusters 2016 Charity Motorcycle Ride was visiting when we arrived!

Left: Standing beneath The Spire.

Above: More memories at the 617 Squadron Memorial, Woodhall Spa.

Below: 'We Avenge'. In fields at the old entrance to Kelstern.

It was miles to the nearest pub.... an old taxiway at Kelstern today.

Petwood Lodge Hotel. After the bleak winter at Kelstern, it looked like a warm,
welcoming place - at first....

My wife Ann and I have returned many times.
Here we are in 2016 for the 617 Squadron Reunion Dams Dinner.

Above; Relaxing with co-author Chris Stone in the squadron bar at Petwood.

Catching up with an old friend: Johnny Johnson, 'The Last British Dambuster'.

At Petwood with Mary Stopes-Roe, daughter of Barnes Wallis.

Another generation of flyers. Back in the cockpit and telling my story to the Battle of Britain Memorial Flight boys in 2010.

I reckon I could still fly her today.

'Ken, this is Lucy....' After seventy-one years, reunited
with someone who meant so much to me.

Lucy showed me the letter my sister had sent her all those years ago....

So much to catch up on. Walking on the golf course
which was once the Coulton family's farm land.

It took me seventy-one years to come back, but I'm very, very glad that I did.

CHAPTER ELEVEN

WE AVENGE

As well as my decoration, I had received other good news. Clarrie was fast on the mend after a thorough examination showed that his legs had been badly lacerated and bruised by the rotating turret, but not actually broken. He was able to rejoin us in just a few days, and after his misfortunes was always very careful about using our on-board facilities!

There had in fact been very little respite for us after that eventful raid. Just two days later we had taken off at twenty to six in the evening to make a return journey to Cologne. We were one of 900 aircraft to drop our bombs in the dark just after nine o'clock, and we were on the ground again at a quarter past eleven. In contrast to the previous operation, the weather this time was relatively calm, and we bombed onto markers from 19,000 feet. Our journey home was, I'm glad to say, uneventful.

I imagined that Cologne must have been in a shambles after such concentrated attacks, but Bomber Command still wasn't finished with the shattered city. After a good sleep and a full breakfast, the next morning we were called for another briefing.

'Right, gentlemen. I expect most of you know the way to Cologne by now ...'

For the third time that week we took off for the city which was becoming one of the most bombed places in Europe. It was still cloudy, but again we bombed in the dark onto marker flares at about nine o'clock at night, and again we returned safely.

The second of November saw us take off as darkness fell, heading for the city of Dusseldorf. It was another raid with nearly a thousand bombers, aiming for this industrial centre which we had been asked to smash. We dropped our high explosives and incendiaries into what was already an inferno beneath us, in an operation which turned out to be one of the last big attacks on the city. Our squadron records, which were written at the time, say proudly that before the war Dusseldorf had been described as 'one of the handsomest and most flourishing towns of art in Germany'. Now though, we had turned it into a 'city of ugly ruins only.' We certainly gave it a pasting that night, and it had been thoroughly mauled by Bomber Command several times before.

But despite the knowledge that I was destroying countless homes, buildings, schools, churches, museums and offices, not to mention countless lives, I am bound to say that I felt, and continue to feel, no remorse whatsoever about what we did; only that it had been necessary to do it in the first place. If that sounds harsh, and by today's standards it may, you must remember the circumstances under which we were operating.

We were led by Sir Arthur Harris, known to most people as 'Bomber' – but to us as 'Butcher' or 'Butch.' That was an affectionate nickname, because he was the man who gave us the wherewithal to strike back at the monstrous aggression of the Nazis. When they first attacked London, Plymouth, Liverpool and all those other English cities and left them in smoking ruins, he was the one who told us 'They have sown the wind. Now they will reap the whirlwind.' We were all for that. Many of us had lost family or friends in the Blitz, and I had had some lucky escapes myself. Our overwhelming opinion was that they had started it – and we were bloody well going to finish it. I can't tell you how strongly I followed the widely held belief that the only good German was a dead German, and when Harris called up thousand-bomber raids, I only thought it was a shame he didn't have two thousand. Any attack made on Germany was justified as far as we were concerned. This was war; it wasn't a game. Across Europe, men, women and children, Jews, Gypsies and homosexuals were being enslaved, gassed, tortured and burned because of the Nazis; and they had be defeated as quickly as possible using whatever means were at our disposal. They were also a long way down the road towards creating nuclear weapons, and they already had the wherewithal to deliver them. Who can doubt that Hitler would have revelled in the sight of a V-2 rocket with a nuclear warhead heading towards our country? After the war, especially after the bombing raids which destroyed Dresden, Butcher Harris was snubbed by Churchill and many of our other leaders, who found it distasteful that such a beautiful city had been destroyed so late in the war. But people tend to forget that we were *at war*; that Dresden had legitimate targets such as railway marshalling yards, and that Hitler had shown no sign of wanting to capitulate. He had to be shown that we would not relent until he was destroyed, that we would pursue with all due vigour our aim of ridding the world of his tyranny. The motto of our squadron was *We Avenge*.

Gelsenkirchen was the next city to receive our attention, in a daylight raid in quite good weather. We found the target quite easily because smoke was pouring from the industrial area around the Nordstern synthetic oil plant, which we were told was a primary aiming point. Despite some fairly intense flak, Noel got us bang on course and we dropped our bombs to add to the conflagration.

Three days later, on 9 November, they sent us to Wann-Eickel in terrible weather, to attack the oil refinery there. From the moment we took off, there was ten-tenths cloud filling the sky, and we flew much of the way enveloped in a white haze. The cloud went all the way up to 20,000 feet, and Noel had to rely on one of the latest bomb-aiming devices, which identified your position using a system of radio beacons. Mosquitos had dropped some of their usual flares but they'd simply disappeared in the murk. As Noel said, 'Bombs gone!' and I started the turn for home, I heard another cry from Clarrie, 'Oh no, looks like some poor bugger's bought it!' Looking to port, I could see a Lancaster stricken by flak, burning and in serious trouble. We looked for parachutes but saw none, and flew onwards grateful on that it had been them and not us. We had all imagined just how difficult it would be to get out of a spinning Lancaster. Getting out of one when it was sitting on the ground was hard enough, but when it was tumbling through the sky with burning fuel spraying around, it would be hellish trying to clamber over the spars and cables to the nearest exit while feverishly trying to make sure your parachute was clipped on and ready. It was no wonder that so few men ever managed to bail out successfully. I'm very glad I never had to try. We later found that two of our squadron's kites had been lost with all their crew.

The raid on Dortmund on the eleventh was another attempt to hit the enemy's production of synthetic oil. During our briefing, the officers had stressed the point that the Germans had lost a lot of the oilfields they had occupied in the east as the Russians advanced, and were becoming increasingly reliant on synthetics. The Hoesch Benzin plant was our target for that night, and by the time we got there we could see it had already been hit. As well as the usual explosions of our bombs, there was a raging fire right in the middle of our aiming point, which we could see quite clearly through scattered breaks in the cloud. We added our contribution to the blaze, and got back home safely.

Unbeknown to us, when we woke up and went to our breakfast the crews of 617 Squadron, the Dambusters, were fuelling up for their next most important raid: the sinking of the *Tirpitz*. In clear weather they found her in a fjord at Tromsø and dropped huge Tallboy bombs which finally sank her. After months of trying, one of the most dangerous battleships of the war had been sunk by one of the most elite squadrons. When the news came out I felt elated, and also slightly envious. It was splashed all over the newspapers, the radio news bulletins talked about little else, and the dramatic footage on the cinema newsreels made it even more exciting. I resolved to apply to join them when my tour of thirty missions was finished. I didn't find out until I actually joined them that it had been their third attempt!

I wasn't called upon to fly for the next ten days, which was fortunate for me as my birthday fell on the nineteenth. With no operations to worry about the next day, I was free to celebrate in the usual way ... I was now the grand old age of twenty-two.

But the hangover from that party had scarcely faded when we were called for our next operation on the twenty-first. It was to be an important raid because it was Ricky's twentieth operation of his second tour. He'd done one tour of thirty already. When you had done that you were entitled to call it a day and come off operational flying duties, but he'd come back for another tour of twenty. He had already announced his intention to leave us to become an instructor, and reckoned he had well and truly 'done his bit'. For his sake, as much as for the rest of us, we each took an extra long time at the tailwheel before climbing aboard.

Aschaffenburg was the target: a night raid to destroy important railway marshalling yards. The weather was awful, cold and cloudy, and darkness was falling as we climbed to join the stream of bombers headed across the Channel. The temperature dropped steadily, and 'brass monkeys' was the gist of our conversation as I tried to get us above the clouds. Clarrie in the back, with a panel taken out of the glass of his turret to improve visibility, was suffering the most. As we got up towards 20,000 feet I noticed the kite beginning to feel sluggish and the engines struggling to push us any higher. Looking across the wings, I could see the tell-tale glitter of a crust of ice forming across their surface. The pressure dropped steadily the higher we climbed, and the thickening ice was spoiling the carefully formed aerofoil shape of the wings so that the air didn't flow over them properly and give us lift. It built up on the blades of the propellers too, until we stopped climbing and were forced to level out, unable to go any higher. The Lancaster felt tired as I tried to keep it at altitude, like a man with a huge pack on his back trying to climb up a mountain but sinking to his knees with the effort. The weight was building up alarmingly, with layers of frozen water adding to the burden of bombs we were carrying, as the engines strained to turn the ice-laden propellers. Ice had also formed on the control surfaces of the ailerons, making them stiff and hard to move, and there was a risk that their mechanisms could freeze up and go completely rigid. I had been iced up before, but this was far worse than I had ever experienced. If it got too severe, the whole aircraft, with us inside, would be unable to maintain height; if conditions were bad enough we could crash or be forced to ditch in the sea. It had happened to many aircraft before us. I had to do something. 'Chaps, we're getting badly iced. I'm going to take us down to try to get rid of it.'

The most effective way to get rid of the ice was to go lower, where the air was usually warmer and the pressure higher; that would hopefully melt the ice away, provided it warmed enough before you hit the ground. It was, however, a huge gamble. If we descended too fast, the ice could still be frozen on the control surfaces and I might not be able to pull up in time. Too slowly, and the ice could become even thicker. I gritted my teeth once more. Just do it. The altimeter unwound as we dropped through the cloud in a shallow dive. The layers of ice on the wings disturbed the air flow, and the extra speed started shaking the kite as it tried to cope with the unusual stresses being placed upon it. Down, down down, into the all-obscuring darkness, and I found myself wondering what the hell might happen to us. We had coped with flak, fighters and searchlights, but tonight Mother Nature was our worst enemy. For a long time nothing seemed to change as we sank lower and lower. I was beginning to think the gamble may not have paid off, when a loud crash against the fuselage shook the kite and lifted my spirits enormously.

'What was that?' demanded Ricky from back at his gun, no doubt worried that his last mission was going to end in disaster. 'Don't worry,' I said, 'It's just the first ice coming off the props. It's exactly what I wanted to hear!' Sure enough, further crashes and bangs followed as bit by bit the sheets of ice peeled off the propellers in the slipstream and flew backwards, some of them hitting the aircraft as they went. While they sounded alarming, they were the most welcome noises I could possibly hear. The aircraft began to respond to the controls again, and the Merlins started to sing as the weight came off the propellers. We had lost a lot of height though, and I wasn't too keen to climb back up only to have the same problem. We ended up over the target at 13,000 feet, but couldn't see anything because of the total cloud cover. There weren't even any marker flares, so Brin made doubly sure of his navigational calculations before we dropped our bombs. The flak which was coming our way reassured us that we were in the right place, and later reports showed that the target had been hit. On the return journey I couldn't put the nose down too far because we were already relatively low, and I certainly didn't want to climb back up and get iced over again, so we headed back home as quickly as we could at a more steady altitude. The cloud kept us safe from too much harassment, and we were down on the ground at Kelstern by a quarter to ten.

I was sad to lose Ricky, despite the fact that ours had never been a close personal relationship. He was terrific at his job but as a senior officer he was somehow above me; he had already completed one tour and was effectively a pro while I was still an amateur. After we debriefed he shook hands with us all, wished us luck, and that was it. He stayed on in the RAF, and eventually became an air traffic controller.

For our next operation, we had a new mid-upper gunner to replace Ricky, although he only stayed with us a short time. Sergeant Thompson took his place for what was to be a very long flight, all the way to Freiburg near the Swiss Alps. None of us had been there before; indeed it was the first time the city had been bombed by the RAF. There was no oil refinery or weapons industry there, but the city was only a short distance from the Allies advancing on the ground, and they believed the Germans could be gathering there for a counter-attack. Despite being very long, it turned into a reasonably pleasant trip, with wonderful views of the moon glistening off the peaks of the mountains, and little enemy activity.

One novelty for us, and for Brin and Noel in particular, was that we were guided to our target using beams from Oboe which were actually sent from motorised caravans attached to the liberating armies. We finally got back to base shortly before half past eleven, after a seven-hour round trip. As a first mission for our new gunner, it could not have been more straightforward.

Our last mission for that month was to return to Dortmund on a daylight raid. This turned out to be a very unpleasant experience. We had an escort of fighters which managed to keep away any enemy aircraft, but the other defences were particularly strong. We arrived over the burning city shortly after three in the afternoon to find it covered in heavy cloud.

As we made our approach, all hell was let loose in predictive flak. One had the unfortunate impression that even though they couldn't see us, they knew exactly where we were. The site must have been very well defended, as walls of the stuff came flying up at us. 'We're on the right line, Skip.' the navigator told me as we got closer. The flak intensified until the sky was filled with the black puffballs of explosions and our kite was shaken around like a toy. We still had no serious damage, despite the regular rattling scrape of shrapnel on the fuselage. It sounded like someone throwing handfuls of gravel against a metal door, and I'm sure other aircraft were suffering in the same way.

Noel was climbing unsteadily down into the bomb aimer's office to begin the final run-in, the kite was shaking, and suddenly there was a bloody great CRASH, followed by a screaming rush of air into the cockpit. As usual, I didn't have any goggles on and my eyes were instantly streaming, blind in the 200-mile-an-hour wind which was punching through a jagged hole in the screen. The noise had risen to a ferocious, deafening roar.

'Are you all right, Skip?' Bill's voice was loud and tense on the intercom, but despite my streaming eyes I felt fine.

'Yes, yes, I just need some goggles, what's wrong?' I shouted.

'Well, look at your hands!' I managed to wipe my eyes, and did so. The backs of my hands, clenched on the control column, were running red with blood. I never wore gloves unless absolutely necessary, and as a consequence my hands were unprotected. I saw Bill looking at me with a degree of horror, and put my fingers up to my face, only to find that covered in blood too. I must have looked a pretty grim sight, but strangely I was in no pain. I wiped my face and hands as well as I could, and the bleeding seemed to stop fairly quickly. 'This is what it was, Skip.' shouted Bill, and reached down onto the floor of the cockpit where he'd spotted a piece of shrapnel the size of a beer bottle which had blown in through the windscreen right in front of my face. It must have missed me by inches, and the shattered glass had caused hundreds of tiny lacerations on my skin. 'Damn!' he cursed, as he picked it up. It was still red hot from the explosion, which must have been very close to our kite. He dropped it on the floor with a clang.

'Any damage? Red, Clarrie, Brin, Noel?'

'All OK here, Skip.'

'Yes, all well.'

'Coming up on the target, Skip.'

Noel's voice reminded me we still had a job to do, and there didn't seem to be any reason not to do it. 'OK, someone get me some goggles. Noel, talk us in.' His calm voice was in stark contrast to the din of the wind rushing in through the cockpit. His cupola was undamaged. Someone pushed a pair of goggles up to me, and with them on my life suddenly became more bearable. We could see the scattered red, green and yellow flares through the dense clouds of smoke which were belching up from the battered city. 'OK, left a bit, steady, good … bombs gone!'

'Right, let's piss off sharpish!'

I swung us away from the danger zone, and pushed the nose down slightly as usual to try to get us home fast. The journey back was noisy as the wind blasted in at us, but thankfully short and free of enemy activity. We were one of the first back as I intended, but as we came in to our approach, losing height with the runway clearly in sight through the smashed screen, we heard a voice over the intercom. 'Hello tower, this is D-Dog, please clear us for immediate landing, request ambulance on immediate standby, repeat, request permission to land immediately.'

The aircraft belonged to P/O Mattingley, and I was sure that he wouldn't call in an emergency like that without very good reason. Although our kite was a bit smashed up, his need was greater. Pushing the throttles open and easing the stick back, I climbed back up with a roar of the engines, to clear the approach to the runway as fast as possible. We could see his kite approaching just behind us and looking badly shot up, but Clarrie told us he saw it make a safe landing. Then it was our turn as we completed a circuit and lined up once more.

Coming into land was a bit nerve-wracking as you were never sure after being hit by flak if the undercarriage had been damaged. On this occasion, the green light was on and I had to trust that all was as it should be. I approached gingerly and set her down as gently as I could, but all was well and we were very glad finally to get some solid ground beneath our wheels. We piled quickly into the crew bus, squashed in on top of each other, and were happy not to see the smashed-up remains of Mattingley's aircraft, which had already been towed out of the way by a tractor. We found out that both he and his flight engineer had been seriously wounded by the same flak which had got us, but that they had managed to nurse the stricken kite back over England. He'd offered the crew the chance to bail out, but they'd rightly trusted him to get them home safely and as soon as they landed they had been rushed to the hospital. Mattingley was awarded an immediate DFC for 'indomitable spirit, superb captaincy and outstanding devotion to duty'. When we got into base I received some quick first aid, but in fortunate contrast to him I was largely unscathed. My face was probably a real sight for the medical staff, covered as it was with slipstream-smeared dried blood, but after they washed me carefully they could see that my only real injury was a cut above my left eye which has left me with a scar which is still visible today – my only 'war wound'! The poor ground crew though were left scratching their heads at the state of our kite, with the smashed cockpit and various holes. They loved that Lancaster, and regretted every moment it was out of their sight. Typically, they did a wonderful repair job and it was ready to fly again very quickly. It was certainly a lucky kite for us that night.

One of the reasons we didn't want to see the remains of Mattingley's Lancaster, or to go and see him in hospital, was that we didn't want to dwell on the fragility of our aircraft, or consider what could happen to us inside them. We would shy away from reminders of our mortality, happy to have survived and ready to head to the bright lights and pretty girls of the closest pub to forget the fires and noise and fear of the operation. The belongings of dead or badly injured men were always gone by the time we got back.

There were, of course, exceptions. I had some very close friends, the ones who regularly came 'in the car' with myself and Steve, and I would have been anxious to seek them out if they had been injured. We were all very sad when Joe went missing, but as he simply failed to return we had no way of knowing what had happened to him.

One of those who was a 'guest' member of our car club was the wing commander himself, known as Wingco Barker. He was a very posh-sounding, well-educated individual who was actually a bloody good bloke. He wanted to be part of our gang, and once invited us to travel to the pub in his beautiful Lagonda sports car. It was a huge machine with headlamps like searchlights and a wonderfully noisy engine. The only problem was that perched up on the high back seats with the roof down, we were exposed to the full slipstream of the speeding car, which the Wingco threw around the lanes like a racing driver, with us hanging on for dear life. Before joining Bomber Command he had been a fighter pilot. That had given him a different vocabulary to many of us, and I remember him drawling 'Angels twenty-four, old boy' when he was speaking about the height of 24,000 feet. He liked to have an informal relationship with us when appropriate, and it was due to his recommendation that many of our medals were awarded.

Steve, meanwhile, had struck upon another cunning scheme. He belonged to a golf club in Grimsby, and often used to disappear there on his days off. I'm sure the fact that it was also the cheapest place to drink for miles around had some bearing on its popularity, and Steve had a wonderful knack of finding the most cost-effective drinking dens available. Unfortunately, just as he was becoming a proper regular there, the owners decided to sell the land and move on, meaning that the wonderful clubhouse with its stacks of cheap booze would be closing too. We piled into his car and drove down there to find they were having a closing-down party, and were virtually giving away the drinks. Remembering my nefarious doings at school once more, I realised we could make ourselves a tidy sum out of the golf club's generosity. Ordering round after round of doubles, we poured virtually all of them back into empty bottles which were going to be thrown out. Every time one was filled, it was taken outside to the car, and by the end of the night we were well pissed but also had a great stash of nefarious liquor in the back. The journey home was an interesting one, punctuated by smashing sounds from behind us as Steve steered erratically around the dark twisting lanes back to base. We made it in one piece, and most of the booze was still safe too. Our king-sized hangovers the following day were tempered by the thought that we had a great supply which would last for ages, and make us a few quid into the bargain. The only problem came a few weeks later when on one of our regular pub trips someone said, 'Bloody hell Steve, your car stinks!' He was right, the aroma of sour spirits pervaded the car and was becoming most unpleasant. It reminded me of a Canadian livery stable, a place where people would leave their horses while they conducted their business about town. The stench of decades of horse piss as you entered instantly made your eyes sting, and it was not a place where you wanted to loiter any longer than necessary. Lifting up the back seat of Steve's car, we soon found the cause of the smell. While we'd got rid of the glass from the bottles which had been broken on our drunken drive home, the booze they had contained had seeped through the upholstery and formed a putrid puddle below. 'Don't worry,' said Steve, 'I'll sort this out!' Off he went, and came back with a drill. A few noisy seconds later, and the mess dribbled out and onto the road. He was that sort of bloke, ready with a practical solution to any problem. He once told me that when he'd applied to join the RAF, he'd invented all sorts of falsehoods and academic qualifications to put on his form. 'They'll never know,' he said. And, as with so many other things, he was right.

Winter began to bite. December 1944 was cold, especially up at Kelstern, where the wind whipped snow up against the mess and the kites. Erks went out onto the runway with shovels to try to clear it away and I think we may have gone out to help them, freezing without our thick flying gear. One Sunday morning there was a church parade, but the bitter cold and inviting mess fire meant that not a single officer turned up. Orders were pinned to noticeboards. 'You WILL go to the church parade next week ...'

The month's operations began with a long-range attack which should have given me the chance at last to be a real Dam Buster. On 3 December we were detailed to attack the dam at Urft in Germany, south west of Aachen, the idea being that we could cause similar damage to that caused by the attacks by 617 Squadron at the Mohne and Eder. We were told at the briefing to treat it as a normal target, but to be as accurate as possible. This time the aim wasn't to destroy industry, but to disrupt the enemy's plans for defence. If we were successful the dam would be breached, and the Germans wouldn't be able to hold the water back deliberately in order to flood areas where the Americans hoped to advance. It was to be a very early start, so there was no pub trip in Steve's car the night before.

We were awoken first thing in the morning, way before dawn, to find a very cold, wet and miserable day. The dispersal lorry hissed over the tarmac with its wiper blades working hard over the windscreen, and we hunched in the back with not much to say. This was a very long way from the sun-kissed glamour of the Spitfire days of 1940! Rain whipped off the wings of the Lancaster as we made our last-minute checks and paid the tailwheel its traditional honour in the dark, before squelching up the ladder to the chilly cockpit.

At a quarter past seven we were airborne, and settled in for what was to be a long trip across occupied Europe. I was looking forward to attacking a different target, and was confident that my crew could have us bang on course for an accurate drop. A new addition was another mid-upper gunner, Flight Sergeant Arthur. We'd hardly had time to get to know him, but he had already made an impression. He had recently completed a full tour with another crew, been awarded the Distinguished Flying Medal, and had asked to stay on. He was a brave, keen, cheeky little chap, who always had a smile and never seemed to be down in the dumps. He quickly became a welcome fixture in our crew, and his pointy, elf-like features soon got him the nickname Gremlin. (A gremlin was the name engineers gave to the malevolent spirits who interfered with perfectly serviceable aircraft and stopped them from working. They even had a cartoon strip in their honour.)

Ahead of us, the Pathfinder Mosquitos flew on to identify and mark the target with the usual flares, but the weather deteriorated as we crossed the North Sea and we couldn't see too much. 'We're over the coast, Skip,' Brin told me, 'and bang on track I think, but I can't see anything to get a fix on.' The miles droned by, and we shivered despite our thick clothes. It was an unknown target for us, which always caused more nerves; what would the defences be like, would they have predictive flak, was there a fighter base there we didn't know about? 'OK Skip, not far now, Noel, standby.'

Just as we were lining up on what Brin said was an accurate bombing run through the cloud, Red started to get an important signal through. 'Hold on, Skip. Noel, don't drop anything! That was the Master Bomber. They haven't been able to identify the target properly. They want us to abort.' After all that way, to be almost on top of the target and then to be called off! 'Oh, and they want us to take the bombs back with us.' Well, that's just fantastic. Hundreds of miles back over dangerous country with thousands of pounds of high explosives – and then I'd have to land it, fully laden. 'All right, Brin, let's get out of here and back to base. Keep us away from any flak, for goodness sake!'

Landing with a full load was not particularly easy. The extra weight meant your approach speed to the runway had to be slightly faster to avoid a stall, and you had to land as near the beginning of the runway as possible. Once you were on the ground you had to slow down carefully, using the brake lever on the left of the wheel on the control column. Too hard on the brakes and you could overheat them; too easy and the extra weight could push you all the way down the runway to crash into the fence or buildings at the other end. I found the best way was to squeeze the brakes on and off repeatedly, rather than keeping them hard on. If you pancaked your landing and came down too hard, the undercarriage could collapse and the bombs could explode, bringing your flying career to an abrupt, if spectacular, end. By the time we got back, most of the rest of the squadron was already on the tarmac, which was still running with rain. The fields and hedges skimmed past as I watched the altimeter like a hawk. Gently, gently, over the perimeter fence, throttles off, stick back, NOW, and the wheels touched gently down into the puddles. Some cautious braking and we were safe, wheeling around to our hard standing for the armourers to inspect the bombs and make sure they were safe. My attempt at being a dam buster, for the moment, had amounted to nothing.

The following day the weather had improved and aircraft from other squadrons were sent to the dam, to rather better success. They managed to blow chunks out of it, but failed to breach it completely.

It was around this time that I applied to join 617 Squadron. My tour was coming to an end, and I knew I would soon be farmed out to a training wing or desk job. That was not at all what I wanted. My ambition was to take the whole crew with me, to use our skill and experience, to carry on and finish the war. I had no intention of coming off operations until the German war machine had been destroyed, and was thoroughly determined to be 'in at the kill'. This was despite the fact that I had started to exhibit an unsettling symptom of my hours in combat, common to many others who had completed a large number of missions.

Imperceptibly at first, and then more seriously, my hands had begun to shake. I first noticed it as a minor trembling when I tried to hold small objects, but as my tour progressed it escalated to the point where I had to be very careful when raising a glass to my lips for fear of spillage. Gripping the rungs of the ladder into my kite or grasping the control column or throttles brought them under control, but using a knife and fork was becoming a little tricky. Under other circumstances it would have aroused concern among the others, but so many of us were now living on the edge of our nerves that it had become an unremarkable condition. I didn't consider it to be fear, because I still wanted to fly on operations; rather it was a sign of the tension leaving my body through my hands. I did my best to ignore it, and told the rest of my crew that I wanted to go to 617 and take them with me as a fighting unit.

We had a meeting to discuss my plan and unfortunately, though quite understandably, my crew had other ideas. They had 'done their bit' as the saying goes, and made it clear to me that once they had completed their tour they would be calling it a day. All of them, that is, except Gremlin, who was becoming a delightful and dependable member of the team. He was up for more. I found it disappointing and yes, a little painful after the trauma and danger we had faced together, but I respected their decisions. Gremlin and I talked more about it, and I found his enthusiasm so encouraging that I recommended him for a commission, which I was delighted he got.

There was the option of staying on at 625, which had become my home – even if it was rather ramshackle and windswept. The attraction of 617 was too hard to resist, however, after the tales of their daring exploits had made headlines across the world. After the Dams raid, 617 had been THE squadron to join. Then they sank the *Tirpitz*, the pride of the German navy, in a daring daylight attack. They were the Spitfire pilots of Bomber Command, the few among us who were getting lauded and praised for the job they were doing. They were also using innovative new weapons and daring flying techniques, as well as hitting really meaningful targets. I felt that if I could join them I could make a difference to the war, although of course I anticipated that competition would be strong to get a place. I approached Wingco Barker, who approved my request for a transfer, and prepared to wait.

My next trip, to Karlsruhe on 4 December, was really only memorable for it being my first time as a 'second dickie' pilot. This was a system which gave new crews a chance to go on their first mission with an experienced skipper, to give practical help and advice in getting there safely and dropping the bombs accurately. Since I was now considered something of a veteran, I suppose I was an obvious choice. Flying Officer Alexander stood next to me in the cockpit, for what turned out to be a fairly straightforward op. Clarrie, Red and Brin were with us, but the engineer and bomb aimer were also newbies. Alexander moved around the cramped space, sitting down whenever the engineer or bomb aimer changed position. The weather was fine, the Germans were reasonably quiet, and it was a good way to begin for the new crew.

The sixth of December, two days later, saw us take off on a very long trip to Merseburg-Leuna, which was about 500 miles from base over some pretty hotly defended areas of eastern Germany. The boffins told us we were after another synthetic oil plant, and we had time to enjoy some lunch before taking off at about twenty past four. I had my usual crew on this trip, which was most welcome to all of us as this was my twenty-ninth operation. The others were just behind me, and we were all aware that our tour was coming to an end. It would have been most unfair to have come a cropper at this late stage, but a foolish mistake by yours truly nearly brought us to a premature end before we had even left home territory.

Our orders were to take off and head towards Skegness to climb to our operational height over the North Sea. It was a day with a lot of low cloud though, and I was worried about the potential for collisions, as 800 of us from many different squadrons all came up through the murk in the same place. My error was to decide that we would climb on our own, away from the crowd, on a different bearing so as to keep our distance from them. I asked Brin to find us a different route, eased back on the stick, and up we went through the clouds. All was going well until we emerged into the sunshine at about 6,000 feet to come face to face with hordes of Halifax bombers, very close and heading straight towards us. I saw one away to our left and climbing on a direct collision course with us, then another, then another until the sky was streaming with them. There were more than 300, heading off on a raid on the railway yards at Osnabrück. Naturally we hadn't been told about them due to secrecy restrictions. The crew had already spotted the danger.

'Whoa, watch out Skip!'

'Where did they all come from?'

We were flying right into their bomber stream, and were a serious danger to all concerned. What a way to end your penultimate operation, killed in a collision with a friendly aircraft just because you'd disobeyed orders! I had to take very swift evasive action, and wrestle us around so we could avoid them and still get back on our own operation. I took us above them then turned slowly onto the same course as they were following.

'Well, that was a bit of a cock-up. Still, a miss is as good as a mile.

We're OK now. Brin, please would you get us back on track. Next stop Meurseburg, and keep us away from the flak.'

'All right Skip.' I could sense the relief, and cursed my foolishness. I had, by not obeying briefing directions, jeopardised the whole crew on almost our last mission together. If we hadn't emerged from the cloud when we did, we wouldn't have seen them at all. It was a dreadful mistake which but for the grace of God would have meant disaster for us and for some unfortunate Halifax crew. Each group of bombers was given its own climbing space to all join up above the cloud later. I'm sure the hand of God was on us that day.

After that close call, Brin plotted our route with even more care than usual. He slotted us between the flak concentrations around Hamburg and Bremen, north of Hanover and then towards Leipzig. His plotting worked well, and there was no real opposition until we reached our target, which was just before that city. When we started in on our run-through, the Germans let loose with a lot of flak, which came streaking up through the clouds in the dark. Explosions in cloud light up the sky for a long distance, as the burst is diffused through the water vapour. In this instance most of the explosions were happening below us as we had come in at 20,000 feet thanks to Brin, while other Lancs were as low as 15,000 and copping most of the flak. 'All right Skip, we're going for those dripping greens,' said Noel in the nose, 'then we should be bang on. Left a bit, steady …' The dripping greens were the flares which were used in cloud at night, so-named because they hung in the air for a long time, dripping green coloured fire down towards the target. 'Bombs gone … there's the photo, let's go!'

It was a bloody long way back, and I knew we had about four hours of flying to do over an alert Germany. I knew that Brin was well aware of the fact, and wanted to be sure that he got back in one piece so close to the end of his tour, but it was now that a new problem manifested itself. It had been a long time since lunch, and my last cup of tea was reminding me of its presence with an urgency which I could no longer ignore. Usually our last-minute tailwheel routine, coupled with intense activity and nerves kept the urge at bay for the whole operation, but this was just too far. 'I'm sorry Bill, but I'm going to have to take a leak. I'll try and do it in a bottle or something.' I didn't want to make the complicated and smelly journey back to the Elsan. Relieving oneself at 20,000 feet in a cramped cockpit is a very complicated business which I had very little practice in though, and I found it even harder than I had imagined. First I had to undo my dark overalls, to get at the flap of my extra thick quilted flying suit. Burrowing down through the gap in the padding, I found the buttons of my battledress. Pulling them open with some urgency, I now had to find the opening in my long johns, which I managed to do after some contortions in my already uncomfortable seat. What my fumbling fingers finally found was about the size of an acorn, shrunk by nerves and the cold, despite the pressure building up behind it. It was certainly not sizeable enough to extend beyond the layers of cloth and padding, but the need had become too great to ignore. Taking the best aim I could, I let go and closed my eyes. Bliss, for a very short moment.

'Oi, Skip, you're pissing on my throttles!' Bill's cry of anguish cut through my feelings of relief, and I realised my aim hadn't been quite as accurate as I might have wished. 'Sorry Bill ...' but I was in mid flow and couldn't simply turn it off. I lurched to my left, and the unwelcome stream soaked the P4 compass instead. Damn. It was an unpleasant journey home, but at least it kept our minds off the flak ...

The last operation of my first tour came two weeks later on 21 December with an attack on the railway yards at Bonn, a city just south of Cologne.

Brin took great care to route us around Cologne for our final approach towards the target, because we knew there would be a lot of flak coming up from its defences. It was very cloudy again, and at 12,000 feet we couldn't get a clear view of the ground or of the marker flares. We dropped on Brin's best estimate of where the target was, but speaking to other crews afterwards I don't think it was the most accurate raid. The real drama began as we put the nose down and turned for home.

'My God, did you see that?! Clarrie, could you get a shot?'

'No chance, did you see how fast it was going? What the hell is it?'

Having failed to shoot us down with conventional, propeller-driven fighters, the Germans had launched their new jet interceptor, the Messerschmidt 262, and our gunners were stunned. They were much faster than anything else in the sky, and they tore into any bomber foolish enough to poke out of the clouds. Following Steve's advice, Clarrie and Gremlin made the kite vibrate with the recoil of their guns as I pointed us straight into the nearest cover.

'I think we got him Skip! He's on fire! He's on fire!'

But the jet didn't seem to be damaged, apart from the huge plumes of smoke and fire shooting out from either wing. It was just going faster, but fortunately too late to catch us as we got safely into the cloud and Brin directed us home as fast as our Merlins would carry us. The cloud became progressively thicker though, and as we crossed over the Channel the prognosis wasn't good.

'They're telling us that there is ten-tenths at base, very low visibility, unsuitable for landing, Skip. They want us to re-route. Details to follow.' That was annoying, as I always preferred to land at our home base. In fact, if we hadn't had the incident with the Halifaxes on our last trip, I might even have tried it. My foolishness had almost cost us dear once, and I decided that it might be advisable to do as I was told for a change.

Hoping an alternative airfield close to Kelstern might become available, I kept on our existing course with Brin's help.

'OK Skip, should be over the coast now. Other kites have been sent to Ludford Magna or Fiskerton, so we'll probably be sent there too.'

That wouldn't be too bad. Ludford was further west of Kelstern, and not so troubled by fog and bad weather. It also had a system called FIDO installed, which was designed to make it easier to land in these conditions.

Soon our destination was confirmed; we were off to Ludford Magna, and we flew blind over the Lincolnshire countryside, following instructions and guidance from Gee. There were several other aircraft also wanting to land, and Ludford was soon back in touch. 'How much fuel do you have? How much flying time left?' The engineers on every aircraft floundering in the fog had to make a quick calculation. We were then called into a queue, stacked up above the aerodrome at 500-foot intervals, each flying a circuit so that we could land as soon as possible when our turn came. Those with the least fuel were called to land first, then the rest of us descended 500 feet, until it was our turn. The lower we got, the harder we searched for the runway beneath us.

Sure enough, a bright orange glow began to appear through the clouds ahead. FIDO was a very simple, if rather expensive, system of burning fuel to light up an aerodrome's runway. To install it, engineers laid lengths of pipe along the length of the runway at its edges. The pipe had a series of holes in it, and when fuel was pumped along it and ignited, flames lit up the landing area and dispersed some of the fog. As we got closer to Ludford I could see the glow separate into twin lines of fire showing that we were dead on track, and at the right angle of approach. Startling among the darkness and fog, the flames made it appear as if we were landing in one of the burning cities we had left behind us. I took care to align the Lanc's long nose exactly in the centre of the runway, with Noel helping with directions from his turret. The smoke and flames licked up to meet us as I took us slowly down.

The final operation of my tour ended in a careful landing amid fog and flame on an unfamiliar airfield, with relief at having made it back safely.

Clarrie and Gremlin were still talking about the jet fighter as we rode in the bus to debrief. 'I saw it on fire! I'm sure it was burning! I saw the flames ...'

'Did you see how fast it was going though ...'

We talked about them to the intelligence officers, and found that countless other gunners had claimed to have shot down an ME 262. To their regret, it seemed they had nearly all been the victim of a common misunderstanding of the time. The 262's jet engines were hugely powerful but quite new, and every time the pilot opened the taps, flames would shoot out from the exhaust, together with dirty black smoke. What we had hoped was a German in trouble was in fact a German going faster and hoping to kill us!

Unfortunately, as soon as debrief was over, I was given some very unwelcome news – and a railway warrant. An officer took me aside and told me my mother was gravely ill in hospital in London, and I was to go there immediately to be with her. I had time to pull off my thick padded overalls, which I left with Gremlin to take back to Kelstern, but very soon I was in a car to catch the earliest possible train. For the RAF to have arranged my travel at such short notice, and at an unfamiliar aerodrome, surely meant that my mother was very unwell, perhaps even dying. I was still wearing my flying gear and carrying my helmet and other equipment in a bag, which got me some strange looks on the platform as I waited impatiently for the train to arrive. It couldn't come quickly enough, and as soon as it arrived in London I ran as fast as possible to the nearest Tube, clumsy in my padded boots. People were very helpful to me as they could see I was an airman, and really couldn't have done more for me. As the train rattled along, all kinds of thoughts were going through my head. Would I be able to see her, was she critically ill, just what was wrong with her? All these questions made me determined to get to Mum's bedside as soon as possible, and I bounded through the doors of the Woolavington Wing of the Middlesex Hospital.

When I finally found her, thanks to the help of some nurses who could see I was in a bit of a state, she was sitting up in bed, recovering from a major operation. My sister Janet was there too, having been released from her army work in the same way as I had been released from the squadron. Mum had a beaming smile on her face, she was so happy to see us both, and I remember how pleased she was to see me in my uniform. She told me she was fine, just a little unwell, and would soon be on the road to recovery. I wasn't convinced by her cheery disposition though, and while she chatted to Janet I had a conversation with one of the other ladies on the ward who had befriended her. This lady knew the real story, and it was devastating news. Mum had terminal cancer. The doctors had operated to see if there was anything they could do for her, but there wasn't. She was fifty-eight years old, and they had just told her she had about three months left to live.

'But be bright, be chatty, be normal,' this lady said, 'She's so proud of you being a pilot, and so glad to see you. Don't let her see you upset, don't let go.'

That was very hard advice to follow, but I did my best as I spoke to Mum again.

'Where there's life, there's hope,' she said. It was heartbreaking, but I smiled and told her how pleased I was to see her sitting up and getting better.

I left hospital in a daze, and went home to see my dad. Again, I tried to be normal, optimistic and chatty, and slept the night before getting an early train back to base. I couldn't afford to dwell on what was happening to Mum, and I tried to push it from my mind as I needed to concentrate on the rigours of my job. This time, when I arrived at the station, I called an RAF car to take me back to base. I was actually glad to be back in a routine, to have tasks to concentrate on, to take my mind off my sadness.

In the event, I didn't fly for several days after I returned from London. One of the reasons for that was the bad weather which was sweeping across Europe, bringing more snow and icy winds, as well as heavy cloud which made operational flying almost impossible. Ground crew and staff on jankers swept the runways and taxiways clear of snow and ice in case we were needed, and some of us helped out, but for the most part we shivered in our draughty huts and tried to huddle closer to the great fire in the mess.

Hitler had other ideas though, and used the cover of bad weather across Europe to mount his huge counter-attack through the Ardennes. As we slept in our chilly but safe beds in Lincolnshire, thousands of British and American soldiers were dug in and under attack in sub-zero temperatures, making holes in icy ground to protect themselves from the marauding tanks. We couldn't offer any air support because of the conditions, and the tanks ground their way forward with limited opposition. It became known as the Battle of the Bulge, as the Germans pushed a huge gap into the Allied lines and caused many Allied units to retreat in confusion. Still we were powerless.

On Christmas Eve we were told, 'No operations for the next few days, chaps.' The weather was still bad over the Ardennes, and the top brass saw no sign of us being able to intervene there. That suited us, because amid the chaos of war preparations were already underway for our Christmas party.

Come the day, and the draughty old Nissen hut which was our mess was transformed into a nightclub. Spruced up in our best togs, we arrived to find the bar already doing a roaring trade, and guests and colleagues gathered around the 'water feature' which was the centre piece for the evening. It was in fact a life raft full of water, decorated with various bits and bobs, with big plants in pots dotted about it ... and it was obvious to those of us who had been there for a while to what use it would inevitably be put! The squadron padre was already well oiled, propping up the bar and chatting up a couple of local girls whom we knew (by reputation only!) to be prostitutes. I've often wondered since whether he knew, and whether he managed to get his end away. Other pretty local girls were dancing with some of our blokes to the music from a gramophone, and the great fire was blazing away, overloaded with logs and creating a wonderful fug. The atmosphere was very happy, enhanced by the presence of the girls and the realisation that we had survived to celebrate another Christmas. I must confess that my main priority was to get pissed, which I proceeded to do with Steve and my other 'car club' chums. Group Captain Donkin performed his party trick of drinking a pint of beer while standing on his head, and there were various other chaotic games and challenges typical of any group of young, sloshed people. We kept our stomachs lined with some of the food which had been laid out on tables around the edge of the mess, and altogether managed to have a fairly riotous time. I remember picking up one of the enormous pot plants from the 'water feature', marching over to the Group Captain, and saying 'Here you are Groupie, Christmas present!' Unfortunately I was only holding onto it by the stem, and as I held it out to him the pot slipped off and landed with a crash on his foot. He reacted very well considering, even though he had to hobble about for the rest of the evening. We all had the greatest of respect for him, and in fact a couple of times he had defied orders and flown with me on operations under an assumed name so that it wouldn't show up on the flight records. He was a qualified pilot in his early forties, and very much wanted to be part of the action. He had flown with me as my Flight Engineer, and always spoke to me as 'Skipper', never 'Skip'. He wanted to understand what we were going through when we went on operations, and was always very sympathetic to the dangers we faced. It was also quite a compliment to have one's senior officer along for the operation, and made me feel rather special.

The evening wore on and became early morning, the fire blazed and a few blokes had got lucky with the girls they had been chatting up, when we realised the Groupie was no longer with us. Had the drinking and the plant pot been all too much for him? The answer, when it came, was unexpected and rather unwelcome. The gramophone scratched to an abrupt silence to the chagrin of the dancers, and the Groupie's voice cut through the chatter and the noise. He sounded far more sober than he had been an hour or so before.

'Right chaps, I'm sorry but that's it for tonight. The party's off. Ladies, please would you leave the mess immediately and make your way home. All flying personnel to the crew room immediately.'

At first I wondered if this was a joke at our expense, but staff were already ushering the ladies out and putting the main lights on. Feeling just about able to navigate my way to the crew room, I joined the crowd heading that way, grumbling and speculating wildly. Why break up such a successful party? Had we been invaded or attacked, was the war over already? The answer came quickly enough when we had settled unsteadily into our seats. Jugs of coffee were being passed around.

'Right gentlemen, sorry to have cut the party short. We have had instructions from HQ that an operation is imminent. We are on standby to go.' Collective groans greeted his announcement. Surely not. We were all pretty pissed and in no state to think about attacking Germany. What could be so urgent that we had to rush into the air?

'The weather's clearing over the Ardennes. They need us to attack in support of the ground troops. I'll be able to give you more details at briefing in the morning. Now bugger off and get to bed. Alone. If you want more coffee I'll have it laid out in the mess. Goodnight gentlemen.'

Suddenly we were far more sober. For most of my crew it would be their last operation, and it was being forced upon us at very short notice on Christmas night. You can imagine my feelings as I forced down some coffee and trudged off to my bed. Moments later, it seemed, we were being roused to action.

I believe we even missed the traditional breakfast as we plunged under cold showers and threw down some more coffee before heading back to the crew room feeling decidedly rough for briefing. Sure enough, when the curtain was drawn back across the blackboard we saw the target.

'St Vith. The Germans have taken it from the Americans and it's in the way of our counter-attacks. Your job is to get over the town and smash up the German troops and armour holding it. Drop from 10,000 feet.'

At least it was a short trip, just inside Belgium, and hopefully not too much flak. We were also to have an escort of fighters, which was always reassuring, and meant that we could approach and drop from lower than usual.

'Weather has cleared over the target gentlemen, and you should have good conditions in your run-in. Good luck.'

Hangovers dissipating, we headed out for a pre-flight check of the kite and its engines before getting kitted up. Finally, at about one o'clock in the afternoon, we got the order to go. Despite it being our last mission together, there was no banter or joking from the rest of the crew. Apart from feeling rough after the night before, I think they wanted to get up, get the job done, and get back again as quickly as possible. Conditions were much as promised, and we felt reassured at the tell-tale flashes of sunlight from the perspex canopies of our escorts. Sure enough, as we approached the target the fighters peeled off to deal with the enemy aircraft which had been sent to meet us, although the Jerries weren't going to let us bomb undisturbed, and sent a lot of flak up at us as we made our approach. We were quite low, less than 10,000 feet in daylight without too much cloud, and I'm sure the enemy gunners could see us as we opened our bomb doors and prepared to let them have it. For what was to be the last time, Noel's calm voice talked me in to the target, which was already throwing smoke and flames into the sky.

'Left, left, steady, BOMBS GONE!'

A moment on course until the photo flash went off, then we were turning away, heading back home for the last time as a crew. While it was sad that we were breaking up, after going through so much together, I don't think any of us got particularly emotional about it. They had done their jobs, and done them well, and were simply relieved to have come through it in one piece. The sun was setting over our port wing as we flew back over the Channel, marking the end of another day, another operation, and of our time together. By the time we touched down at five o'clock it was dark.

CHAPTER TWELVE

A NEW YEAR

As I awaited news on my transfer, I was kept busy flying 'second dickie' operations with scratch crews who needed to get some experience. The usual procedure would be to take a new pilot up with your established crew, but as mine had all left, with the exception of Gremlin, I took entire crews who were new to the job. That was to prove a risky business, and I missed the coolness and skill of Brin, Bill and the rest very much.

It began on the very first day of the new year, 1 January 1945, and caused the return of the fear which I thought I had left behind me in that sunny country lane months before. New Year celebrations in the mess had been limited, and the day began as normal as I helped the new crew to check over our kite and its engines before repairing to the mess for the traditional fry up. The view out of the window was most discouraging though, as sleet and rain from a glowering sky was driven in by a gusty wind. Flying in these conditions would be dreadful, and I expected ice to cause problems at very low altitude.

Feeling less and less sanguine about the whole affair, we reported to the crew room for briefing. Target Nuremburg, a long flight across the well defended heart of Germany. The weather man had no good news, only doom, gloom, ice, low cloud and everything you didn't want. Surely, I thought, they won't send us out in these conditions. The operation was urgent though, and orders were to get out and get on with the job.

I remember getting dressed in my flying gear with a feeling of mounting dread, which I tried not to show to my novice crew as we were bussed out to our kite in the driving rain. We spent an extra visit to the tailwheel for good luck, rain dripping off the wings and guns as the skin of the aircraft glistened black in the low light.

We got aboard, and over the noise of the rain I heard the crew settling into their positions behind me as we prepared to start the engines. Ground crew looked up at us from outside as they sloshed about arranging chocks and starters. Sitting in my cockpit, with my mask covering much of my face, my fear grew and grew.

For the first time on an operation I felt really frightened, and dreaded what was coming next. I had never experienced fear of what lay ahead in my previous ops, as we were so busy attending all that had to be done before take-off, and then we were in the air and fully occupied. This time it felt different. Still we hadn't had the order to start up, and I remember watching the kite before us through the streaming windscreen to see if its propellers would start to turn. We just waited and waited, until a little green Hillman car came slowly along the line of waiting aircraft. Someone was shouting and gesticulating out of its window, and quickly the message came through: 'Take-off postponed – wait for orders.' A new twist to the tension. The rain battered down on the perspex of the cockpit, drumming with noise and blurring our view of the outside world. The wind shook the kite as it rushed across our great wide wings. I thought of the other airmen in the hundreds of other kites across the country, waiting on their fate like I was. Were they feeling fearful too?

For myself, I was now petrified. It was worse than walking down the lane to Elsham Wolds when I joined my first squadron. The fear came and stayed; I was just sitting there with the frights, on and on for over an hour. It was far worse than being lost in the fog, far worse than being attacked by fighters or flak, far worse than feeling the kite dragged down by layers of ice. I gripped the steering column to stop my hands shaking from the cold and from the fear. The radio stayed silent. Surely we wouldn't take off, surely they didn't need us, surely the weather was too bad. I thought of my mum, I thought of my friends, I thought of Steve, in one of the hulking black aircraft close by. Whatever must my new, inexperienced crew be thinking? I hoped my dismay wasn't apparent to them. Still we waited.

Suddenly, radio silence was broken as my earphones crackled to life. 'Stand down gentlemen. Operation cancelled. Repeat, operation cancelled.' I let out a huge breath, and my grip on the steering column relaxed. I was overcome with relief and tiredness after one of the longest waits I had ever endured. With shaking legs I climbed back down the ladder and onto the bus back to the changing rooms, then headed straight to the mess for a drink. Steve was the first person I saw there, and we drowned our relief with a pint. I told him how frightened I had been.

'I was shit scared too,' he told me. 'Everyone was. Bloody awful weather, we should never have gone out.' It was kind of gratifying to know that I wasn't the only one. The following day, some of our squadron did take off to attack Nuremberg with 500 other kites, and helped to destroy a large part of the town.

On 4 January I was to get airborne for the first time with the same crew. The target was to be Hanover, and the Met Officer informed us at briefing that it should be pretty clear all the way to the target. We were to take off in the dark, and I hoped that the navigator had paid attention to the route we were supposed to take to avoid the flak concentrations around Bremen and Hamburg.

Mercifully, I felt no fear as we ran through our pre-flight checks, and we were soon ready to go.

We lumbered up into the night at about twenty to seven, by which time it had already been dark for a couple of hours.

I explained what we were doing in detail to the second pilot, Flying Officer McPhail, and to the rest of the crew. Fortunately they seemed quite capable, although understandably they were nervous. We crossed the enemy coast at exactly the right point, and slotted through the flak-free corridor just as the briefing had described. Soon we realised that navigation to Hanover would be quite straightforward. From 20,000 feet, on a clear night, we could see the city burning from a hundred miles away. First a red glow suffused the horizon, then as we got closer the brightness of the flames intensified until we could see the hot yellow core of the centre of the city, surrounded by a ring of smaller, less intense fires. We opened our bomb doors, a statement of our intent to add yet more fuel to the inferno. Smoke was pouring up into the sky and creating a haze which was lit by the flash of more explosions, and desultory flak bursts were peppering the sky around us. The bomb aimer, Flight Sergeant Cooney, kept calm as he talked us in to the target, and I was glad the night fighters were staying away. As we flew over the burning heart of Hanover, I heard his voice as the aircraft jumped. 'OK Skipper, that's it, bombs gone.'

As usual I put the nose down as we turned away from the stricken city. I knew that we had done a good job that night, and there could be no doubt that our bombs had found their mark. McPhail went on to fly more successful operations with his crew.

My next mission, on 7 January, couldn't have been more different. It was another scratch crew needing an experienced pilot to go along to oversee their abilities and make sure they were up to the required standard. At the briefing they appeared to be paying attention, and as we took off just after six o'clock in the evening the navigator gave us the right headings for our target: Munich. Unfortunately Munich is a very long way down into Germany, almost into Austria, and we would have to fly close to several cities which we knew had heavy concentrations of flak and fighters. We had been advised at the briefing to go around Essen, Dusseldorf and Cologne, and down between Nuremberg and Frankfurt. It would be nearly a nine-hour round trip, and our fuel tanks were filled right to the top. For a new crew with an inexperienced navigator it was a tall order, especially as the weather quickly became less than welcoming. As the Met Officer had predicted, we were soon in ten-tenths cloud and had to rely on the calculations of the navigator hunched over his table behind us. Compass bearing, airspeed, wind speed, wind direction, altitude, all had to be taken into account when working out where we were. On some occasions we were able to use one of the RAF's direction finding devices such as Gee, but the reliability of that system deteriorated the further away you flew from base. The navigator's timing and direction to the enemy coast was spot on, but the clouds then quickly obscured our view of the ground.

We droned on, trusting the navigator as we were obliged to do. Every now and again his voice would come through my earphones. 'Alter course Skipper, bearing one one two degrees'. As far as I could tell, he was following the directions given to us at the briefing. After about four hours in the air, over enemy territory and in the cloud, we heard 'OK Skipper, twenty minutes to target.'

The bomb aimer had been shovelling Window out of his hatch, and now began to prepare his equipment to drop our load. At about half past ten, the navigator came through again. 'Skipper, we should be coming up onto Munich soon. Ten minutes to target. We could open the bomb doors now. Bearing to target one seven five degrees. One minute behind schedule, just as you asked.'

'Well done, thanks Nav.' I duly adjusted our course, and began to scan the horizon for any signs of activity. There were none. I pulled the lever on my right. 'Bomb doors open.' The bomb aimer was in the nose, preparing to operate his release switches and peering through his sight. 'Coming up on target Skipper,' said the navigator, 'one minute to go.'

I stared ahead into the cloudy darkness, searching for any sight of flares, flak bursts or light from a burning city. Despite my best efforts, all remained inky black cloud as far as the eye could see. The bomb aimer's voice came through. 'This isn't right Skipper. I can't see anything but clouds. Where the hell is Munich?'

'We should be right over it right now,' said the navigator in a plaintive voice, 'Ready to drop our bombs. Can't you see it?'

It was evident even to the bomb aimer's inexperienced eye that we were most certainly not right over it, or perhaps anywhere near it. The total lack of enemy activity, marker flares or signs of bombing meant only one thing. We weren't over Munich, we were lost, 400 miles into Germany, above the cloud and in the dark.

So what does one do in a situation like that? I had never needed to consider the question before. Perhaps I had been fortunate in having Brin as navigator in my previous crew. Always calm, quiet and utterly dependable, he had never failed us on an operation, no matter how bad the conditions. I gritted my teeth and resisted the urge to swear. Shouting or getting angry would not help, and I certainly didn't want to scare the crew by appearing to panic. Stay cool, THINK! The situation could be a lot worse, as we still had plenty of fuel and all engines operational. The first priority would be to get rid of our payload, which hopefully would fall somewhere into Germany.

'Right, bomb aimer, we're probably somewhere close to target. Drop the bombs and we'll work out an easy way home.'

'Understood Skipper … Bombs gone.'

I felt the relief from everyone as the kite lifted, freed from the thousands of pounds of explosives and suddenly more agile as the bomb doors closed.

'Right, Nav,' I called, 'I'm altering course to 300 degrees magnetic. That should take us back over the North Sea eventually, with a bit of luck over the Westerschelde area. Keep trying the Gee box later, we may be able to get a fix from that.'

'OK Skipper. I'm really sorry, I thought we were in the right place, I don't know where I went wrong.'

After thirty-three operations, I was lucky to have had enough experience to make a rough guess of where we may have been and the best way to get us home. Steering just west of a northerly course would, sooner or later, bring us away from Germany, and if necessary we could drop down low to get beneath the cloud and have a look for recognisable landmarks. Until then, with no definite fixes, we would have to stick to that bearing; with the inevitable drawback that our carefully plotted course between all the flak hot spots would be useless. We would just take a straight line home, and hope for the best. In the meantime, the darkness and cloud would be our friend if any night fighters found us. I pushed the nose down slightly to bring us up to well above 200 miles an hour, reminded the gunners to keep an eye out, and settled in for a nervy flight home.

The cloud enveloped us, and it felt very lonely up there, knowing that the nearest friendly aircraft could be hundreds of miles away, and unsure of where we were. The Merlins droned on reassuringly though, and our engineer kept regular checks on our fuel. For the moment, until we reached the coast in a couple of hours, all was as well as it could be under the circumstances.

Bang! Bang! BANG!

Without warning, blossoms of orange fire were bursting all around, and shrapnel rattled off the skin of the aircraft as the explosions shook us. An intense barrage of flak had our range perfectly, and we were getting a pasting. From the cries over the intercom I knew that the others had seen and felt it too, but thank goodness there hadn't been any serious damage. I recognised that we were being attacked by predictive flak, and that there would soon be more on the way for us to fly into. I immediately eased the stick hard over and forward to change course, to avoid the salvo of shells which I knew would be shooting up to intercept us. The anti-aircraft guns were linked together with a kind of computer which calculated how high you were and which direction you were flying in, meaning that they could track your progress across the sky and aim their shells into the airspace into which you would be flying. The only defence was to alter course and height quickly, so that the barrage missed you. If you did that effectively, you could look out of the cockpit into the space which you would have occupied had you stayed on course, and see the explosions go off harmlessly.

I started to weave around the sky, counting the seconds. It takes about twenty seconds for a shell fired from a flak gun to reach 20,000 feet, so you need to change heading and height every ten seconds.

The flashes of the next salvo reached us, but they weren't so close this time, bursting exactly where we would have been if I hadn't taken action. Keep moving. In the meantime, the crew were understandably nervous.

'God, that was close.'

'Shit, there's more coming!'

I needed to reassure them, so I started a bravura commentary on where the next bursts would come. It was a kind of showing off, but also kept me focussed on making sure I went the right way to avoid the attacks. Soon another group of guns, also using predictive technology, joined in and my exertions had to be even more determined. I was also trying to keep us more or less on the bearing for home.

'Going down hard left, watch up there to starboard, five seconds, four, three, two, one ... there they go!' as another series of explosions broke through the clouds.

'Now breaking right and climbing, hold on, watch down there, here they come ... missed us again!'

It was incredibly tiring, hanging in my harness, keeping my eyes all over the sky to spot the next burst while calculating where the following one may be. The Lancaster has a wonderful all-round glass cockpit, and I twisted and turned in my seat to keep the best watch out. We climbed and dived, turned hard in every direction as the explosions came, sometimes close enough to feel the shake of their shock wave and hear the telltale rattle of shrapnel. My adrenaline was firing like hell, and I was sweating into my flying suit as I fought to save the situation.

'Up there, here it comes ... ha, they'll have to try harder than that!'

'Well done Skipper!'

'Going left hard, watch out ...'

More turns, more dives, climbing, pushing and pulling the stick, kicking the rudder pedals with gritted teeth and a pounding heart. As suddenly as it began, the attack stopped and we burrowed into the clouds towards comparative safety, breathing hard into our oxygen masks. I don't know how long it had been, but it certainly felt like an hour. Realistically though, if it had been a large city, it had probably taken no longer than ten or fifteen minutes at the speed we were travelling. Brin would have logged the incident had he been there.

'All right, I think that's it. We aren't home yet though. Nav, keep trying on the Gee box: Gunners, keep your eyes peeled.'

Breathing a little more easily, I got us back onto level flight, on the same heading of 300 degrees. There were signs the weather was improving, and the cloud started to thin out. While that made flying a little easier, it also made us an easier target for any enemy fighters. Fortunately the two gunners seemed to be on the ball. The peace wasn't to last though, and just as we were starting to feel we would be OK, another bout of flak came up to meet us. Once more the kite shook with explosions, and fragments pinged off the wings and fuselage.

'Not again!'

'OK lads, going hard down to starboard ...'

The adrenaline had hardly subsided from the last time, and as I eased the stick forward I automatically started scanning the sky for the next burst. There it was, high up to the left, bingo ... pull back up, over to port a little, *bang*! There's the next one, down to the right, ten seconds, nine, eight, ease it down to the right, hold on lads, *bang*! Missed us again, back up, start the count ... a few breathless minutes later and we emerged unscathed; the attack hadn't been so bad this time. I imagined we had perhaps gone over the edge of the defences rather than through the middle. Still we were in cloud, although it was thinning steadily, and still the navigator didn't know where we were. I settled back onto 300 degrees.

'Everyone all right?' Their relieved replies assured me that all was well.

'Engineer, any damage?'

'Don't think so, Skip. Fuel is still good, no signs of any leaks. I think we're OK.'

'Right, keep your eyes out chaps, any sign of land, any landmarks, anything you can get a fix on. Nav, any luck with Gee?'

'Nothing Skipper, sorry.'

'All right, keep trying. We're going in the right direction so you might get something soon.'

As we went on we were gradually losing height as I kept the stick ever so slightly forward to give us the extra speed. It was well after midnight when, peering through the perspex, I noticed the cloud was becoming patchy beneath us until suddenly it parted to give us a clear view of land. Bingo! From a combination of experience and good luck I recognised the rocky peninsula on the southern edge of the North Sea.

'Nav, that's the Westerschelde just approaching. We'll be over the sea in a minute. Changing course to three ten degrees. Can you get us a fix yet for Kelstern?'

Behind me, he fiddled once more with the dials on his equipment.

'I think so Skipper. Yes, we're getting something now, it's easier now I know where we are …'

In moments we had the right course, and dropped lower across the sea as we mercifully left the flak behind. Landing was an anticlimax and we were the second kite home, well before most of the others. We touched down at seventeen minutes to three in the morning. The mood on the bus back to debriefing was subdued, as we all realised how lucky we had been. When I spoke to some of the other crews I realised we weren't the only ones who had run into trouble, as there had been a lot of fighters over the target to greet those who had actually made it there.

As for us, I guessed that the first flak barrage could have been from the defences around Stuttgart, and the next from the edge of a town in the Ruhr, further north in Germany. It was the first time I had been in such an exposed position, and, I hoped, the last.

I had to report our unhappy experience to Wing Commander Barker, because the crew, in particular the navigator, simply hadn't been up to scratch. They disappeared in short order.

By some strange quirk of fate I met the pilot of that crew many years later in Jersey. He remembered the incident, and told me they had all been posted to another squadron after some extra training, apart from the navigator. They had continued operations successfully, and all survived the war.

I was understandably nervous about my next mission, which was to be another 'second dickie'. Usually one would take a new pilot with an existing, experienced crew, but again this time I had a kite full of newbies apart from Gremlin in the rear turret. They were Canadians, which reminded me once more of my time with family in that country.

Fortunately, their first op proved to be fairly straightforward, despite some low cloud. We set off just after seven in the evening heading for Leuna, and by the time the navigator, Fl Lt Jones, said we should be coming onto the target we could already see the red glow in the sky from markers and the burning oil plant which was being attacked. We had a straightforward drop from 20,000 feet just before midnight, and headed back without too much opposition. Later intelligence reports showed that we had severely damaged the plant, and in fact after the war Albert Speer (Hitler's armaments and production minister) said it was one of the most damaging oil production raids his country had suffered, so it was a great success all round.

News of a bigger success was soon to follow. I was notified that my application for a transfer to 617 Squadron had gone through. I had been deemed sufficiently experienced to join the most famous squadron in the country, and you bet I was excited about it! My posting was scheduled for the middle of February, and I had one more operation to do with 625 before taking some leave and preparing to take on a new challenge.

I was determined to get this mission on 1 February over with as safely and as efficiently as possible, even though it was another with a scratch crew of inexperienced airmen. Take-off was late in the afternoon, and we had time for a proper breakfast before checking the kite and all its systems. Briefing officers told us our target as Ludwigshafen, a town on the Rhine with important railway yards and bridges. We were airborne at five to four, and the crew were effective and reliable as we headed off with the setting winter sun away across our starboard wing. As instructed, we approached at 16,000 feet and again found the target was visible from miles away as a red glow which quickly grew to a bubbling cauldron of flames. The novice bomb aimer talked me in without any fuss, and we did our bit to add to the destruction. The defences were very thin on the ground, and my last journey home with 625 Squadron was a simple one. Others weren't so lucky, and fifty-six airmen from various squadrons didn't come back.

Before my posting to 617, I had a period of leave, which I of course used to visit my family in London.

On my return to the squadron, I was preparing for my move to 617. Due to my imminent departure, I missed out on two raids which were important for different reasons. On the night of 13 February the squadron took off into the dark loaded with high explosives and incendiaries to take part in one of the most intensive attacks of the war. Operation Thunderclap was the mission to flatten Dresden.

That night 800 Lancs took off from England, and the devastation they caused was such that Churchill tried to distance himself from it after the war. My pal Steve was one of the pilots, so was Joe Cunliffe; a couple of the new crews I had taken on 'second dickie' flights were part of the operation too. They all completed their missions successfully, and landed back at base leaving a terrible firestorm raging behind them. As daylight revealed the devastation, more than 300 American bombers went to the city to finish the job. Dresden was completely ruined – a warning to the Germans to surrender or they would get more of the same. I was sorry after the war to hear so many people decrying the attack. To my mind it was a legitimate target, with the aim of killing Germans and destroying their transport and production centres. I'm also sure that if they had managed to complete the atomic bomb, which they were very close to achieving, they wouldn't have hesitated in using it on us. That said, I am glad that I didn't have to go on the raid and destroy all those lovely buildings.

The following day, 14 February, after their nine-hour round trip to Dresden, the squadron was sent into the air again, this time to Chemnitz to the east. It was a continuation of Operation Thunderclap, although Bomber Command didn't consider it to have been as successful.

Only one squadron aircraft failed to return that night. It was Joe's. He was flying with the same crew which I had taken to Ludwigshafen. The squadron records say there had been no news of him after take-off, and that he simply 'failed to return'.

Four days later I was posted to 617 Squadron.

CHAPTER THIRTEEN

DAMBUSTER

Leaving 625 was a day of mixed emotions. Its draughty, windswept huts had been my home for several months, and I had longed to see its welcoming runway lights at the end of many missions. The atmosphere was wonderful, with supportive and encouraging senior officers, a great mess and of course my comrades. It was going to be particularly hard to leave Steve, my mentor and now great friend who had taught me how to stay safe in the sky and have fun on the ground. From now on, there would be no drinking partner, no front seats in the theatre eying up the ladies in the chorus. This was war, and, as with the loss of Joe Cunliffe, we had to move on like ships passing in the night. It was a hard parting though, as we had shared so much together over the past few months. We shook hands before I headed to the car which would take me and Gremlin to the station.

In the train on the way we talked mainly about the challenge ahead. We wondered who would join us in our crew. The two of us had never really socialised, and there was certainly none of the debate over girls and beer I had shared with Steve on similar journeys.

There was to be no walking with a kitbag on my shoulder this time, and we were met at the Woodhall Spa station by an RAF driver in the ubiquitous green Hillman 10 saloon car. Woodhall Spa was a small, well kept village and I was pleased to see a couple of pubs. On the short drive down a straight, tree-lined road conversation fell away, and I found myself reflecting on what I had let myself in for. I was excited to be joining the most famous squadron in the RAF, the best there was, the equivalent of the Spitfire pilots I had so admired five years before. After all the near misses and dangerous missions I had completed I was confident that I could live up to the task, and looked forward to some interesting raids. 617 was, after all, an outfit which had built its reputation on pinpoint accuracy attacking essential targets. After the Dams and *Tirpitz* raid, it was for me simply THE place to be.

My anticipation seemed to be confirmed as the car turned left and swept through the gates. I had left behind a dreary, exposed hillside base, miles from the nearest pub, where having a comfortable night's sleep meant putting your bed as close as you dared to the fire without actually setting light to yourself. Here I was greeted by a valley of rhododendrons which opened out to reveal a magnificent, sprawling, mock Tudor building with white walls studded with black beams. A wide terrace looked out over thirty acres of beautifully kept gardens. The driver told us how it had been built by a wealthy heiress during a painful divorce. She had wanted a country retreat where she could enjoy the company of her animals – hence the name Petwood Lodge. The whole place radiated a traditional, old-fashioned, comfy feeling. As the house had been expanded, the great and the good had come to visit. King George VI was a keen tennis player and had enjoyed the courts there; Lady Mountbatten was a firm admirer, and other aristocrats found it a perfect site for a getaway. In a link to early aviation, the Marquis of Douglas and Clydesdale, who had flown over Everest, once landed his private plane in the grounds. We felt as though we had moved from the workhouse to the Ritz.

A batman hurried to take our bags as we stepped under the carved stone archway into the dark and ornate entrance hall. Tudor and Jacobean styles met, with a carved oak staircase and panelling, and sumptuous, deep-red decor. Doors led off right, left and centre, down intriguing corridors and stairways.

'This way, please Sir. Sir.' said the batman, lugging our gear up the staircase towards our room. Gremlin, now an officer, was to be sharing with me. After some twists and turns, we arrived. As the batman bowed out and the door closed quietly behind us, we looked first at the comfortable beds and tasteful furnishings, then at each other.

'Not bad in 'ere, is it Skip?'

He was right. So far my 617 Squadron dream was being entirely fulfilled.

We unpacked, and decided on a drink in the bar to meet some fellow officers. I slid my hand down the polished wood of the staircase as we went down, feeling like the lord of a well appointed manor house as my feet sank into the carpet. Turning left at the bottom of the stairs, we followed a murmur of voices down one of the corridors, and came to the mess bar. It was a small, dark, wood-panelled room which extended away to our left, with the bar further down on the opposite side. A fire burned in the grate on our right. Opposite us a noticeboard was fixed to the panelling, with details of raids and photographs of successes. A broad window at the far end let in some natural light, which was enough to illuminate a large tree branch tied above the bar counter. Apparently it had come through the nose of one of the squadron's aircraft when it was flying very low indeed, but everyone had lived to tell the tale and now showed off the branch as evidence of their lucky escape. A few officers were sitting on the bar stools or standing up chatting as we entered, ready to make friends. At 625, whenever a new chap turned up, he would be greeted at the mess with smiles, handshakes and a pint. I fondly recalled Steve's friendliness to me when I first arrived, shaking with nerves, at 576.

But as Gremlin and I walked in, smiling, expecting a similarly warm welcome from the six or seven officers there, to a man they ignored us. Turning their backs with indifference, continuing their conversations without giving us a second glance, they gave us the complete cold shoulder in a way calculated to cut us to the quick. These men, whom we regarded as famous heroes, didn't want to know us at all. If Steve had been there I'm sure he would have tried harder to strike up a conversation, but we were too unsure of ourselves. Perhaps, we thought, we had better keep quiet until we had proved ourselves in this elevated arena. I wasn't to know at that point that most of the pilots and crew who had taken part in the legendary Dams and *Tirpitz* raids had either left or been killed, and the squadron was made up largely of replacements. As I sipped a subdued beer, I felt a chill which never truly left me for my whole time in the squadron. Beer finished, I saw there was no immediate need for my presence on the station that afternoon, and resolved to go for a walk to clear my head and perhaps become acquainted with the surroundings.

In fact, I didn't walk very far from the base that day or any day in the future, and it was a decision which changed my life. Turning right out of the Petwood main gate, then right at the first junction, I found myself wandering up a road lined with low, well kept hedges bordering farming land. It wasn't long until I came across a grassy track on the right leading up to a farm. As a city boy I was curious, and headed up through the white gate to see what might be going on. Ahead of me I could see the farmer's cottage on the right with a cowshed on the left, and beyond that a large pond. A chap with his back to me was filling two enormous wooden buckets with water from the pond, and I watched as he hooked them onto either end of a yoke before balancing them across his back. The yoke sat over his neck and shoulders, spreading the strain and allowing him to carry the heavy load quite easily. I'd seen contraptions like this in picture books, but never in reality.

'Hello,' I said, 'could I have a go on that?' I was keen to try out this novel arrangement. Before I knew it I was helping to water the cows, while the farmer's wife began the process of milking them. His name was Mr Coulton, but he told me to call him Bob; his wife Lucy was known universally as Mrs C. After a short while we were joined by their two daughters, Lucy and Joyce, arriving home from school, trailing after them their pet pig on a short piece of rope. They were astonished to see a uniformed RAF officer from the very upmarket officer's mess next door with a yoke around his neck watering their cattle! They weren't shy at all, but had plenty of questions for me.

In due course the milking was done, and I was invited in for a cup of tea. We entered the cottage straight into the main room. On the right hand was a door into a large pantry; on the left a door which I believe led to a staircase. The main feature on the left was a very large fireplace, which held a black kettle on a stand which swivelled. Mrs C pushed it, swivelling it into the fire to bring the water to the boil. A large table and a doorway to the kitchen completed the room.

As we drank our tea I got to know my hosts a little better. Bob was a little taller than his wife, at about five feet eleven: stocky and strong as befits a farmer, without carrying too much weight. He would never be known as a man of letters, but he was a man with much knowledge who was bright and capable enough to create a good living for his family and who, with his wife, had produced a warm, loving home. Mrs C was tall and slim, with the telltale hands of a lady who assisted with the many farm chores that helped to keep the wolf from the door.

I lingered with them, drinking tea in the kitchen, playing with the children, and laughing at their antics with the pet pig. As I waved goodbye that evening, with an open invitation to return, I realised I had inadvertently stumbled upon a warmth and humanity I had been missing. Petwood felt cold by comparison, despite the opulence of my surroundings.

The following morning it was time to discover who would make up the remainder of our crew. After a full but cheerless breakfast, Gremlin and I boarded the bus which would take us to the crew room. Petwood was a little distance from the airfield itself, and it was a longer drive than we were used to. We tried, without much success, to make small talk with the other chaps on board.

Once in the crew room, we found that our crew had already been allocated. Unlike my first squadron when we had a chance to meet lots of individuals and size them up before making a decision, the powers that be had already made it for us. Just like at school when you wanted to see if your name was on the team sheet for the football match, we looked at the lists stuck up on the noticeboard. Flight Sgt Johnson W (Bill), Flying Officer Richardson WS, Flight Lt John Rumgay, Flying Officer Slater J, and Sgt Farino H were to be the people who would be relying on me for my piloting skills. I, of course, would be relying on them to tell me where we were going and to make sure we got there and back in one piece. They were all experts and had many sorties behind them, and Flight Lt Rumgay was actually the bombing leader for the squadron.

He was tall and good looking with a shock of brown hair, a bit full of himself due to his exalted position, and rather difficult to control, but nonetheless an excellent bomb aimer. Bill Johnson was a quiet, efficient flight engineer of medium height and pleasant disposition. Flying Officer Richardson was a small chap with fair hair – a wiry type with a lot of experience who was good to have aboard. Gremlin was as keen to meet them as I was. We managed to pick each other out among the seventy or so guys milling around in the hut, and made brief acquaintance over a coffee before getting our briefing orders for the day.

'Proceed to Wainfleet Sands ...'

We had to learn the art of dropping single bombs on pinpoint targets. When bombing a city you might be loaded with a dozen or more bombs which were to be dropped in an area which could be several acres in size. 617's speciality was to drop single, very powerful, bombs onto individual targets such as bridges, battleships and dams.

For the next two weeks we were kept busy in the air as we flew mission after mission to the RAF bombing range at Wainfleet, where I had first learned my trade with the old crew. This time though, we were expected to demonstrate much greater accuracy. Starting with individual ten-pound bombs, we flew in towards the targets at low level, using our new-style bombsight to help.

In order to achieve the accuracy required, there were some important differences in our manner of approach to the target. For the sight to work correctly, it was essential to maintain a straight and level course for ten minutes on the final run-in. We were given careful lectures on the new Stabilised Automatic Bomb Sight, or SABS, which promised to drop our explosives right on the button if used correctly. Preparation began about twenty minutes before we were over the target. The bomb aimer and navigator used compasses and landmarks on the ground to work out which way the wind was blowing, and how fast it was. Sometimes even the rear gunner got involved, sighting landmarks running along the barrels of his guns. As they were calibrated to 360', he was able to pass the degree of drift to the navigator. This was a complicated procedure known as getting a 'three drift wind'. For the bomb to fall correctly, the right wind details had to be fed into a box attached to the sight. It also automatically took note of our altitude and airspeed. We knew it as the 'magic box', and it controlled the movement of the sight and when the bomb was released.

The visual part of the sight was a piece of glass about three inches wide and eight inches long, attached to a box in the front of the bomb aimer's nose compartment. A cross in the shape of a sword was projected onto it, with the blade of the sword pointing in the direction in which we were flying. When we saw the target ahead, the bomb aimer would switch on the light to illuminate the sword. He would then call, 'left, left, steady …' to direct the kite so that the target lined up with the end of the sword blade. As a result of the information about wind we had put into the magic box, plus the details it was receiving about our airspeed and altitude, the target should run right along the blade towards the hilt of the sword. When it reached the hilt, the bomb aimer pushed a button and called 'bombsight on'. Immediately, the glass of the sight started to tilt forward so that the target remained in the centre of the hilt, and when it reached a certain angle of tilt it automatically tripped the bomb release mechanism.

It all sounds very good, and no doubt managed to get our bombs much closer to the target, but the cost was that we had to maintain that straight and level course for ten minutes to make it work. That of course would make us a far easier target for anti-aircraft guns, and sitting ducks for any marauding fighters. Nonetheless, aided by my crew's considerable expertise, I was enthusiastic about the chance to use new technology to attack the Germans and challenge my own skills. It was also encouraging to think that the RAF had sufficient confidence in my abilities to trust me with what was then top secret and very expensive equipment, and I finally felt as though the long, frustrating hours in the air above the plains of Canada were truly paying off. I tried my very best to get things right, enjoying the challenge without putting too much pressure or expectation on myself, as pressure leads to stress which leads to errors. They constantly evaluated our bombing at Wainfleet, and checked where our bombs landed. Flying Officer Richardson was very exacting, as he was already experienced and knew the drill. We were required to have a margin of error of about twenty-five yards.

The meticulous nature of our training was hard but it quickly began to pay dividends. Within two weeks we had tightened up to the extent that we could be reasonably confident of dropping a full size bomb in exactly the right place for the maximum effect, which was just what they had in mind for my first mission on 9 March.

First though, I had to get used to a new aircraft. The Lancaster was a wonderful kite, as I have described, but the new version we were to use was quite different. For a start, it was a different shape. I remember first seeing the modified Lancaster on the apron, next to our conventional Lancs, and wondering where the mid-upper turret was. In the place of its usual protruding glass blister with twin machine guns, was simply a smooth continuation of the fuselage. There were no bomb doors, which had been removed to allow the fitting of the huge bombs we were to carry. Indeed, all of the fixtures and fittings of the bomb bay had been taken away to give a smooth, empty space beneath the fuselage. Inside, I found that the armour plating which was meant to protect me and the crew from shrapnel and bullets had been removed. I didn't mind that particularly, as I always believed that if you were going to get hit then you were going to get hit, and the armour was purely an attempt to make you feel better about your chances. A lot of the radio equipment had been taken out too, and we rarely flew with a wireless operator because the advent of VHS radios had made it far easier to talk to base over much longer distances. The engines had also been upgraded, to Merlin 24s with paddle bladed props, to give us more speed and power. Also very noticeable was that all of 617's Lancasters looked NEW! Compared to our old kites at Kelstern which had been patched up, dented and scratched, these were in lovely condition with no holes. One by one, they were converted into the new, powered up and stripped down Lancaster designed for our particular operations.

The result was a joy to fly. The loss of hundreds of pounds in weight, the smoother fuselage due to the missing turret, and the extra power from the engines turned the Lanc into a faster, more manoeuvrable kite which was at the cutting edge of bomber technology. That was, of course, until it was loaded with one of the monstrous bombs which it was designed to carry. The Tallboy was designed by the explosives genius Barnes Wallis, who had designed the famous bouncing bomb which had proved so successful on the Dams raid. It was twenty-one feet long, nearly filling the bomb bay, and weighed nearly five and a half tons or 12,000 pounds. It had a thick steel case filled with two and a half tons of an explosive called Torpex, which was hugely powerful. It had been designed to crack particularly hard targets such as bunkers and armoured battleships, where traditional bombs might simply bounce off. The idea was that they would fall in a very accurate arc when they were released, due to their aerodynamic shape and the fins on their tails which caused them to spin as they dropped.

When they hit the target, their hard, pointed case would plunge through steel, concrete or earth, before exploding well below the surface to cause maximum damage. They were known as 'earthquake bombs'. These were the brutes which had been dropped by the squadron on the *Tirpitz* to such great success and acclaim, and had also been used against U-boat bases and V-weapon launch sites. It was the most powerful conventional bomb in existence, although little did we know that its successor was waiting in the wings. Unfortunately their cost was in proportion to their power and availability, and we were under strict orders to return with our bombs if we couldn't get a clear run at the target. As a precision weapon, one couldn't simply drop them in approximately the right place; clear weather and a straight run-in were essential. We practised and practised until we were deemed to have reached the necessary proficiency, and then, with little warning, on 9 March the first mission was upon us.

It began in a very similar fashion to those I had undertaken at 576 and 625. The pre-operation drill was a full breakfast of bacon and eggs before we were called to briefing. We had details of the weather, which they hoped would be clear, possible flak concentrations and fighter stations, and the course to steer. The Squadron Commander, Group Captain Fauquier, would be flying with us. He was the one who drew back the curtain over the board to show us our target; the viaduct at Bielefeld. It wasn't a distant target, lying halfway between Münster and Hanover, but we could expect strong defences because it was a vital link between the production centres of the Ruhr and north-east Germany. The RAF had already tried to destroy it he said, and was hoping that our Tallboys might finally do the job. I studied the maps and technical details carefully in order to familiarise myself with the target, while the rest of the crew concerned themselves with their own preparations.

Bielefeld viaduct was a vast and impressive feat of engineering, and was in fact two viaducts built next to each other seventy years apart. Each carried a twin track railway line, one traditionally used for passengers and the other for freight, hundreds of yards over a valley. They were of great strategic importance because if the line could be cut there, it would force supplies heading from the factories to the front to take a far more circuitous route.

Until that morning I had received very little attention from the man who led us, but my impression so far was not favourable. Fauquier was Canadian, with a brusque, almost rude manner, who seemed anxious to make a name for himself in the same way that Guy Gibson had done after he had led the Dams attack. He had little time for his subordinates and made no effort to inspire any kind of loyalty or affection in us; he simply expected us to defer to him and do our duty.

His words at the briefing were exciting to me though, and it was plain that the viaduct was exactly the kind of target we had prepared for, which gave me a feeling of excitement and anticipation as we went through the usual pre-flight checks. Our Lanc was yet to be converted, and it would have to operate at the very top of its ability. Just twenty of us were taking off that day, for a raid on a far smaller scale than those I was used to. Compared with the thousand-bomber raids I had been on before, there was far less chance of a collision. We queued up on the tarmac, the powerful engines making the kite shake as we opened the throttles when the green light flashed at the controllers hut. The Merlins roared in protest at the heavy load of our Tallboy, but the tail came up and we were airborne without too much trouble, just before twenty to three in the afternoon.

'Climb to 10,000 feet, Skipper, heading 120 degrees,' came the navigator's voice. Up we went, lugging the weight of our load towards the meeting point where our force would converge before heading across the North Sea. I remember wondering what would become of us if a group of enemy fighters attacked our little formation, in broad daylight and so heavily laden. I certainly didn't want to start pulling hard evasive dives and turns.

In the event, my concerns came to nothing. We approached the town of Bielefeld as expected without much opposition, took our three drift wind reading and fed it into the magic box. Unfortunately though, things weren't going to plan ahead of us. During our morning briefing the Met man had told us the weather should have been clear, but as we got closer we could see dense cloud formations exactly in our way. The bomb aimer began his preparations anyway, trying to fix the target on the glass cross and talking to me on the intercom: 'Left, left … no, lost it again … right …' The cloud was making accurate aiming impossible. The bombing controller, in another kite ahead of us, told us to circle for a time in case it cleared, and we did so while at the same time keeping all our eyes peeled for any attacks by fighters. After a short time, though, the VHF spoke again. 'Abort the mission. Repeat, abort, there is too much cloud. All aircraft return to base with your bombs, repeat, return to base.' How frustrating! After all the training and all the miles we had flown, to be called off because of some clouds. In my previous squadrons where we were dropping lots of bombs on a widespread area, we would have released our load on marker flares and had a fast flight home. This time though we had to save our valuable bomb for the next mission and make our way back fully laden. Fortunately there was little opposition, and we were soon back over the North Sea where inevitably the cloud had thinned out. I now had the challenge of landing with our huge Tallboy hanging beneath our belly. Luckily, with an undamaged kite and calm conditions, we touched down without any difficulty.

To my regret, I wasn't detailed to take part in the operation which finally toppled the viaduct.

On 13 March, some of the squadron took off to attack it again, but had to turn back once more because of the weather. Two of them were, for the first time, carrying the successor to the Tallboy, which it was hoped might bring success. Astonishingly, it had only been properly tested that same morning at a bombing range in the New Forest, before being loaded onto aircraft at Woodhall Spa that afternoon.

If our Tallboys offered destruction on a level never seen before, the Grand Slam upped the stakes even higher. Designed by Barnes Wallis, it weighed ten tons to the Tallboy's five and a half. Its twenty-six foot length was suspended beneath the modified underbelly of the Lanc's fuselage, and a chain protruding from each side, including a release mechanism, was joined underneath to hold it in place. It promised a difficult take-off even for our souped-up kites, which would be strained to their limits by its weight. One of the two Grand Slams was to be dropped by Group Captain Fauquier himself, and I clearly remember how pleased he was at the thought that he would be the first to drop one of these new weapons. He was frustrated at having to turn back with it, but he would get another chance the following day.

That mission, on 14 March, gave rise to one of the best known stories about Fauquier, which was recounted to me with glee by countless pilots and crew later that evening. He was still determined to be the first to drop one of the new bombs in combat. His kite was all loaded up with what we were now calling 'Special Store', as was that of Squadron Leader 'Jock' Calder. As they warmed up their engines on the runway just before take-off, one of Fauquier's engines failed. He sent an urgent radio message to Calder, ordering him to abort his take-off so that he and his crew could purloin Calder's aircraft to complete the operation and thereby grab the glory. Calder however was not to be taken in, and apparently gave him what we termed the 'Nelson treatment'; i.e. he pretended he hadn't heard the order and took off anyway while the Group Captain and his crew were running across the field towards them. The story went around the mess and ground crew like wildfire, and we all had a jolly good laugh at Fauquier's expense. He was doubtless even more put out when it was revealed that Calder's bomb had helped the operation to succeed where so many others had failed, and the squadron leader was awarded a bar to his DSO! Later photographs revealed that the earthquake bombs had done their work. While they hadn't scored 'direct' hits, they had fallen very close to the viaduct, and caused such violent earth tremors and underground craters that the arches had simply collapsed. The term they used was 'camouflet', which means the ground supporting the arches simply gave way beneath them, which was exactly the result the bombs were designed for. There was great cheer in the mess that night, except for Group Captain Fauquier!

My next operational flight was on 19 March, an early morning take-off against the Arnsberg viaduct. As with the viaduct at Bielefeld, it was an essential route for war materiel to flow to the German front. Its wide arches carried a railway line over a waterway, and if it could be destroyed it would be another nail in the coffin of the retreating Jerries.

We awoke around dawn to make sure we had time for breakfast and to check the kite over, before briefing and take-off in the early morning light. The forecast was good, with clear weather which promised us a good view of the target. It would be cold, so we kitted up with all our thermals as usual before signing Form 700 to acknowledge the kite was airworthy. As we took off at about a quarter past eight I hoped that I might at last be able to use our Tallboy in earnest, and show that my place in 617 was justified. Climbing steadily, we joined the gaggle of Lancs and headed across the North Sea for the short penetration into Germany. Arnsberg is in the north of the country, and we would pass close to Duisburg and Essen, both hotly defended areas. Our carefully plotted route kept us away from most of the flak though, and before long the navigator came over the intercom. 'Ten miles to go Skipper. 11,000 feet steady.'

'Righto. Bomb aimer, standing by.'

'OK Skipper. That looks like it straight ahead. Checking the wind now. Navigator, Gunner, here we go …'

I got us pointing as closely as I could to the target, which I could already see in the distance, exploding in clouds of smoke and spray.

'Bombsight light switched on.'

The target was on the tip of our sword. Now it would run down the length of the blade towards its fate as we flew closer and closer.

'Steady, right a little … steady …' Once again an eternity of waiting. Every sense alert, concentrating on staying exactly on course, height, speed, no time to look for fighters or ease the discomfort of my tight straps. 'Bombsight on …'

Flak started to come up at us, bursting in the clear sky in malevolent black puffs. I did my best not to let the near misses divert me from my straight and level heading. Ahead of us, other Lancs were dropping their bombs, or circling away from the target ready for the journey home.

Dead straight now; holding the kite as stable as possible as the glass of our bombsight began its slow swivel. More flak to be ignored; shaking us slightly but not enough to put off the inevitable. Nearly there, nearly … We flew straight towards the rising plumes of smoke from earlier bombs. We had to stay straight and level for a dreadful ten minutes, a sitting duck for the enemy, no chance to take evasive action, just grit your teeth and keep right on. Just do it. The flak got worse, having our height and range perfectly. Keep it straight. Five minutes. More flak, bursting very close and showering us with red-hot sharp pieces of metal. Two minutes. Come on. One minute. Shaking, gripping the stick tight to keep it steady and on track.

'Almost there Skipper, almost there …'

'Come on, come on!'

'Nearly …'

An agony of waiting.

'Bomb gone!'

He didn't have to tell us. The automatic release mechanism had worked perfectly, dropping the five and a half ton bomb from underneath the kite. The effect was immediate. Without the weight of the bomb dragging beneath it, the straining Lanc was suddenly freed, and it leapt into the air like a supercharged lift. We were all pressed hard into our seats, our stomachs churning, and the altimeter wound on several hundred feet before settling down again. Our bomb aimer still managed to keep an eye on our Tallboy as it arced downwards towards the target.

'Ohhhhh that was close! About twenty yards off the end of the viaduct! It looks pretty badly smashed up though, especially at the west end. Reckon it's done for. Hope we got a good picture.'

As we circled to turn for home I managed to look out of the cockpit down onto the viaduct. It was covered in smoke, but I could see huge craters all around it and what looked like severe damage to the structure itself. The southern approach in particular looked as though it had received a direct hit.

'Not bad, we got the bugger this time. Navigator, let's get home now.'

'Righto Skipper. Bearing three five zero to join the gaggle and get us past Essen, then we'll turn west.'

Five and a half tons lighter, the kite responded beautifully as I set her for home. The loss of the bomb's weight made such a difference as we flew easily north, avoiding the flak hotspots as instructed and landing safely back at Woodhall Spa. I had passed my first test as a pilot in the famous 617 Squadron, joining the ranks of men I had viewed as heroes when they destroyed the Dams in 1943.

There wasn't long to wait before I was in action again. This time, on the 21st, it was an even earlier take-off, against the Arbergen railway bridge over the River Weser at Dreye, Bremen. On the positive side, we thought as we looked at the tapes stretched across the blackboard in the briefing room, it was a relatively short flight into northern Germany. Bremen was a well defended target though, and we would need careful navigation and some luck to avoid the flak over the city and the nearby coast with its naval defences.

Another early alarm call, another bleary eyed breakfast before trooping to the briefing, making final preparations and struggling into our thermals once more. Take-off was into cold, clear skies at five to eight, and we were all hoping for a quick return to give us the later part of the afternoon off. After a very short flight, we crossed the enemy coast safely and were soon on our run-in again. This time the flak was intense as we came in over Bremen, and thunderous explosions were going off in the sky all around us, peppering the sky with black. The city below us was clear, even at more than two miles up.

'Steady, steady ...' again the interminable waiting. They were throwing the kitchen sink at us this time, no doubt aware of our target. Ahead of us, I could see the first bombs throwing huge spouts of smoke, soil and water hundreds of feet into the air, and other Lancs lining up as we were for their approach.

Straight and level. Ignore the flak. Thirteen and a half thousand feet. Ignore the shaking and the rattling of shrapnel. Follow the bearing. Keep her straight. The bridge ran slowly down the sword of our bombsight.

'Bombsight ON.'

Nearly there.

'Ohhhh, no, did you see that? Someone's bought it, Lanc on our port side!'

'That looks bad, hope they can get out!'

I couldn't see it from my canopy, and I kept my eyes on my instruments and the oncoming target. Behind us a stricken Lancaster was dropping out of the sky some distance away, with flames pouring from one of its wings where flak had found its mark. I concentrated on our bombing run, but Gremlin in the back had a clear view.

The Lanc was doomed, falling in flames until he saw it crash to the ground with a huge explosion, probably from its bomb going up. Our bomb aimer in the nose, meanwhile had all his attention on the tilting bombsight.

'Any moment now ... steady, here we go ... bomb gone!'

Again the lurch and leap upwards as our load fell away, with the bomb aimer giving us a running commentary.

'It's looking good, looking good … blast, can't see through the smoke, but I think we're more or less on target … there it goes! Not far off Skipper, very close, but don't think it was a direct hit … let's get out of here!'

I didn't envy him, lying face down looking at the flak coming straight up at him but unable to move until his job was done. I needed no second bidding, and pulled us round to get out of the danger area as quickly as we could. Below us the railway bridge was being rocked on all sides by Tallboys and Grand Slams, and finally succumbed. Two of its main arches collapsed, pulling the railway line to pieces and wrecking the enemy's chances of using it to transport anything for many years. Our celebrations were muted by the oily black plume coming up from the crater in a field nearby, where the remains of the wrecked Lancaster were still burning.

When we got back, I found that the downed aircraft had been flown by Bernard Gumbley, known as Bob, a New Zealander who had shared a beer with myself and Gremlin on several occasions after returning to Petwood on the crew bus. He had been one of the more sociable officers in the mess, with plenty of experience on operations. Apparently he had been shot down by a German jet fighter which had managed to avoid our escort, perhaps after taking a hit from flak. I had an affection for the people of New Zealand because of my cousin Len Trent VC, who came from there. He had won his VC for brave flying, but had been shot down and was now in a prisoner of war camp. It was sad, but this was war, and these tragedies happened. As before, we had to get on with the job and turn the leaf over to the next page. Bob Gumbley's place, and that of his crew, would be taken by a new intake of men keen to prove themselves at 617. I headed to the welcoming warmth of the farm for the rest of the day, after a warning to us all from Fauquier: 'Don't relax too much. Another operation tomorrow.'

At least this one wasn't quite so early. A period of good weather had settled in, and we had the luxury of clear skies all day. After bacon and eggs, we were bussed to the crew room for ten o'clock.

'It's another bridge today, like the one we smashed up yesterday. Target: Nienberg. It's another essential transport point for the Jerries, so we need to take it out. It will again be well defended, so get in, get your bombs dropped and get out again. Your outward route will avoid Bremen, and likewise on the way back. Good luck.'

My crew had been slightly altered, and on this trip F/O Daniels was to be our bomb aimer. I didn't really know him, but he seemed to be both confident and competent as we prepared, and I hoped he would be easy to work with during the stress and danger of our run-in to the target.

Fauquier would lead the attack with my usual bomb aimer in his kite, and he was one of the first to take off into the early spring sky shortly before midday. We formed up into a loose formation, or gaggle, surrounded by a protective screen of fighters. Flak came up at us as we crossed the enemy coast, but it wasn't too much trouble.

We stayed in our gaggle until we were getting near to our target, and then received orders from Fauquier over the radio.

'We will bomb in three phases. Sections four and eight, hold back and stand by.' We circled a distance away from Nienburg, watching the first wave of attacks. The bridge was easy to spot, even from 10,000 feet, as we could follow the winding River Weser and see where it bulged next to the town.

As the first bombs fell, we saw the now familiar sight of vast plumes of smoke, debris and water surging into the sky after shockwaves burst out from where the Tallboys and Grand Slams fell. Fauquier circled in his Lanc calling out instructions and comments. The first wave finished their attacks, with several near misses but no definite hits.

'All right second wave, your turn, take your time, let's have a good show.'

I turned us onto our attack heading, following the calls from the bomb aimer once more. The Weser unwound beneath us, with its series of smaller villages leading us in towards Nienburg on the left. The bridge was soon out of sight below me, and only he had a clear view of it as he watched it creep along the blade of his sight.

'Bombsight on … steady … going along fine, really good …' Any concerns I may have had about our new bomb aimer had gone, as he talked us in calmly and carefully.

Ahead, flak was bursting all over the sky as I held her straight. I gritted my teeth as it came closer and started to shake us again.

'It's looking good Skipper, keep it like this, good, yes ...'

The glass of the sight was slowly tilting, as more shells came flying up from the town on our left. As we had been warned, the defences were thick and accurate all around Nienburg, and it seemed they were all aiming at us. We had the uncomfortable sitting ducks feeling again. Holding the kite steady on our bombing line was becoming very difficult as the explosions caused shockwaves in the air around us, and I gripped the control column even tighter. Just do it.

'Standby, standby, nearly there, come on ... bomb gone!'

Again the feeling of being in a very fast lift as the weight left us, but the bomb aimer still had his eyes glued on the target as we flew upwards.

'There it goes, looking good, looking good, yes, yes ... *BANG!* Ohhhh, bingo! Right on the button, Skipper! We've hit the bloody thing smack in the middle! A perfect shot! Oh, that's fantastic ... hold course for the camera!'

'Bloody good oh, let's hope the photos come out all right!'

We all cheered for a few moments, and I looked forward to seeing the pictures which would prove we had scored a direct hit. I was brought back to earth by the navigator.

'OK Skipper, steer three five zero degrees, we're going back between Bremen and Hamburg, two and a half hours to base.'

Instructions were coming through for the other kites in the third phase to turn around and bring their bombs back, although some others in our wave did drop theirs to complete the destruction.

We felt elated in our kite, and I was particularly happy. For the first time I had flown hundreds of miles to a pinpoint target, and made a perfect drop to destroy a vital enemy asset.

When we got back to Woodhall Spa shortly before five o'clock that evening I found that four other crews had claimed hits on the bridge, although our bomb aimer was adamant that it had been our Tallboy which had smashed it straight through the middle. I resigned myself to the fact that we were sure of our hit, and what was most important was that the bridge had been destroyed, no matter who by. Time to forget about it, and try to unwind for what was left of the afternoon.

Just twelve hours later, in the early hours of 23 March, I was rudely awakened to find that we had to get out on another operation. An operation which was to be memorable for unwelcome reasons, and prove a sharp contrast to the success at Nienburg.

After a quick pre-dawn shower and shave, we made our drowsy way to briefing at 05.45. Today's target was to be another bridge, this time at Bremen, which was far closer to the coast and therefore a shorter flight. After the usual target, routing and weather details, I got the news that I would be flying one of the new modified Lancs on operations for the first time, and carrying a ten-ton Grand Slam. It was exciting news, and I took a good look at my new aircraft before getting in. The bomb, painted dark at the nose and a lighter colour in the tail, looked vast as it hugged the underside of the fuselage. Squadron records show that I had a Tallboy, but it was certainly a Grand Slam in a modified Lanc, with just the five of us on board.

I ran through the take-off drill carefully before we pulled onto the runway at first light. I could feel the extra power from the enhanced engines shaking the airframe, but also the enormous drag of the bomb beneath our belly. Other crews with Grand Slams said they saw their wingtips bending upwards by several inches as the airframe flexed under the load. At a quarter past seven, with the darkness of the sky streaking with red as the sun rose, I got the green light and pushed the throttles to their limits, feeling the effort of the Merlins as they heaved to pull us along the runway. Because of the weight I had to be sure that we were going fast enough to take off, so I kept her down on the runway until we reached 110 miles an hour. Finally, almost at the end of the runway, we lumbered into the air, joined the gaggle of other Lancs and flew over the North Sea as set out in our briefing.

At about half way towards the enemy coast, we began to climb towards our operational height of 12,000 feet. The engines, with their new wide-bladed propellers, responded well and we were soon past 6,000 feet.

'OK chaps, climbing now. Better turn on the oxygen, Bill.'

'OK Skipper, all on.'

I waited, but to my dismay there was no tell tale series of puffs against my face as I breathed. The others evidently had the same problem.

'Skipper, I'm getting nothing from my oxygen. It's not working.'

'Same here Skip, nothing here either'

'No, nor me, no oxygen.'

Damn, this was a real problem. We all knew from our training in the decompression chamber that if we went too high without our oxygen supply, we would lose our ability to think straight and could even pass out if we went high enough. On such an auspicious day though, with our new kite and Special Store, I didn't want to miss out on the operation. I kept us climbing on course, and debated what we could do.

'All right. How about if we climb up to 9,000 feet, where we can probably cope without the oxygen, and carry on to bomb from there? We won't tell the Flight Commander, just do it?'

'Yes, OK!' immediately came from Gremlin in the tail. I knew he trusted my judgement and it was good to have his support.

'Yes, we can make it, we'll be careful.' came from the others, and I was confident we could succeed. But then the bomb aimer shouted us all down in no uncertain terms.

'No way. Not without oxygen. That's against the rules, against procedures. We have to turn back.' He was a stickler for doing things by the book, and he wouldn't be budged. I resolved to take it to higher authority, and used the VHF radio to call the Flight Commander.

'This is K-King reporting a failure of oxygen. Repeat, oxygen failed. Requesting permission to climb to 9,000 feet and continue to target.'

'Hello K-King, negative, repeat negative. You cannot proceed on this operation without oxygen. Go back to base, repeat, go home.'

With a heavy heart, I apologised to the rest of the crew – apart from the bomb aimer, who was satisfied with the outcome of my conversation.

Peeling off from the gaggle, and feeling rather exposed to be alone with our heavily laden kite, I tried to work out how we might make a safe landing.

'Navigator, course for home please. I'm going to keep up a little more speed to give us enough lift over the runway.'

Luckily we had clear skies and not too much wind as we lined up for landing. I'd called up to warn them we were coming in with a bomb on board. The ten-ton weight of the device dragged us inexorably down towards the airfield. We were in the realms of the unknown, because hardly anybody had ever tried to land with a Grand Slam before. After all, hardly anyone had ever needed to before!

It was common sense to add a little speed to the approach, so I kept us about five miles an hour more than usual, gliding in low over the perimeter fence. It was looking good. I wanted to touch down at the very beginning of the runway as I knew we'd need as much distance as possible to enable us to lose speed before it ran out, so at the earliest opportunity I pulled the throttles back and dropped us down towards the tarmac. The kite floated on though, and passed the point where I had hoped to touch down, causing a few muttered curses before she finally settled with a gentle bump sixty feet further down. Now the wheels were on the ground, we had to rely on the brakes to slow us down before we ploughed through the fence at the end of the runway. I knew that if I simply jammed the brakes on they would burn out under the load, so I made myself squeeze and release them repeatedly as we hurtled down the track. My efforts weren't enough though, and the weight of the bomb dragged us forwards like a runaway train. The end of the runway was fast approaching, and I knew there was no way we would be able to stop in time before we ran through the fence. Once more I had to do some very quick thinking, and pushed with my left foot to give us full left rudder. I gave the left brake a quick squeeze at the same time, and the Lanc started to swing dangerously to the left which could develop into a ground loop hard enough to make the undercarriage skid, twist and collapse even though it had been modified and strengthened to cope with our heavy load. If that happened, we would be left sliding and spinning along the ground on the bomb which was fastened to the underside of the kite. As the turn began to tighten, the tail of the Lanc was lurching around and the tyres were squealing in protest at being abused so badly. We were almost skidding along sideways towards the end of the runway, carrying a ten-ton bomb, and I could see the airfield whizzing sideways across the cockpit glass. Before it was too late I reached out with my right hand and jammed the port outer engine open right up past the emergency gate to full throttle, to try to get the utmost power to counteract the swing. There was a roar as the engine responded, the view from the cockpit suddenly stabilised and became steady, and I quickly closed the throttle again. All was suddenly peaceful, and I found we were now proceeding along the taxi path at a sedate four miles an hour. Breathing an enormous sigh of relief, I allowed my fingers to relax their death grip on the control column. I wondered if the rest of the crew had realised how close we had come to disaster. My answer came very quickly, when Gremlin piped up on the intercom.

'Ha ha, that was funny, did you see those workmen at the end of the runway? They were running like hell to get away from us! Serves them right, they get an extra ten shillings a day in danger money!'

I pulled us onto our hard standing, switched off the engines, and sat still for a moment to allow my nerves to recover. I took a deep breath.

'Right boys,' I said, 'I'm buying you all a drink.'

A bus came to pick us up after we had climbed with shaking legs down the ladder to terra firma. Our Grand Slam sat smugly under the kite, and would have to wait for another day before it could be dropped in anger.

We explained our aborted mission to the debriefing officers in the crew room, changed, put our flying gear away, and repaired to the mess bar, still talking about our near miss.

'Right, five beers please ...' I had got this far when a shout went up from my right.

'Hey Skipper, come and have a look at this! It's fantastic!'

Wondering what all the fuss could be about, I went over to look. There were three photographs pinned to the noticeboard, each with 'F/

Lt Trent' written along the edge. The first showed the bridge at Nienburg with a hole in the middle, the second showed a great splash as the bomb hit the water beneath it, and the third showed the bomb exploding and the bridge taking to the air. It was proof positive of our claims to have smashed the Nienburg bridge, that our bomb had been the one to get a proper bullseye. After what we had just been through it was a great result, and we troubled the barman for rather more than just one drink! The beers that day were some of my very few at 617 Squadron, because I now had other, more relaxing ways to unwind – at the farm.

CHAPTER FOURTEEN

A COUNTRY LIFE

Since that first day when I met Bob Coulton and his family I had become a regular visitor to Brackenwoodside Farm. It very soon became my second home and I would spend all my free time there, away from the base until I was needed. Until then my life in the RAF had been a continual round of training, operations, nerves, pressure, parties, drinking, the theatre, girls, training, operations … and it was becoming a real strain which had already manifested itself in my shaking hands. The farm, on the other hand, exuded stability, warmth, peace, and above all – love. My guardian angel had guided me into a place of happiness, where just along the road was war and all those things which involved killing people and trying to stay alive oneself. I stopped drinking excessively and found solace in doing all the little jobs there which helped me to unwind.

I was often there at six in the morning before operations or training to milk 'my' cows or generally help out, and headed there immediately after any operation which finished in daylight hours. Before landing I would circle tightly over the farmhouse and waggle the wings of my Lanc. Little Lucy would run inside calling, 'He's back! Kenneth's back,' and her mother, with her lovely soft northern accent would call back, 'Gooood!' Sometimes I would arrive still trembling with nervous energy after a dangerous trip, and before I had the chance to tend to 'my' cows Mrs C would pack me off to their spare room. 'Leave the cows alone,' she'd say, 'You get off to bed. You need a good sleep.' I would drift off gratefully in warmth and comfort with the roar of engines and bang of guns forgotten.

Bob grew potatoes, produced milk and eggs, and kept hens running free around the yard which had to be penned in every night. Twenty or so guineafowl slept up in the trees away from marauding foxes, and the pet pig followed us about under the impression it was helping with whatever chore we were undertaking. I was with them at the time of year when the potatoes were being harvested, and watched Bob store them all by the side of the road. They were piled into a long heaped line covered with a layer of grass and soil, and then another pile of potatoes laid next to them, and another layer of earth, repeated all along the length of the road. It was known as a 'clamp', and was a means of storing the harvest until it was sold. Gradually the piles diminished as they were bought.

There was also a very large sow. She had given birth to a full litter of piglets which had been sold off, all except the runt, which had become the children's pet because it was barren and appealed to their good nature. One day the ominous decision was made that the time had come for the sow to be turned into bacon (which was against the law in 1945 without the authorities' permission), and I was involved right up to the hilt.

I didn't much enjoy the nasty part of seeing Bob cut her throat and drain her blood, but once that was over the process became quite an adventure. We fetched several large buckets full of water from the pond. These were brought to the boil in a copper over the kitchen fire. Bob and I had a dipper like a small ladle each, and a sharp 'scraper'. The dipper was used to pour the boiling water over a small area of the carcass, before using the scraper to remove any hair and clean the skin. This was a very time-consuming but highly satisfying task, as we were left with a nice clean pig! When every part was ready, a butcher's hook was pushed into each back leg and she was hoisted up onto the branch of the oak tree in the yard. Bob dragged over a large bath and positioned it below, before opening up her tummy with a well sharpened knife and scooping out everything which was inside. Together with the head, it all went indoors for Mrs C and the girls to prepare. We were left with a large piece of pork hanging up on the tree, which we washed with more water from the pond and left overnight to cool off. As luck would have it, I wasn't required for training or ops the next day, and was able to be back at the farm bright and early to see what happened next. As a city boy who had previously only seen bacon in a butcher's display cabinet, this was proving to be a real eye-opener!

Bob began the process by cutting the pig down the middle with a small hatchet, giving us two 'sides'. He then chopped them into quarters, giving us two hind legs, two fore legs, and two large pieces of back and belly. I helped him to trim further the big pieces which were to be used for bacon, as the girls carried away the trimmings to make sausages.

Mrs C had prepared several buckets of seasoning mixture which contained mainly salt, as well as saltpetre, sugar and pepper all stirred together. Bob and I spent most of the day rubbing it into the flesh of the pig until every single surface had been covered, taking care not to miss a single nook or cranny. Mrs C told us to use a little extra saltpetre on the areas where the thigh and leg bones were visible.

Inside the cool pantry was a low, flat, stone bed which had been covered with the mixture from the bucket. Together we carried the pieces of the butchered pig inside and laid them skin side down before sprinkling more of the mixture on top, until all the exposed surfaces were well and truly covered. The legs and shoulders were laid down next and covered with more seasoning, the last piece going skin side up. Two weeks later the whole lot would be turned over and re-seasoned. Our work done for the day, we repaired to the simple kitchen for a much needed cup of tea before remembering to milk the cows.

That was a skill which took a long time and a lot of patience to master. The first time I tried it Bob showed me how to sit on the little stool with my head pressed into the cow's side, so you had an early warning if she was going to misbehave. You had to wash the udder carefully, before pulling gently at the teats to bring out the milk. The squeezing motion is difficult, as you don't simply pull and expect an instant result. A particular motion involving the thumb and a forefinger, plus a rolling movement with the wrist, is the best way to keep the cow happy and ensure a constant stream of milk into your bucket. It took me a while to learn, and Bob gave me two just two cows to look after because I was so slow. For many days I had sore wrists as I gripped the control column of my Lancaster, because of my inept attempts at milking!

The work was also having an unfortunate effect on my battledress. From slopping pails of water to mucking out cows, from shovelling dung to butchering pigs, as well as the splashes of milk, it wasn't the best way to keep your uniform spotless. Add to that the unpleasant sensation of bugs crawling along my forehead as I milked with my head pressed against the warm flank of the cow, and I'm sure I would never have passed an inspection should our officers have been unkind enough to hold one. In the meantime, my crew would have to suffer the whiff of dried blood and curdled milk whenever I pulled off my fleece-lined flying suit. I didn't care though.

One day Mrs C decided she wanted to cook a guineafowl for dinner. The birds were always running about the place, and weren't shut in at night, making them very difficult to catch. We trooped outside into the yard, and Mrs C spotted one in a tree very close by.

'That's our dinner,' she said, 'Let's have it down.'

Bob turned and walked back to the house where he disappeared for a moment before emerging with a double-barrelled shotgun. To my dismay, he passed it to me.

'You can do it,' he said, 'You're in the RAF so you must be a good shot.' The fact is I had never fired a gun in my life, and didn't really fancy the idea of taking a potshot with a great big shotgun at the innocent-looking bird just a few feet away. If I missed, I would certainly make a proper fool of myself. I tried to pass the gun back to Bob, but he insisted – no, it had to be me.

The bird was perched on a branch about thirty feet off the ground, possibly asleep or simply surveying the farmyard in peace. I reared the weapon, looked along the barrel, sighted the poor creature, took a deep breath, closed my eyes and pulled the trigger.

There was an ear splitting *BANG!* and I nearly fell over backwards with the recoil, while watching the unfortunate bird fall straight down from its perch. Well, I thought, feeling proud of myself, that was a pretty good shot – that'll show them. Bob immediately ran forward and collected the kill, which was somehow showing signs of wanting to get up and fly

211

away. Closer inspection revealed that I had almost completely missed it, apart from one pellet which had hit it in the foot. I think it had fallen off the branch in sheer fright at the noise, or maybe it was just laughing at my terrible shooting. I, a member of the much-vaunted 617 Squadron, who could drop a twenty-three-foot bomb onto a thirty-foot-wide bridge from more than two miles up in the sky, couldn't hit a bird with a shotgun at five paces.

I had my revenge though. It tasted delicious.

It wasn't long before I turned up at the farm one day and Mrs C asked me if I fancied a piece of bacon. The meat from the sow had cured to perfection and was hanging from hooks in the living room in cotton bags, all except the back and belly, which were exposed. She cut a rasher about fourteen inches long, which was a little on the fatty side until cooked to perfection in a sizzling pan over the fire. Thick, crispy and smelling divine, it was out of this world. I had no idea what the girls had been doing under the guidance of Mrs C with the contents of the sow's tummy, but the sausages which also appeared were simply superb. After the repetitive food of RAF messes, this was indeed a treat.

I have no doubt that meeting these wonderful people changed my life. Instead of living from one operation to the next, and drinking in between, I now had a reason for living. They gave me a glimpse of what life could be like after the war, and the optimism that maybe I could have a kind, calm and loving home of my own. All of a sudden I believed I had a chance of surviving the war. 'I might get through this,' I thought. I had never thought that I wouldn't, but equally I had never thought that I would either; you simply had to take each operation as it came, to see what happened. Dwelling too much on the future was rash, in a service which had lost half the young men it had sent into the sky. I had never had a home life like this. When I was young my parents were always concerned with the shop, making money, balancing the books and dealing with customers. When I was older I was at boarding school, and from there I had gone almost straight away into the RAF. The Coultons gave me a family, life and a reason to live it, and I can never thank them enough. They were some of the happiest days of my life.

CHAPTER FIFTEEN

SPECIAL STORE

My next raid, on 27 March, was a novelty for me for two reasons. Firstly, the target was very interesting, and secondly I actually got to drop my first Grand Slam.

After quite an early alarm call and the usual breakfast, my crew and I found we were once again listed on the board for operations.

At first glance, the route markings on the large map in the briefing room showed that we were returning to Bremen, but as the intelligence officer filled us in it became apparent that our target was slightly to the north-west, right on the banks of the River Weser at Farge. We were to attack a submarine base. This was a new one for all of us, so we listened with great interest to what he had to say.

It was a massive concrete building which had been under construction by slave labour for two years. At more than four hundred metres long and a hundred wide, it would be easy for us to spot, even from altitude. Inside they were preparing to build the very latest U-boats, which could sail up the river and out into the North Sea ready to attack our shipping: a very real threat even at that late stage of the war. The site was very heavily defended and incredibly strong, with walls four and a half metres thick and a reinforced roof which was up to seven metres deep, leading straight out onto the river. Intelligence had known about the project almost from the beginning, but had decided not to attack it until they knew it was almost ready to go into use. Their reasoning was that it was using up vast quantities of steel and concrete which would otherwise be used to build tanks and bunkers in front of the Allied armies invading Germany.

Due to the formidable thickness of the roof, they realised that a raid with conventional bombs might simply scratch the surface – but an attack using Grand Slams and Tallboys might do the job very well.

As we examined the maps we saw another positive element to the operation: the location of the target. It was a few miles to the north of Bremen, with its bristling flak emplacements. Hopefully that would mean we could make our drop and have time to turn before the worst of the anti-aircraft fire could be directed at us.

We took off at just after twenty past ten into clear skies, twenty of us forming into a gaggle over the North Sea and flying the now well-known route towards Bremen. After a few doglegs to avoid hotspots, we were soon following the Weser in a line at 14,000 feet with good visibility. The enemy fighters were leaving us alone, and we were quickly into our straight and level flight to check for wind and get the bombsight prepared.

'Got it clear Skipper. Dead straight now. That's it. Bombsight ON.'

Ahead, the first Lancs were dropping their bombs on the enormous submarine base, some Grand Slams and some Tallboys. I saw a couple of very near misses, in the river and on the land surrounding the building. There was at least one direct hit which we saw smash right down into the roof at the western end, before we got so close that the target disappeared from my sight under the nose.

'OK, that's it … steady … whoa, there she goes!'

If the aircraft had leapt when we dropped a Tallboy, it was nothing compared to what it did when we let go of the Grand Slam. Relieved of its ten-ton weight, the souped-up Lanc shot upwards like a rocket, pushing us all into our seats while the engines blared with noise. I felt as though I was being squashed down to just a few inches tall as my head pressed down through my shoulders; my arms felt like lead on the control column. Fortunately there was no other kite above us, or it could have been disastrous. The bomb aimer managed to keep an eye on the progress of our Grand Slam as it fell, but had some bad news.

'It looks like it's on target Skipper, but there's too much smoke and water in the air. Can't be sure … it looked pretty good though … OK, photo's taken, let's go!'

I needed no second bidding, as we were getting uncomfortably close to the main flak defences of Bremen which were throwing up a lot of shells in our direction.

'Come on Skipper, home time!' came from Gremlin in the back.

A fairly steep turn to starboard took us away from the worst defences, and I climbed slightly higher to join the stream of bombers heading north. Gremlin could now see the last few kites as they lined up to attack.

'There's more going in, don't know how they can see what they're aiming at, it's all covered in smoke … there goes another Grand Slam … looks like that was a close one too … reckon we've done it!'

The journey home was straightforward, untroubled by fighters, and all of the twenty kites which had taken off landed safely. I was very glad not to be carrying my bomb home and I had time to enjoy the performance of the enhanced Lancaster. It was so powerful and full of fun, as light as a feather to fly, and felt like a single-engined fighter. A true dream machine.

Later photos showed that we had dropped two Grand Slams dead on target, and smashed two great big holes right through the roof of the submarine base. The damage was so bad that the Germans had to abandon it, after two years of work and thousands of tons of concrete and steel used up. Another job well done.

It was soon after this that I received more bad news from home. My mother was now seriously ill, and I was to have more leave to go to visit her. The three months allocated to her by the doctors was coming to an end. I had written to tell her about my new friends the Coultons, and she in turn had written to them. Before I left, those wonderful people loaded the boot of my car with bacon, potatoes, eggs and all sorts of farmhouse treats to take back to my family.

I arrived at home wearing my smelly battledress to find my mum weaker than she had been but downstairs, resting as much as possible but still helping with the post office books. It was terribly sad, as she had terrific courage and kept saying, 'While there's life there's hope!'

I think she knew she was dying though, and when she felt well enough she set about giving the whole house a thorough spring clean. It was as though she wanted to leave everything clean and tidy for my poor dad, who would have to carry on after she went. She even gave my dirty uniform a good scrubbing, and returned it to me free of the dirt and stink of the farm. She was always so proud to see me with my wings.

Five years of war had had their effect on the shop too. There was now almost nothing left to sell; cigarettes and confectionery were all strictly rationed and the customers who came in were there to collect their pensions or the allowances made to the wives of servicemen. Sometimes someone wanted to buy stamps or send a telegram or postal order, but the business was really suffering.

When my leave came to an end I left with a heavy heart.

In the meantime the squadron had been in heavy training for its next missions. One was to another U-boat pen, this time in Hamburg, and was deemed to have been a success. In a continuation of the naval theme, our next target was to be a battleship.

617 was already known for its daring and ultimately successful attacks against the *Tirpitz*, which I had marvelled about while in main force the previous November. Despite fierce resistance they had managed to sink the mighty vessel, seen as a major threat to Allied shipping. The news had been celebrated all over the country, and now I had my chance to take part in a similar raid.

It wasn't all cheery faces though, when the curtain was pulled back on the map board at briefing. The ribbon showing our outward route stretched for miles across the North Sea and Denmark, all the way over to the Oder See just above Stettin. It was a change from heading to the Weser or the Ruhr, but it was months since I had been on such a long operation.

The battleships *Lutzow* and *Prinz Eugen* were anchored in the canal at Swinemunde, and were considered important targets. *Prinz Eugen* had been involved in the sinking of HMS *Hood* earlier in the war, and the *Lutzow*, a heavy cruiser, had sunk tons of naval and merchant ships. Both had been targeted for destruction several times during the war, but had been lucky enough to fight off the ships and aircraft sent to hunt them down. Naval anti-aircraft fire was known to be accurate and well disciplined. Fauquier left us in no doubt that despite the long range of the operation, we were the boys to finish the job. While several of our kites were to carry Tallboys and Grand Slams, I was back in one of the older kites carrying twelve 1,000 lb bombs, which they probably hoped might penetrate the decking of the ships.

Take-off was at half past eleven in the morning, and the Met man had promised that the clear conditions over Woodhall Spa would continue all the way to our target.

Unfortunately as we crossed Denmark we started to notice some cloud, and by the time we approached our destination after nearly four hours of flying it had joined up to form an impenetrable layer. After a couple of turns over the target to look for a break, the outcome was much to be expected.

'Abandon target, repeat, abandon target, return to base.'

All that way for nothing! It was a very long and cold journey back, and we didn't land until half past six.

Two days later, on the 15th, we tried again, this time taking off in the early morning light at half past eight. Again we flew for long hours over Denmark and again, unbelievably, the cloud closed in – this time well before the target, sending us home once more with our tails between our legs. We were all fed up with it, and determined to get the job done if we could. We were told, 'Go to bed, get some rest. We'll try again tomorrow.'

For our third attempt on the *Lutzow* and *Prinz Eugen* on the 16th, we had a mid-morning take-off after being assured that this time the target would be clear. We bloody well hoped so, after the problems of the past few days, and were ready to get stuck in.

This time the cloud stayed away and the enemy coast over Denmark glistened in the noonday sun. Reassuringly, it also glistened off the wings of our fighter escorts as they patrolled around us ready to take out any enemy planes sent to intercept us. Unfortunately, however, they didn't have enough fuel to take us all the way to our target.

Our route took us over variations of land and sea, as we flew over the north of Germany and its Baltic peninsulas. Still the weather was clear. Right, this was it. Even though we weren't dropping Special Store, accuracy was important because we were at 13,000 feet. Spotting the targets was quite easy, as they were anchored at the mouth of a very prominent canal. Inland was a very large lake, and the canal led in an almost straight line to the sea. To make the attack, we simply had to spot the canal, follow it to the ships anchored by the sea, and drop.

However, the cloud of our previous two attempts had hidden us from the anti-aircraft batteries both on the ships and on the shore, and this time they were waiting to give us a very interesting few minutes. As we lined up to make our bomb run there was a frightening amount of fire coming up at us from all possible angles.

'Bomb doors open! Bombsight light ON. Left a bit Skip.' Holding the kite straight, and listening to the bomb aimer, I was glad to have something to concentrate on to take my mind off the danger. Ahead of us I could see other Lancs lining up for their attack, and raining bombs down on one ship in particular. As we got closer and closer, straight and level, the flak increased in intensity until it became a storm of explosions all around us.

'Bombsight ON.'

Our previously pristine Lanc was shaking and rattling to the impact of shrapnel, with the occasional louder crump as larger pieces smashed into us. Still we hadn't let go of our bombs, and all of us were silently yelling at the bomb aimer to let the bloody things go, even though he had to wait for the automatic sight. The other Lancs around us were experiencing similar problems, and I could see them bucking and heaving around the sky as the black explosions shook them.

Just 100 yards ahead of us was V-Victor, piloted by Squadron Leader John Powell. Like us his bomb doors were open in preparation for the release of his load of thousand-pounders, and like us he was flying as straight and level as possible to get an accurate drop. In the face of the curtain of flak being sent up by the enemy gunners though, it was inevitable that one of us would get seriously hit and I watched in horror as a sudden explosion tore off half the port wing of V-Victor and wrenched it to one side.

'Christ!' Bill yelled out in alarm and dismay as the stricken Lancaster went into a flaming spin. Unbeknown to me, his best friend Henry Felton was the flight engineer on that aircraft. I was torn between watching my instruments and watching V-Victor as it dropped burning out of the sky, but I had to concentrate on the job in hand.

'Bombs gone!' shouted the bomb aimer, and we lifted in the air still buffeted by flak.

'Any parachutes? Has anyone got out?' Bill was shouting, breathing heavily into his oxygen mask as he craned over the cockpit to see what was happening to his friend's kite.

'None yet, none, sorry ...' Gremlin had a clear view of the burning Lancaster as it fell towards a wood near the target.

'Come on, come on, get out ...'

'Photograph done. Looks like we might have hit her, we straddled right across her bows. Let's get out of here!'

'There's a 'chute! Very low though ... don't know if he's OK ...'

I eased the stick back to pull us around. I was relieved when I felt the controls respond readily, as I had been worried what damage might have been caused by the numerous flak hits we had received. As we arced around to take up our homeward bearing, we saw the wreckage of V-Victor go straight down into the edge of a wood and disappear in a series of earth-shaking explosions as her fuel and bombs went up. Behind us, the *Lutzow* was shrouded in smoke and plumes of water as she burned from our attack and still the sky was black with the puffballs of flak. I pushed the throttles open as far as I could and followed the navigator's course for our first leg back to base. Slowly we left the flak and explosions behind for a sombre flight home. We landed at five to nine that evening, and during debriefing found that we weren't the only ones to have seen V-Victor go down. None of Powell's crew had survived. We were later informed that the *Lutzow*'s bottom had been ripped out by a Tallboy and she sank into the shallows of the canal.

The following day, the news reached me that my mother was dying. A forty-eight hour pass was arranged and I left once more for London as fast as I possibly could. My mother had been so important in my life that even amid all the death and destruction of the war, I was desperate to see her.

She was dying of the awful condition which had blighted her life since that day I had seen her in hospital. She had fought it every day and worked hard to leave the house and the shop accounts ready for my father, who would miss her dreadfully. She had always shown such love and devotion to him, and it was touching to see how she thought of his future even when she only had a short time left.

As the train rattled south, I gazed out of the window and looked back at the too little time I had spent with her.

When I was growing up she had always been busy with the shop and the post office, helping Dad with the accounts and stock. To make sure JJ and I were well cared for they had employed a lady called Mrs Wolving to look after us, and do some simple cooking and cleaning in the house. At bedtime she would bathe us and put us to bed, and my mother would come upstairs and kiss us goodnight.

From the age of eight I had been at boarding school, and spent much of my holidays playing in the sand at St Osyth, which limited the time I had with her even further. In fact, I had spent relatively little time with her as a child or as an adult. I'm sure this lack of a really close relationship must have influenced my attitude to life. I never really got homesick, never lay crying in my bed like so many others when I was at boarding school, but nonetheless when I was with her we had some magical times together and I loved her very much. She was a great sport, time spent with her was precious, and she gave JJ and myself an ability to cope with life and all its problems as they passed us by. I was devastated to think that she would no longer be around. I had recently received notice that I had been summoned to the Palace to be awarded my DFC on 29 April, and I so wanted her to be with me.

From the station I ran home as fast as I could. Mum was in her own bed, while my father had to mind the shop downstairs. JJ was with me, as was a close friend of the family called Percy. As we sat and watched over her, she was barely conscious as she slipped away. She whispered 'Bye-bye Percy,' which drifted into 'Bye-bye Li...' to my dad Lionel. Those were her last words, and she stopped breathing soon after. Dad came upstairs and we all knelt down to pray for her and recite the Lord's Prayer. I was desolate, but had to leave to go back on duty while Dad made arrangements for the funeral.

Although we didn't find out until after the war, Mum's wasn't the only death in our family that spring. My Canadian cousin from Pathlow, Frederick Bernard Trent, who we all knew as Bernard, and who I had last seen when I was training in Canada, had joined up and gone through all the training just as I had. He had just joined 431 Squadron to begin operations, and as usual flew his first mission as 'second dickie' – just as I had. On 22 March in an aircraft piloted by the very experienced Jack Duggan DFC, he flew towards the target, a railway yard at Hildesheim. Shortly before they arrived, a flak shell crashed into their Lanc and set off the bomb load they were carrying. It was a great loss for the family, and I remembered Bernard with fondness as a great tall, strong yet gentle man whose party trick was to lift a heavy table with one hand from the bottom of one of its legs.

The war was fast approaching its end, but as the Russians squeezed the life out of Berlin and the Western Allies pushed across Germany on a broad front, there was still work for us to do and I had to put my poor mother out of my mind for another operation on 18 April. The islands of Heligoland, in the North Sea close to where Germany meets Denmark, were to be our next target. We all knew where they were, as we had flown over them on our way to attack the Lutzow. At the morning briefing the Intelligence Officer explained that they held important gun batteries which could fire on Allied shipping heading around Germany towards the port of Cuxhaven. They had to be destroyed, and since they were in reinforced bunkers they would have to be attacked with Tallboys.

Thankfully Heligoland was only halfway between our base and our previous destination of Swinemunde, which made for a much quicker trip. We did need very accurate navigation though, because the islands are very small and in the middle of the sea; there could be no following rivers or canals to the target this time. The Met man got it right though, and following careful bearings the gaggle was able to spot the cliffs below the target quite easily between scattered clouds. The gun batteries were perched at the top of high cliffs, giving them a commanding field of fire out over the sea. Flak batteries around the bunkers sent their usual greeting up to meet us, but it was far less severe than we had experienced before, and we were able to begin our timed run-in without too much trouble. Several kites had dropped their bombs before we arrived but most, it seemed, had undershot, crashing into the cliffs or the water. There was plenty of smoke and dust flying up into the air.

'What do you reckon bomb aimer? Can you see the target?'

'Think so, Skipper. Steady on, just as you are. Bombsight ON.'

We were on a perfect heading, at 10,000 feet, and approaching well.

'That's missed …'

The bomb aimer was commentating on the other attacks which he could see ahead of him.

'And that one; it's gone into the cliffs …'

'Let's get ours on target then, if you can see it …'

'Yes, steady, steady, BOMB GONE!'

This time I had prepared myself for the lurch as the great bomb was unleashed from beneath us, and I kept us steady as we waited for the photo to be taken.

'OK, photo done, time to go!'

'Did we hit it?'

'Not sure Skipper, it looked good but I didn't see it hit because of all the smoke. Let's hope so.'

A straightforward flight back over the sea and we were back at base in the early evening. The photos looked good, and this time we all came back.

Three days later I had to go to my mother's funeral, which was one of the worst days of my life. I made the now familiar train journey in my best uniform, wearing my wings and medal ribbons she had been so proud of.

The shop was closed for the day, and all the relations arrived there including Mum's best friend who we knew as Aunty Tim. My sister JJ looked magnificent in her WAC uniform, and I'm sure she wanted to do Mum proud just as I did. With terrible sadness we climbed into the black limousine which took us behind the hearse the short distance to the church. On shaking legs I followed her coffin up the steps of the building which to my amazement was packed with people, many of them Mum's regular customers at the shop. Somehow I held myself in check during the service, but when we followed the pall-bearers with the coffin out of the church I lost it. I started to cry uncontrollably, which I found dreadful. Here was I, an RAF officer in full uniform with wings and the DFC on his chest, blubbing – at a time when the stiff upper lip was expected in even the worst situations. I felt I had let us all down by displaying such weakness. I tried to get a hold of myself while the coffin was placed back in the hearse and we drove to the City of London Cemetery at Wanstead, a long, slow drive on a dark and threatening day. On arrival, the pall-bearers shouldered Mum and took her to her burial place followed by myself, JJ and the rest of the family. I gripped JJ's hand as the coffin was lowered down, only to lose myself again when the first handfuls of earth were gathered up and thrown down onto the coffin. It was to be the last time I would be physically close to my mum, who had gone at just fifty-eight years old. A major part of my life had gone forever, but the memories of her are still with me and will remain with me until my dying day. Thank goodness crying is considered more acceptable in this day and age.

Just a week later, I was expected at the home of the king, Buckingham Palace; before that I had an appointment at the home of Adolf Hitler.

It was 25 April 1945 and although I didn't know it at the time, it was to be my last offensive operation. We were called to the briefing room at a very late hour, and sat chattering and waiting for the briefing to start.

The station commander came in to the sound of scraping chairs as we all stood up, waiting for the news of where we were to go this time. With a dramatic flourish the Intelligence Officer pulled back the curtain over the oversized blackboard. The telltale strand of wool snaked across the map in a different direction to any we had flown before. Some 600 miles to the south-east, it appeared to end somewhere in the Bavarian Alps.

'Berchtesgaden,' said the officer. 'Hitler's hideaway. Your aim today is to take it out.'

We craned our necks and muttered in disbelief. Why was it important to take out Hitler's house when everyone believed he was in Berlin, surrounded by Russians?

'This isn't just a holiday home for Hitler. Since they built it in 1939 it's been extended to become a place from which he could, if necessary, run the war. There are communications, railway lines, barracks and support services, and goodness knows what else there. Our concern is that it will be used by fanatical Nazis as a last redoubt, a final fortress to prolong the war and cause many more casualties. We want it flattened.'

'You'll be carrying Tallboys. Your kites won't have the range to carry Special Store that far. We're not expecting too much fighter opposition, which is just as well because it's out of range for our escorts.'

As we stood up to go, my mind was racing. For the first time in any operation I really couldn't see the point in what we had been asked to do. Fifteen of our kites flying all that way with five-and-a-half-ton bombs each to knock down someone's house right at the end of the war seemed an odd and rather petty mission. Having studied the map, I certainly couldn't see how Adolf could possibly transport the hardware he'd need to mount a last stand in such a mountainous area. Nonetheless, orders were orders, and I prepared for the raid with just as much care as the others. After squeezing into our flying gear, we were on board and ready for take-off shortly after 4 a.m.

It was a beautiful morning, and I clearly remember how the sun appeared over the horizon as we climbed to meet it. Here we were, in all the splendour of the dawn, while it was still dark on the earth 20,000 feet below us.

The flight was a very long one, and some time before we arrived over the snow-capped peaks of the Bavarian Alps I was astonished to see that we were joining up with a much greater number of Main Force bombers. I was perplexed, as there didn't appear to be any obvious targets in the area. Our task was a very accurate one, to drop on the actual Eagle's Nest, which meant we had to get a very clear picture of exactly where it was.

As we approached, though, it became clear that identifying the site would be no easy task. The Alpine peaks stretched out before us were glorious; a picture postcard view which seemed ill-suited to our warlike intentions. Mountains topped with white hid deep, dark valleys, many of which were in shadow in the morning sun. There were a few similar-looking villages dotted about, but for the most part it was a vast, unpopulated area, and certainly not the kind of place to have to make an emergency landing. As the Main Force bombers left us and we stooged around trying to identify the Eagle's Nest, I was very aware that our time would be severely limited as we were towards the end of our range.

'Where the bloody hell is it?' Rumgay, the bomb aimer, was getting frustrated at our inability to find exactly what we were aiming at. We weren't the only ones trying to find where we should drop, and our navigator was trying hard to identify our run-in point. We knew we were in the right area, but that wasn't good enough.

'Hold on, I think that's it … yes, that's it, got it. OK, left a bit, we're nearly bang on it … bombsight light on!'

Pleased to be back on track, I made the correction and we began our ten-minute run-in. While the magic box did its work, ahead of us the small complex of Adolf Hitler's mountainside home grew closer. We'd all seen the newsreels of him there before the war, greeting politicians on the terrace which looked out over a spectacular view, and now we were intent on its destruction. All was going well, five minutes into our run-in and no flak or fighters yet. Steady.

'Bombsight ON!'

The target disappeared under the nose as we got closer, uninterrupted by flak, and it was shaping up to be one of the more simple operations I had taken part in. Steady … steady … any moment now … steady … come on … surely it should have dropped by now … steady … I was tensing myself for the kite's leap upwards as the bomb dropped, but time seemed to stand still as we flew onwards.

'What the hell's going on?' I asked, 'What's happened to the bomb?'

'It's hung up, it didn't drop,' came the reply, meaning that the bomb hadn't released when it was triggered, and was still attached to the kite.

'All right, never mind, keep your eyes on the target and we'll go back for another pass, see if it works.'

Suddenly I was aware of Rumgay climbing up out of his space in the nose, pushing past the engineer and making his way towards the back of the aircraft. Because I was concentrating on flying, I didn't immediately understand what he was doing. When he came back a few moments later, I asked what was going on.

'The release didn't work,' he said, 'so I pulled the emergency release lever to get rid of it. That damn thing doesn't work either though.'

I was appalled. Instead of telling me, the skipper, what he was going to do, he had taken it upon himself to dump our bomb miles off target when there was still plenty of time to go around again for another run. To make matters worse, our five-and-a-half-ton Tallboy was now lodged under the belly of our kite with the emergency release lever pulled, and quite possibly fused to go off. I wanted to haul him over the coals right there and then for his irresponsible behaviour, especially because, as Bombing Leader for the squadron, he really should have known better. We were under strict instructions that the Tallboy was an expensive item, to be used professionally and accurately, and brought home if it wasn't used. I was really wild with him but I bit my tongue. I believed it was very bad practice to have an argument on board the aircraft while still over enemy territory, when everyone on board needed to work together. Tight-lipped, I asked the navigator for a course for home, as Tallboys exploded behind us and we turned north-west. I had to maintain all my concentration for our approach and landing at base, as my guess was that a gentle landing would be an advantage when carrying a five-and-a-half-ton bomb which could fall off at the slightest provocation.

The trip back was uneventful, leaving me to stew on what had happened. Thankfully, when we got to Woodhall Spa our approach was perfect. Passing gently over the perimeter fence, I set her down softly right at the start of the runway and had plenty of time to slow down and bring us to a standstill.

My first action on climbing down the ladder was to berate the armaments crew who had loaded our Tallboy. Their work had evidently not been up to standard that day, as the chain with its release mechanism was still firmly fixed around the bomb and to the kite.

My mortification at missing out on our attack was relieved somewhat at debriefing, when it emerged that very few of the squadron had actually achieved any success. Out of fifteen kites, five bombed other targets, three came back having never seen the target at all, and two, including ourselves, had hang-ups. Another two dropped on unidentified targets but saw no explosions, and another ran out of time in the target area and had to drop his bomb in order to catch up with the gaggle of aircraft heading for home. I resolved to have it out with Rumgay if we were called for another mission, but Berchtesgaden was to be the last. It wasn't the most auspicious way to end my operational campaign, but it did mean that we were both spared any confrontation.

CHAPTER SIXTEEN

BUCKINGHAM PALACE TO NAUGHTY NAPLES

It had been months since I was awarded the DFC for helping to save the lives of the Halifax crew in their life raft. Since then I had been parading about with the medal ribbon sewn onto my tunic, with some mixed emotions. Of course I was very proud to wear it, and enjoyed the feel-good factor very much. To begin with it was impossible to walk without sticking one's left breast forward, but this soon wore off and the whole incident, including the gong, was forgotten in the stresses and pressures of operations. There was always an unsettling feeling, though, that the whole thing only came about as the result of a mistake, and that while there had been seven of us in the crew only I had come out with the award.

In the meantime the powers that be had been watching my progress, and decided to give me a Bar to the DFC because I had done a few more ops and was still enthusiastic to get to grips with the enemy. I wasn't going to argue!

When you were awarded the immediate DFC it was customary to be invited to Buckingham Palace to be presented with it by the King himself, and for months I had waited for a letter confirming the date for this auspicious event. I had very much wanted my dear mother to come with me, because I knew how proud she would be to see her son in his officer's uniform presented to His Majesty. She was so excited and desperate to come that we even contacted the authorities to explain her state of health, and request that the date could be brought forward.

Sadly, it was not to be. The invitation was for 29 April, but it arrived too late to show it to her as she died just a couple of weeks before.

The invitation specified that I could bring two guests. Of course one would be my father, and we also asked Mum's best friend, Aunty Tim.

I was given leave to go home just before the ceremony, and drove down to London in my Austin from Woodhall Spa. I stayed at home with Dad in a strange atmosphere. We were very excited about going to the Palace of course, but so sad that Mum wasn't there to share it with us.

The next morning, the day itself, I got up very early to prepare my uniform. It was my best kit, not the one I had been rolling around in on the farm! First to get attention were my shoes, which were polished to get the very best shine possible, before reaching for the button cleaning kit. The most important part of that was the Button Stick, a flat piece of brass about six inches long with a five inch slit in it. That would slide along a line of buttons to protect your uniform as you attacked them with liberal doses of Brasso until they glowed. A clean shirt and tie completed the ensemble, and Dad gave me a final once-over with the clothes brush before we set off to pick up Aunty Tim from Victoria Station just a stone's throw from the Palace.

She was there as expected at ten o'clock, and at exactly half past as requested we drove past the Victoria Memorial and up to the gates of Buckingham Palace. Police checked us through, and we were waved through into an inner courtyard where we were allocated a parking space.

Hoping that my buttons and shoes were still shiny, I presented myself to an attendant who led us through a doorway and into the Palace. Strangely, I remember no feelings of fear or awe as all of this happened, perhaps because I was used to living on my nerves by then, and was ready to take life as it came – although I can't say the same for my father and Aunty Tim!

We were led into a large, brightly lit room full of chairs ready to receive people. Evidently I wasn't the only one to be recognised that day, as others were arriving too. The chairs had a central aisle between them, which led to a little podium where the King would receive us. All around the walls were fabulous paintings and gilded fittings, exactly as you would imagine in a Palace, but at the same time it felt welcoming and not at all austere. We took chairs on the right of the room, in the second or third row.

'May I ask what decoration you are to receive?' another official asked, taking my details on a clipboard. I told him, and he fixed a special clip beneath my wings to make it easier for the King to attach my gong.

All about was an excited murmur of conversation until the equerry mounted the steps to the podium. We listened in respectful silence.

'Good morning. I'd like to run through the procedure for today's ceremony. When your name is called, please march to the podium. Wait for the King to speak to you, and if you speak to him please address him as 'Your Majesty'. He will pin your medal on your chest, and may wish to have a few words with you. When you have responded, please WAIT for his Majesty to offer his hand to be shaken, and most importantly, kindly DON'T squeeze his hand. His Majesty shakes thousands of hands every week, and repeated strong handshakes could damage his right hand. Thank you.'

As he left the podium conversation grew again, as we waited in anticipation of the King's arrival. Suddenly, without any fanfare, he was there and we all craned our necks to see him. He was dressed in full uniform with all his medals on show, and I noticed that he had quite a few more than me! The equerry started to read through the list of names, and each time a soldier, sailor or airman would march stiffly up to the dais, salute, and receive his decoration and perhaps a few words. A gentle handshake, and they marched back to their seats and smiling relatives.

Before I knew it, I heard 'Flight Lieutenant Ken Trent, DFC.'

'Just do it,' I thought, and marched with all the vim I could muster with the eyes of the room upon me, up to the King. I imagined Mum watching over my shoulder as I came to a smart stop, and shot up the best salute I had ever made. My DFC was handed to the King, who hooked it carefully onto the clip on my uniform.

'Congratulations,' he said, 'and thank you for your outstanding efforts.'

I was aware of his hand being held out and remembered to take it carefully. A gentle shake, and I was marching back to my chair, with my dad and Aunty Tim beaming at me. I was very aware of the silver cross flashing on my uniform, and as the proceedings came to an end I stood up feeling a little self-conscious but of course very proud. When it was all over we were invited through into an adjoining room, where we were offered tea and a piece of cake. Everyone was trying to be terribly polite but really it was just like a bunfight at a local parish hall, balancing your cake in one hand and tea in the other while making awkward conversation.

My dad and Aunty Tim were thrilled with the whole adventure, although of course it was tinged with sadness at the loss of my mum. Their pride in me was obvious, and I'm sure my dad was glad to think that my expensive education may not have been entirely wasted after all. As we scoffed our cake and drank our tea, I looked around at the opulent surroundings, the gold, the paintings, the velvet and the plush carpet, and realised that I really didn't belong in such formality. I would much rather have had a piss-up with the boys in the mess at 625. I was far more comfortable in my scruffy battledress milking a cow on the farm, or taking off into the darkness at the controls of my Lancaster, than in best dress making small talk in a palace. I was quite glad when we finally left, with Aunty Tim and Dad chattering way in the car about what they had seen.

Nine days later the war in Europe was over.

I had survived, where 55,000 of my Bomber Command comrades had not.

The war in Japan was still going on, however, and I was caught up in the desire to do my duty to get it all over with. I volunteered for Tiger Force, a bomber group which would be sent to the Pacific to take the war over mainland Japan.

While we waited for our chance to carry on the war, High Command found some other jobs for us to do. So it was that we were called to the briefing room one day to find the piece of red ribbon on the blackboard stretching hundreds of miles due south across France and down towards

Italy. Where on earth were we going?

'Gentlemen, we've been asked to go to Italy to help repatriate some of our Prisoners of War who need to come home. They've had a tough time out there, and we're going to be the taxi service to bring them back.'

We were to be part of Operation Exodus, where bombers which were no longer being used would bring home prisoners who had spent a long time behind German wire. It certainly sounded worthwhile, and easier than the bombing raids I was used to, and I looked forward to seeing a liberated France from my cockpit. The weather forecast was good, and we took off with a full load of fuel into blue skies after making as much space as possible for soldiers in the kite. Our destination was Pomigliano, an airfield northeast of Naples.

It was a strange feeling, flying over countries which up until now had represented danger and death to me. We all kept a good lookout, but as a matter of habit rather than in the expectation of anybody attacking us. I could look down and enjoy the sight of towns, rivers, hills and cities in the afternoon sun, instead of sweating into my suit waiting for the first burst of flak or command to 'Corkscrew left'.

On we flew, almost due south, until we approached the north of Spain and the Pyrenees before turning east and across the Mediterranean to Italy. Having never been there before, our navigator made sure he was spot-on in finding our way. On arrival we had hoped for an enthusiastic welcome from the Brown Jobs we were due to be ferrying back the next day. Instead, soon after climbing down from our kite after a very lengthy flight, we were told to parade on a small square and face a pep talk by a Warrant Officer Parkes. He was a small man with an enormous voice, and he wasn't afraid to use it. The troops all knew the Italian city as Naughty Naples, and he was very keen to ensure that we didn't get up to any mischief during our free evening. I will never forget his final words of sage advice …

'The ladies here all have the Black Pox, so my advice is to put it between your legs and mark time!'

Not to be put off, a bunch of us decided to go into town that evening just to see what all the fuss was about. None of us had much cash, so the plan was to go in, have a look around, maybe a beer or two, then back to base, preferably without the Black Pox! We soon found out that ladies were the least of our worries, and that in fact we should be far more concerned about the children. There were hundreds of them roaming the streets, often in ragged clothes, but they were all on the make. Every single one of them wanted to trade or change money, and between them I reckon they ran the black market in Naples. Anything you wanted they would offer, crowding around you, waving packets of cigarettes and bundles of cash, everything from Lira to ladies, and they wouldn't take no for an answer. They were also very bright and sharp, and as soon as a deal was done they took off and disappeared into the crowd. The reason for that quickly became apparent when one of our number unwisely changed some money with one of the little urchins. He got well and truly diddled and lost a lot of money, realising far too late that the little tyke who had offered him such a good deal had long since scarpered. 'Where is the little bugger?' he cried, pushing between the hordes of other kids and scanning the street. Of course there was no sign of him, and his partners in crime were hardly like to grass him up, were they?

Bitterly, he swore revenge while we chuckled, a strapping great airman plotting to get even with the ten-year-old lad who had outsmarted him. He wrapped some torn paper in the few notes he had left to make up a fake bundle of readies which looked like the real deal until you looked closely. Unable to find the original criminal, he decided that revenge would be just as sweet if he took it out on another one of the street-savvy urchins. What a mistake! As soon as the kid realised he had been ripped off he started shouting the odds at the top of his voice and all his mates joined in. It was an unbelievable sight as hundreds of scruffy kids came pouring out of every doorway and surrounded him, demanding retribution as he tried to fight them off and prevent their nimble fingers slipping into his pockets and relieving him of everything he had left. Twisting and turning, he tried to get rid of them but they were shrill and insistent that he should cough up his cash. Eventually they chased him until he managed to slip into a Salvation Army building, but if he thought that would deter them he was in for a surprise. Far from dispersing in frustration, the crowd actually grew as more and more kids arrived from every direction, hundreds of them surrounding the building. There was no way he was going to get away without giving in to them, and eventually this man, who had braved the darkness, fighters and flak of Nazi Germany, had to capitulate to a pack of angry Italian kids and give them all his money. Not that we laughed, of course …

The following morning I collected the cargo manifesto detailing the names and numbers of the servicemen I would be taking, and led them out to our Lanc. I had to get on board first, as I would never be able to get to my seat past all of them as they crammed into every available space. When all twenty-five were on board, we took off. It was an unusual distribution of load for me, and I readjusted the trim after take-off to account for it. Climbing slowly, we headed west and crossed the Spanish coast three hours later before crossing the mountains again and heading north. The only problem we encountered was numbness of the nether regions after such a long flight; otherwise it was wonderful to fly over a safe and unoccupied Europe once more. The men all got back safe and sound, and appreciated their quick return to Blighty.

A day or two later, and we were off to Italy again.

Our route was to be much the same, and I looked forward to another evening around Naughty Naples. We went through the usual pre-flight drills at Waddington before turning onto the runway, opening the taps and taking off. We were climbing away onto our course and settling in for a long day when the navigator came over the air.

'Skipper, we've got a problem. The Gee box isn't working. We won't be able to get a proper fix. It's completely U/S.' He meant it was unserviceable.

'That's fine,' I said, 'We know the way, it's easy enough, we can do without it.'

But he was unhappy about flying without what was an important navigational aid, and insisted we turn back.

'We have to get another one. Latest KRs (King's Regulations) say that

234

we aren't allowed to fly if the Gee box is U/S. Take us back to base and we'll either get a new Gee box or a new kite.'

Reluctantly I eased the stick over again, and followed his heading back to base. As we came in to land, I felt the kite give a little swing to one side, which I automatically corrected and gave no further thought to, as it landed smoothly.

After waiting for the ground crew to plug in a new box, we taxied back to the runway and prepared to get going once more. Up went the throttles, off came the brakes, and we were rolling down the track. We were at about eighty miles an hour, too slow to take off but too fast to stop in time, when the kite turned suddenly to the right. The runway disappeared and we were bumping over the grass at full throttle in the wrong direction with very few options to save the situation as we headed fast towards the perimeter fence. I realised immediately that one of the engines had failed. With no time to look out at the propellers, I had to quickly guess which one and take action. Because of the violence of the swing, I was almost certain it had to be the starboard outer, as the two engines on the port wing were acting against the remaining starboard inner, pushing us around and off the runway.

I frantically adjusted the controls as I was bounced up and down in my seat. Full left rudder, feather the starboard outer, both inboard engines through the gate to emergency power, as I knew we had to try to get airborne.

'Wheels up!' I shouted. Bill pushed the safety catch and pulled the lever.

The crew hardly needed me to shout 'Emergency, emergency, crash positions!' as they already knew we were in desperate and unpredictable trouble. My view of the ground was now obscured, and we were dragging along with the nose up and the tail down, while I relied on instruments to see if we had managed to take off at all. It was like a punch-drunk boxer trying to beat the count, staggering to get up on one knee. My left leg, pushing as hard as possible on the rudder pedal, was killing me and I knew we were in serious danger. To relieve the strain on my leg I reached for the rudder trim wheel with my right hand and started to turn it.

It wasn't enough. The kite was just managing to clear the fields below by a couple of feet when the right wing, without its second engine to give it lift, stalled and dropped.

In a moment the wingtip dug into the ground, which caused the whole kite to begin to cartwheel. Since we weren't on a hostile operation I wasn't wearing my harness, and as the cartwheel began we were all getting thrown around. Despite that I managed to reach for the cage which covered the ignition switches, flip it up and cut the ignition to all engines, hoping that would reduce the risk of us catching fire. The kite was pivoting up and over the right wing tip, and in moments the nose would smash into the ground. I grabbed for the best available handhold, which was the handle just above the windscreen which I would usually use to pull myself up into my seat. The engines fell silent as the ground rushed up to meet us, and I pushed my head as hard as possible against my hands, hoping they might do something to cushion me from the inevitable impact. It came immediately, as the nose ploughed hard sideways into the earth, bending and tearing the front cupola away. The kite crumpled with the force of the crash, mud flew up into the shattered cockpit from the gaping hole in the nose as we decelerated, and my head slipped off the cushion of my hands with the impact. Eyes wide open, I saw the artificial horizon come up to meet my face, only to be smashed back up again as the cartwheel continued and my whole body was thrown against the side of the canopy. All I could hear was a deafening grating, tearing sound, as our once-beautiful kite was shaken to pieces around us. Luckily for us she didn't flip over but came down with another crash as the tail hit, to slide along the ground on her belly. Miraculously I was still more or less in my seat.

My instructions to all my crews previously had been that if I shouted 'Emergency, emergency, jump jump!' then they would never be able to get out of the kite as fast as me. Imagine my surprise when I went for the emergency exit just above my seat only to find my head going into someone else's bum! I scrambled out after him as the aircraft finally slid to a halt, and sat on what remained of the nose watching him run away, slowly realising that I was still alive. The crackling of the dead engines as they cooled down penetrated the sudden silence.

The propellers were bent out of all recognition and covered with clods of earth.

Most of the other crew members had managed to get out of their own exits and were about twenty-five yards away, looking up at me perched above the wreck of our aircraft. Surprisingly there was no smell of fuel, just a warm breeze blowing across our faces. Looking back over the rear of the kite, I could see the furrows where we had torn up the field, and in the distance was the muddy figure of our Gremlin running towards us. Sliding down the side of the wreckage I joined the rest of the crew a safe distance away, and breathlessly exchanged our stories of survival. Gremlin had been particularly lucky. As the tail of the kite had flicked toward the ground in the cartwheel, his rear turret had been pivoted sideways ninety degrees. When the tail hit, the turret doors had burst open, spewing him clear out of the wreckage and into the muddy field. There was nothing wrong with him that a good shower wouldn't cure!

It seemed we had all been extraordinarily lucky, with no real injuries to speak of. I had a slight strain to my neck which was a little uncomfortable, but it could have been so much worse. We all wandered together over to the field gate, where an ambulance had arrived with a concerned crew who rushed us to the sick bay to be checked over. It didn't take long for us to be given the all-clear and released as fit to fly again. In my later life I was to suffer chronic pain in my back ending in a major operation, and I always wondered if this crash could have been the cause.

After a couple of days to recover, we were detailed for another Operation Exodus mission; this time to Bari on the east coast, just above the heel of the boot of Italy. Fortunately, take-off and landing were without incident, and we found the welcome at Bari far more friendly than it had been in Naples. Having an evening off, a bunch of us decided to go into town for a good time and discovered a wonderful drink called Tia Maria which cost just a pound a bottle. We had never come across it before and it tasted very good; consequently we drank several bottles of it between us and brought several more back to take home. A good time was had by all as they say, but unfortunately the following morning we had to pay the price. I awoke feeling dreadful, very rough and under the weather. I simply wasn't used to drinking such strong spirits, and they were having their revenge. I managed to hold myself together through briefing, and not give away just how badly hungover I was. I listened to the Met man.

'Should be fairly straightforward this morning. Low cloud will break at about 5,000 feet, to give you clear skies pretty much the whole way back.' That didn't sound too bad.

A bus took us, all with throbbing heads and queasy stomachs, to our kite, which was sitting on the tarmac looking as though it disapproved of our conduct. As we got out and stretched our legs another bus filled with soldiers who were to be our cargo arrived. The officer in charge, who would be travelling with us, presented me with the all-important cargo manifesto which carried details of exactly who would be on the flight. I didn't really pay it any attention because a serious situation had just arisen.

'Sorry Sir, but I can't take off just yet. Where's the nearest toilet, please?'

My stomach had just lurched again and I need to relieve myself quickly. Burdened with my flying gear, I hobbled across the airfield to the nearest convenience which was just a long, rough plank with holes cut in it over an open ditch. There were no screens or anything to give you any privacy, and the smell emanating from the well-filled ditch was utterly nauseating.

When I finally finished what I had to do and managed to rearrange my layers of clothing, I staggered back towards the aircraft feeling very green. I was met by the officer, who handed back to me the cargo manifesto which he had found blowing about the airfield. Not exactly the way to instil confidence in the boys who were waiting to get on board, I'm sure! Chastened, I climbed the ladder and pulled myself blearily into the seat.

Aware of my fragility, I took extra care over my pre-flight checks before pulling onto the runway and taking off.

As predicted there was low cloud above us but I kept climbing, expecting it to clear at 5,000 feet. When we got to that altitude, though, we were still deeply enveloped in thick cloud with no sign of it thinning out.

'I'm going to take us up higher,' I said, 'to try to get out of the cloud. It's bound to thin out soon.'

So we climbed higher … and higher … and the kite started to shake alarmingly as we approached 10,000 feet with still no break in the clouds. We couldn't go any higher because the twenty-five chaps crammed into the back didn't have any oxygen supply and would quickly pass out. It was also getting very cold. The whole scenario was becoming very worrying as the turbulence increased to severe. I wished I had my harness done up, as my poor hungover head and stomach were being tossed up and down and from side to side by fierce up-and-down draughts.

'OK Navigator, this is no joke, I'm going to take us down as low as I can to try to get out of this. How low can we go and still stay safe above any hills?'

'You might be able to get to 3,000 Skip, that should be OK …'

'All right, let me know when we've passed the coast and are over the sea and we'll go even lower.'

I started our descent, but quickly realised that it would be far harder than I expected to get below the danger. We had unwittingly flown into a cumulonimbus cloud even worse than the one I had experienced over Germany. One moment I had the stick forward in a dive but was being pushed UP at a rate of knots, the next the current changed direction and we were violently forced downwards beyond the ability of the Lanc even to hold its altitude. The stick was being shaken around in my hands, and it took all my efforts to keep us on an even keel. I wanted to lose height, but to do it safely and in a controlled fashion, otherwise we could find ourselves pushed straight into the sea. I couldn't imagine what the poor soldiers in the back were going through, although I felt pretty dreadful myself due to the ongoing effects of the Tia Maria.

Suddenly we burst through the bottom of the cloud a few hundred feet above the sea, to see a huge water spout reaching up into the cloud about 500 yards to the right. In that moment, everything became calm and safe again as I could clearly see the bottoms of several more cu-nim clouds and steer around them.

'OK Navigator, I'm going to stay at 200 feet until we clear these clouds. I will be taking a few detours to avoid the worst of them but I'll try to stick more or less to your original course.'

'OK Skipper, just give me a moment to pick all my stuff up off the floor …!'

It had been a very hairy time. Those cumulonimbus clouds are more dangerous around southern Europe and the Mediterranean than they are closer to home, and we were very, very lucky to have escaped without any serious damage. Eventually the cloud cleared and we were able to climb again to our recommended cruising height. As we approached England, another problem presented itself.

'Skipper, you do realise that if we land at Woodhall, we'll have to get everyone checked by customs?'

Ah, yes of course, customs … and us with several crates of Tia Maria on board.

'I understand, Navigator. Any suggestions?'

'Well Skip, we could always head to Woodbridge …'

That was a great idea. Woodbridge was a base regularly used by aircraft in trouble because of damage or malfunction. Its runway was extra wide and extra long – and more to the point it didn't have any customs.

'OK, let's have the bearing …'

I got on the radio to Woodbridge explaining that we had been in a big storm and were worried about the effect it may have had on our aircraft. One of our engines was overheating and we had twenty-five POWs with us. Permission to land? Of course.

We touched down without any problem, and taxied to a hard standing in relief.

Piling out of the kite, we all milled around while waiting for the bus to take us in. The soldiers had all survived the ordeal, and some told me that the storm had been like driving over very rough ground in a tank. As the bus pulled up, a corporal got out holding a white form.

'You don't have anything to declare do you sir?'

'Oh no.'

'Very good, Sir. Please sign here ...'

A quick signature and we were home, although it would be some time before I could bring myself to taste the contraband Tia Maria.

We allowed them to check our 'faulty' engine before returning to our own base the next day. We found that two other aircraft from other squadrons had experienced bad trouble in the clouds. Legend had it that one had been lost, while another managed to struggle home with a broken back, after the mid-upper turret had been sucked right out of the kite, along with the unfortunate gunner.

We were also detailed to carry out several other operations over Europe in the weeks immediately after the war ended, but these would be best described as 'sightseeing' tours.

High Command thought it would be a good thing for ground crew, armourers and anyone else who had contributed to our efforts to see just what we had achieved. So it was that we took off with a bunch of crew, or 'erks' in the kites, to fly over the Ruhr and other bombed areas to see just what they looked like in relative safety, at low level and in daylight. They were called 'cross country' flights. Instead of having to clench my hands over the steering column and grit my teeth flying into a storm of flak while dodging searchlights, this time I could drop down to two or three thousand feet and have a good look at what remained of our targets. Sure enough I could clearly make out smashed sidings and railway yards, shattered factories and installations, and of course devastated homes, shops, churches and roads. It amazed me, as I banked to survey the sea of rubble which was once the heart of Cologne, that anyone could have survived there. We had certainly done as Bomber Harris had asked, and brought destruction on a huge scale to the Germans – which to my mind was no more than they had deserved. I remember looking down and thinking to myself, 'However will they be able to make that right again?'

It was strange, leaving the Ruhr behind and setting a course for home, to be able to fly in safety and tranquillity without having to look for clouds where we could hide from fighters.

The Exodus and Cross Country missions dried up after a week or two and I cooled my heels at the farm while I waited news of my posting, milking and watering the cows and trying to come to terms with everything that had happened to me. Life at 617 had changed dramatically now that there were no exciting missions to be flown, becoming safer and routine. Fauquier left, to be replaced by Wing Commander Grindon. He was of medium height, wearing wings but no other medals. He had spent the war shining an office chair. For those of us hoping to go on to Tiger Force he organised endless training, usually repeated 'bombing' missions over Wainfleet which we now knew like the backs of our hands.

As things wound down, we became aware that we wouldn't be staying at Woodhall Spa much longer. Plans were afoot to move us to a station which was operational in times of peace as well as war, so that Petwood could return to its previous atmosphere of calm. Saying goodbye would of course mean leaving the Coultons and their farm behind, which I knew would be a real wrench for all concerned. I resolved to give them a real treat before the unhappy day came about.

While chatting to Bob and the family over tea one evening I realised that he had never owned a car, and scarcely ever left the surroundings of his farm and the neighbouring village. I resolved that the whole family should have a day out, and on my first day off operations after that, I turned up to the farm especially early. They were all up already in the dawn light, and we went straight to the sheds to water and milk the cows before piling into my Austin and heading to Skegness. Bob helped me out with directions but neither of us were sure of how to get there, and it was little use following the road signs which were few and far between anyway. Many of them had been taken away during the war. We eventually found our way though, with the girls sat in the back singing, 'Ken's car can go very far!' as we chugged along the lanes towards the sea.

It was a magical day for me, wandering along the front and sharing their wonder at the waves and the sand, playing games with the girls and eating ice lollies. After all the nerve-shattering tensions of action, it was ever so nice to have a little hand to hold, and to hear the sound of children's laughter as we strolled along.

Lunch was in a fish and chip shop, and I remember Bob, a practical man, insisting that everyone ate everything they had been given. 'We've paid for that, it's been paid for, you eat it …'

Before we knew it, it was time to get back in the car and head for home. Bob was concerned about the cows, which had to be milked again before the end of the day. More singing as we drove back, into the setting sun and towards an uncertain future, at the end of a day I will never forget.

CHAPTER SEVENTEEN

FROM BOMBER BOY
TO BARMAN

Sure enough, the news soon came that we were to move to RAF Waddington. While not a huge distance away by today's standards, it meant my cosy existence at the farm would have to come to an end. On 17 June 1945 the unhappy day came, and the goodbyes were long and tearful. I was able afterwards to make the odd visit in my car, but could no longer simply pop by at the end of an operation or on days when we couldn't fly.

I concentrated instead on settling in to my new base. Waddington was a comfortable, established RAF station, far less posh than Woodhall Spa, with a well-run informal mess in which Gremlin and I felt far more at home. I remember it as DIT DIT DIT DAA, DIT DAA – Morse code for WA, the airfield call sign.

On the first morning I came down to the usual breakfast, only to find some of the other officers tucking into a far more hearty plateful than mine, seeming to feature mushrooms as a primary ingredient.

'Those look nice,' I said to a friendly looking type. 'Where'd you get them?'

'You can pick them yourself,' he said, 'just go down to the perimeter of the airfield and there are loads of them growing. Cut as many as you want, bring them back, and give 'em to the cooks – they'll sort them out for you.'

The next morning, bright and early, I did as he suggested and found myself a rich harvest of tasty mushrooms which were delicious fried up with my breakfast. It was also a nice way to get myself out and about, and in touch with the soil the way I had been at Bob's.

Life at Waddington went back to the routine I had lived with before I went on operations for the first time. There were interminable training missions to Wainfleet, and plenty of classes to go to in order to prepare us for life in the Far East. The weather conditions would be different there, and we had to learn all about the wind and climate changes and how they might affect our aircraft. It would be hot and clammy too, and I remember in particular a lecture on personal hygiene!

It was all becoming rather routine, and without the distraction and calming influence of the farm I went in search of a little more excitement. My first move was to trade in my nice reliable Austin for a very flashy convertible MG which was bright red and had a fabulous little engine. It cost ninety quid, and led me into all sorts of scrapes, including one which was to have another profound effect on my life.

In order to keep its thirsty pistons running, I used Steve's old trick of popping into service stations in my uniform and asking if anyone had any spare petrol. When they saw my wings and medals, people were usually very keen to let me have a gallon or two, which I poured into a two-gallon metal can in the boot if the tank was already full.

One evening I was in the car with a friend of mine from the squadron, heading out for a good time. We went to the White Hart in Burton upon Trent, which was a lovely pub serving fantastic local beer. I remember the cellar being below the level of the nearby river, and all the barrels of beer were kept nice and cool there. The landlady kept us topped up by going down the steps with an old enamel jug which she filled from the barrel, before returning to slop it into our empty glasses.

Heading back, we were nearing Derby and I was driving pretty fast in my flashy new car. My mate was showing off too, standing on the passenger seat with his head above the windscreen enjoying the slipstream. I was weaving in and out of the traffic, which seemed keen to avoid us, when I felt a tap on my shoulder. Looking across I saw him standing on the seat and waving his arms, looking as though he was having a great time showing off to the people on the streets. I gave him a thumbs-up, put my foot down, and listened to the wonderful roar of the engine as we sped even faster. The next thing I knew there was a strong thump on my shoulder and the muffled sound of shouting. Looking over again, I could see my mate pointing wildly towards the back of the car. A quick glance showed me just what was upsetting him; the boot was on fire, and flames were blazing out behind us like a rocket. I reacted instinctively by slamming on the brakes as hard as I could and bracing myself against the steering wheel. My friend of course had nothing to hold on to, and was flung over the windscreen. As I screeched to a stop I looked over to see him with one foot scraping along the road, one hanging over the screen, and both arms wrapped around the left headlamp to hold himself up – unharmed, although with a few choice words to say ...

I jumped out and ran to the back of the car. The boot had fallen open, and there burning fiercely was the two-gallon fuel tank. The rubber seal on the screw cap must have perished and allowed petrol to drip down onto the hot exhaust.

'Look out!' I yelled, as I wrapped my hand in a rag and grabbed the handle of the can. I pulled as hard as I could to yank it out of the boot and throw it away, but the handle just popped off in my hand as the solder which had attached it to the can had melted. I was left holding a very hot piece of metal and watching my beloved new car turn into a bonfire.

Just as the blaze was taking a real hold, around the corner came a lorry laden with sand. The driver took one look at us and pulled over.

'All right mate, let's get some sand on it quick!'

We all grabbed shovels and, getting as close as the heat would allow, started chucking loads of dark red sand into the boot and over the back of my once-lovely car. Slowly the burning can was covered and the flames flickered and died. I stared ruefully at the lovely red paintwork which was all blistered and cracked. There was sand everywhere, and the whole car was a write-off. As the adrenaline ebbed away, we looked at each other and asked a couple of obvious questions ...

'What are we going to do with it now?'

'And how are we going to get back to base?'

The answer to the first question came from another truck driver, who towed the wreck to the side of the road for us. Mournfully we trudged off down the street, intent on drowning our sorrows before finding a way back to Waddington. Besides, a pub would have a telephone, and we could call from there and maybe arrange a lift.

The first we came to was right on the Derwent Bridge, a two-storey red brick place called the Royal Standard. Pushing our way inside in our blackened uniforms, we must have looked a real sight, and the locals certainly took notice of us! In one corner was an old lady who was well dressed, covered in rings and jewellery, and surrounded by others who seemed to be hanging on her every word as she held court. We had to tell our sorry tale, and it didn't take me long to discover that she was known as Grandma Parnell, and was the mother of the famous racing driver Reg Parnell! Her daughter was the landlady of the Royal Standard. Reg's sister Gladys ran another pub with her husband Dick, and the help of their daughter Peggy, who soon caught my eye. She was tall, friendly and fun with a lovely bright face. It wasn't long before I had her laughing at the story of my car, and before you know it I had asked her out on a date. After an exciting evening I have no idea how we eventually got back to our base, but I know I couldn't wait to get back to Derby to see her. Somehow I managed to cadge enough lifts to see her quite often, and we quickly became attached to each other. The pub they ran, the George, was in the centre of Derby and I became a regular there to the extent that I even helped behind the bar when they were busy. It quickly became another family for me, as her parents liked me and encouraged us to be together.

The war was still going on though, and in between trips to Derby I was kept occupied with training and learning more about what was happening in the Far East. Japan had been beaten at sea, her outlying islands had nearly all been taken, and despite having little hope left she refused to surrender. Most of us were certain that the only way to defeat her was to invade, and we were convinced that we were preparing to fly missions in support of an invasion. By this stage, I just wanted to get over there and get the job done and the war over so I could start to make a new life for myself. The peace I had found on the farm, and my flourishing love affair with Peggy, meant that I was really starting to look forward to it all being finished and making my own way in the world. We were all itching to get going, to end the interminable training and do our job in Japan.

And then, totally out of the blue, two aircraft ended the war on their own. On 6 August the Americans dropped an atomic bomb on Hiroshima, followed by the destruction of Nagasaki on the 9th. The sheer power of the new weapons dwarfed even our Grand Slams, and it seemed incredible that just one aircraft and one bomb could devastate a city far more effectively than the thousand-bomber raids I had been a part of. A new chapter was written in the history books as the Japanese surrendered, and the bomber war changed forever.

I happened to be on leave at the time, and was at home seeing my dad. We drove as far as we could into town, then joined the thronging crowds at the Victoria Monument in front of Buckingham Palace. There were thousands and thousands of us, cheering and waving, and I remembered how proud I had been to go inside and receive my medal a few months before. Dad told me that if we got separated he would put his hat on top of his stick and wave it in the air, just as he had when we had come as a family to cheer the coronation. As the people of London celebrated around me, I felt happy and rather elated that I had survived it all, and 'done my bit' with some success.

On the way home in the car our way was continually blocked by cheering, singing, flag-waving people. At first it was fun but after a while Dad and I were getting a bit fed up with it all and just wanted to get home. We came around one corner at East Ham and the crowd just packed around the car, laughing and yelling and forcing us to stop. For some reason they took it into their heads to start rocking us from side to side, and our little motor was suddenly being thrown about all over the place. He wound down his window.

'What the hell are you doing?' he shouted, as we tilted alarmingly. Enough was enough. I pushed the door open and heaved myself out of the car with as much dignity as I could muster.

'Stop it! Leave us alone!' I yelled, in my best parade ground voice, which proved to be very effective. As soon as they saw my uniform with its wings and medals and heard me yell they let go of the car immediately.

'Sorry Sir, no offence, just having some fun, the war's over!'

I slept at home that night wondering what the future would hold. Even though the war was indeed over, I was dismayed to find that the RAF expected me to keep training and preparing for a move to the Far East. Now that I had done my job and defeated the enemy I wasn't at all interested in staying on for no discernible reason. I had originally signed on to extend my service by three years, but quickly withdrew that when I realised what I might be letting myself in for. It didn't take a genius to realise that hundreds of thousands of servicemen and women would very soon be surplus to requirements with no-one to fight, and they would all be out looking for whatever jobs they could find. I didn't want them to get there ahead of me, so I told the RAF I wanted to go at the earliest opportunity.

My permanent address was now The George Hotel. Peggy's parents approved of me, and when I moaned about having to go back to base one evening and they offered me a room there instead, I needed no second bidding. Just like the farm, when I wasn't needed on station I was in my new car and off to Derby just as fast as I could. My new car was a sixty quid Ford 8 which looked lovely but had a knackered engine. It managed to use as much oil as petrol, and smoked very badly, but fortunately it had a big boot, into which I could fit three five-gallon cans. One of those was always full of oil because I would have to top her up if I was on a long journey. As before I kept her full by cadging fuel at roadside cafes, and I hoped my previous incendiary experience wouldn't repeat itself. The whole thing stank of oil and petrol when it was loaded up and I often wonder how I didn't blow myself up lighting a cigarette while I was driving.

I pulled pints, mopped the floor and generally made myself useful in return for the generosity and warmth of my new-found family. My romance blossomed, and it wasn't long before I offered Peggy a ring and we were engaged. It left me with a dilemma. What was the point in training at Waddington for a war which was already won? When the fighting was on I was dedicated to doing my best to help my country win. Now it was finished I didn't see any reason to go on risking my life.

I was moaning about my situation one evening to Peggy's father, Dick, when he came up with a simple solution. 'What you need,' he told me, 'is a sick note, telling them you've been taken ill and couldn't possibly endanger your health by flying an aeroplane. I think I know just the chap …'

The following day we went to a certain doctor he knew, a regular at the pub, who seemed quite happy to sign me off for a week or two.

That was it. For the next few months I suffered a variety of ailments thanks to my friendly doctor, whom I kept well lubricated with booze for his pains. Gladys (Peggy's mum) took my sick notes to the food authorities to make sure they could draw my rations, while I carried on living a 'normal' life in the pub picking up enough in tips to pay my way when necessary, but saving as much as possible towards building a little capital for myself.

I knew it couldn't last though, and one autumn day I heard through the grapevine that the squadron was getting ready to fly off to the East. Not wanting to miss the chance to say goodbye to those who had become my friends I pulled on my uniform once more, hopped into my car and sped off to Waddington.

Back in the mess, I was having a beer with a couple of the chaps when the Flight Commander suddenly turned up. 'Ken!' he said, 'Wonderful to see you old boy, wonderful to see you looking so well. Do hope you're feeling better!' I managed to compose my face into a martyred smile, having forgotten that I was meant to be at death's door. 'Such a shame you'll miss out on the trip.'

I admit to feeling a bit of a cad as he was so solicitous of my well-being, but I couldn't very well tell him that my whole illness had been a sham. Instead I assured him that I would watch them go with great regret, and indeed I stayed around to watch them roll over the tarmac and lumber up into the sky. 'What a lot of silly buggers.' I remember thinking. Apparently they got as far as India before realising they really weren't needed at all.

While they were off I was busy organising another day trip to Skegness, but this would be very different to the one I had enjoyed with the Coultons. Every week I would collect money from regulars at the George with the promise of a great day out at the end of it. I forget how much I asked them for, but it was to be enough to hire two buses and their drivers, and give us a good time at the seaside. I didn't do it to make money; rather it was a chance to do something useful and fun for the people who had befriended me during hard times. Every week I collected their coppers and silver coins, entered it religiously in a book and paid it in to a specially opened bank account. Somehow I always had more than I thought there should be, but any surplus went into the account with the rest. By the middle of September the money was all in, the weather was wonderful and we were ready to go; although it was a very early start! At six in the morning the two buses rolled up outside the pub in the dawn light, with queues of excited pub-goers waiting to get on. I saw with some satisfaction that the coaches had been supplied by the Trent Bus Company.

Once aboard, amid laughing and singing, I began to dole out the first of the day's surprises. Everybody got thirteen shillings and sixpence back from the money they had paid in, which was surplus to expenses. On top of that all the smokers got a packet of fags liberated from the pub's rations. They cheered and laughed as we pulled out of Derby, and became even happier when I unveiled the other surprise: a stack of crates of booze. Beer, whisky, gin – you name it and it was there. It wasn't long before they were cracking open the first bottles despite the early hour. Even the driver of one coach joined in, and our route to Skeggy became rather zig-zag in the last few miles! Added to that was the need to stop every ten minutes so that people who had drunk too much beer could let some of it out again behind a convenient bush …

Once we got there everyone piled in a big jumble out of the coaches, most of them clutching a bottle of some kind, and headed off to the shops and the beach in giggling groups. My main memory of that day is charging about trying to keep tabs on everyone, because we all had be back at the chippy at five o'clock for a fish and chip supper! I was scared I would lose people or leave someone behind, so I was very relieved when they all finally turned up, somewhat the worse for wear, and tucked into their grub.

Of course we still had crates of booze stacked up on the coaches, and the drive home turned into an epic journey of drinking, toilet stops, singing and laughing. It was simply a monumental mobile piss-up with loads of people having an awful lot of fun, recounting stories of the day's adventures and telling tall tales of what they'd got up to. The driver who had been drinking was persuaded to relinquish the wheel to someone who was sober, and happily joined the throng in the back. We were scheduled to be back at the George at midnight. When we finally rolled up to its doors, honking, shouting and laughing, it was four in the morning. Everybody had behaved themselves, everybody had enjoyed themselves, and the whole thing had been an enormous success. The George's owners were very happy, while the punters themselves said it was the best piss-up they had ever had; to show how much they appreciated it they had a whip round and presented me with £50, which was an enormous sum of money at a time when you could buy eight gallons of petrol for a pound.

Having stretched the sick note wheeze about as far as I could, I thought I had better report for duty in order to be considered for demobilisation. 617 having departed, I was duly posted from Waddington to a different squadron on a base whose name I won't mention in case they decide to come after me all these years later. It was obvious from the moment I arrived that they didn't have a clue what to do with me; I was, after all, a bomber pilot with no-one to drop bombs on. A rather stuffy officer showed me around, while at the same time trying to come up with a job I could usefully do while waiting for my number to come up. Then he had a brainwave.

'I know,' he said, 'I've got the very job for you.'

He led me to a large office. As he opened the door I could see it was lined with shelves upon which were packed boxes and boxes of files, all higgledy-piggledy with no semblance of order.

'These are all our squadron signals from the last five years,' he said. 'Important documents. Be a good chap and get them sorted out, ordered and tidied away.'

As the door closed behind him I had a closer look around the room. Ragged bits of paper poked out of torn folders, sagging shelves groaned under the weight of heavy files, and the desk was strewn with paperwork of all description. The only clear surface was the chair. This certainly wasn't how I had imagined my RAF career coming to an end, shuffling papers in a dismal, chilly office. I sat down behind the desk. Across the room there was an unwelcoming fireplace, black and empty with no sign of warmth. What on earth was I doing here I wondered, as I ferreted in my pocket for my fags. Lighting up and taking a deep pull on my cigarette, I picked up one of the dusty bits of paper from the desk. Apart from a few scribbles it appeared to have no significance whatsoever. I scrunched it into a ball, took aim, and chucked it into the fireplace. Drawing deeply on my fag again, I watched the burning tip flare brightly in the dingy room. Realisation dawned with exhilarating clarity.

I reached for the nearest folder, and soon the office was a warmer, brighter place.

Two weeks later I was lounging back in my office chair with my feet on the desk, reading a paperback and smoking a cigarette when there was a knock at the door. I hadn't even taken my feet off the desk when the officer who had given me the job came in. Scrambling to my feet I fought down a sudden surge of panic. He paused for a moment as his eyes swept the room.

'My goodness me!' he said, surveying the shelves on which remained a very few, well ordered folders. 'You've made a fine job of that! Well done! Knew we could rely on you! Carry on.' With that he made a smart about turn and shut the door behind him.

If only he had taken the trouble to inspect them, he would have found every single remaining folder completely empty. Their contents had been 'filed', very carefully, up the chimney.

Not long after that my demob number came up and with mixed feelings I headed once more to Uxbridge, on 17 June 1946. Like so many thousands of other men, I signed the forms releasing me from service and into an uncertain future. At an austere counter I was offered a choice of demob suit, which I deliberated over before choosing the least terrible: a pinstripe grey double-breasted affair, whose sleeves had to be altered to fit me. As I walked out a civilian again, I felt sad to leave the life of danger and excitement I had led as a young man. When you have experienced the nerves, exhilaration, terror and comradeship of life as a bomber pilot, the idea of a mundane life behind a desk seems uninspiring and pointless. But what else could I do? I'd never really had another job. Dad was selling his shop so there was no position available there for me.

I went back to John Knights, where I had worked at the outbreak of the war while waiting to join up. I had been a boy then, but now I was a man and I wanted more from my life. The company had been very kind to me, even presenting me with a silver salver in appreciation of my deeds in the air, but when I walked back in I knew I couldn't stay. They offered me a position at far less than I had been earning in the RAF, and looking around the office I saw men who had fought in the First World War still sitting at their desks the way they had been for the past twenty-five years. It wasn't for me. The question of course remained: what WAS for me? I knew how to fly powerful aircraft and drop bombs accurately, but those skills were in limited demand in peacetime. I needed to earn enough to feed and house myself, as well as to save towards a more worthwhile future.

I decided to ask advice from my Uncle George. He lived in London and worked as a tallyman, someone who went door to door selling things on the never-never. He'd made a great success of himself with a Rolls Royce car and a nice house, so I thought he might be able to offer me some opinions on how I might start. Many times during the war I'd turned up on his doorstep to be welcomed with open arms – my nephew the war hero. This time I was asked into the house, but I think he thought I was on the make, and somehow he managed never to speak directly to me. It turned out as I feared; that very many men like me were looking for a way to start their lives afresh, and perhaps he didn't want to be burdened with anyone at that time. After dinner the family went upstairs to bed one by one with no invitation for me to stay. I took the hint, dozed until dawn in a chair in the living room, and left quietly without disturbing them. I never went back.

The George beckoned and I returned to keep alive my relationship with Peggy and her family, and also to make a few quid to keep me going. In order to make anything of myself I knew I needed capital so I jealously saved every penny I made. No job was turned down, whether it was serving drinks or mopping out the toilets, and I managed to put away a little amount which might be enough to start me off. I became very good at getting tips out of people by holding lots of coins in my pockets to jingle. When someone was due some change I made a great show of rummaging through it all, counting it out very slowly and carefully … 'That will be one and six I owe you, Sir … just a moment, I've got it here somewhere …' until they finally sighed 'Oh, just keep the change.' It all added up, and I could use it when an opportunity arose. But an opportunity for what?

CHAPTER EIGHTEEN

ARMY BLANKETS AND DODGY BACON

O nce more, fortune was on my side when a chance meeting with a solicitor called John Bar, an ex-RAF man, led me to find a small general store with a flat above at a reasonable cost in Chaddesden. I was very green at first, but with the help of the former owner 'Pop' Martin I managed to start turning a profit by working from 8 a.m. until 8 p.m. seven days a week. It was hard, hard work but I knew I had to stick at it in order to make it a success. It may have been good for business, but my determination to work every hour of the day quickly drove myself and Peggy apart as I had no time to spare for her between working and sleeping, and very sadly we went our separate ways. I missed her and her lovely family, but I couldn't risk failing at my first enterprise.

While we struggled to make ends meet, I kept an eye out for other opportunities to make some extra cash – and so it was that I became the owner of 3,000 army blankets.

I had heard through the grapevine that a wholesaler in Nottingham just happened to have the blankets, which were in very short supply after the war. They were very high quality American Army goods, a light silver in colour and lovely and soft. British Army blankets were far more coarse and uncomfortable. Because of rationing nobody had seen this kind of quality for years, and I realised I might be able to turn a good bit of profit on them. My dad lent me the huge sum of £2,000 to buy them, which was a serious financial risk to us both. I loved the danger of it though, feeling a thrill of nerves which I had been missing since I was on operations. Dad was visiting me when the delivery lorries arrived outside. Until then I hadn't really appreciated just how much space 3,000 blankets would take up, and we were taken aback to find that they completely occupied the shop and the house. Every single room was filled with wool from floor to ceiling – even the bathroom! Visiting the toilet required you to adopt a crouching position facing away from the lavatory, then reversing slowly until you could sit down, hemmed in by piles of blankets. Getting out again was equally complicated as there was no room to turn around. Half the stock ended up in our little garden as every available space was completely stuffed.

It was all worth it though, as we sold the lot in just five days and made a handsome profit. It was my first taste of taking a chance in the world of business, and the danger and excitement of it had me hooked from then on. I distinctly remember my dad saying, 'Fools rush in where angels fear to tread!'

Speaking of danger, I nearly found myself in serious trouble thanks to the black market dealings of a former RAF man I vaguely knew. He came into the shop in overalls and loitered about furtively, seeming to want a word with me. I was too busy dealing with customers though, and by the time I had finished he had gone, saying he would 'look in later'.

Dad and Pop Martin came in shortly afterwards, and Pop told me that the Food Inspector was on his way to visit the shop. Although the war was over, rationing was still strictly enforced, and it was the Inspector's job to make sure that shopkeepers were playing by the rules. I said we'd better offer him a cup of tea, and Pop volunteered to go to the kitchen. He came out with a strange expression on his face. 'You are a cool one!' he whispered to me when he came back out. I found out afterwards that there were four sides of Canadian bacon on the kitchen table, which the RAF chap had obviously left! I was aghast, but Pop just laughed – he had been joking about the Inspector's imminent visit to try to wind me up. He was quite thrilled to think we could give some little extras to his old customers who had gone without through the war. Naturally, they were not to tell a soul, because it was completely against the law, and discovery could shut down my fledgling business and land us all in the clink.

Two or three weeks later I was woken up very early on a Sunday morning by someone throwing stones at my window. I got out of bed and opened the sash, to see a lorry parked outside. A stranger called up to me in a hushed voice, 'I have two bags of sugar.' I immediately replied 'I AM CALLING THE POLICE!' and he scarpered pretty sharpish. I couldn't risk getting tied into the black market, and was very relieved to hear soon afterwards that the RAF man and his accomplices had been arrested.

The shop was progressing, but I knew that in order to reach its potential it needed some work, and so as well as working during opening hours I found myself helping to extend our selling space. It was exhausting, especially as my housekeeper moved on, but somehow I had the energy occasionally to go out. It was at a dance at the Derbyshire Royal Infirmary that I met a nurse called Bertha Chafer, known as Cherry. She was a brunette who seemed keen on me – while my main interest, I'm sorry to say, was that I needed someone who would cook, clean and help in the shop. Within a month we were married and very soon after that she was pregnant.

Even while my new wife was preparing to have our child, I was ambitious for more success in business. Looking about the area I realised that the local newsagent was making more than I was, and I thought perhaps that kind of shop might be better for me. I sold my establishment for a good profit to a chain called Perks Stores after making them believe there were several other interested parties, paid off my debts, and had enough left to start again. Our wonderful baby Ann was born, and while I was delighted, it didn't distract me from my obsession with work.

I found a place in Ripple Road, Barking which looked suitable, and made a deal to buy it and the flat above. Now I had to learn how to organise newspaper deliveries on top of my other business, which was challenging to say the least. I would open up at five to take the bundles of papers off the lorry, then mark them up for the delivery boys. By six the shop would be hectic with customers and I asked Cherry to help me out but she was completely unsuited for it. With our baby asleep upstairs we would try to deal with the rush. A sea of faces would be looking impatiently at us, and all I wanted to do was to get their money and get them out of the door. All they wanted was to get their shopping and get to work. Cherry though would deal with them so slowly that it drove me mad. 'Newspaper, there you are; packet of razor blades; oh yes, here are your cigarettes, would you like some matches ...' and she would add it all up very carefully with a pencil and paper before asking for the money and slowly counting out the change. My approach was different. 'Paperbladesfagsmatchesoneandsixthankyouhere'syourchangenextplease' and so on. Later in the day there would be another rush as people headed home from work, and we didn't close until 8 p.m. It must have been very hard for her, and I confess I gave her no support with our baby as I drove myself ever harder to grow my business. Soon the opportunity presented itself and I bought my second shop: another newsagents in East Ham.

It was the same story, flat out work, and I managed to persuade my sister Janet to help run it. Turnover was high, but so were the hours, and eventually I realised that something had to be done. Taking another risk, I sold that shop, took the profits from it to buy a house where we could live with our new baby, Jane, and took a risk buying a bomb-damaged newsagents which was scheduled to be demolished, in a very good pitch in Poplar.

I loved living there because it was at the heart of a really lovely community, centred around the local church. The place was always buzzing, and was under the care of half a dozen Fathers, known to all and sundry as 'The Farves'. They had a couple of vans and organised all sorts of day trips for the local kids, to parks and the seaside, and were always surrounded by happiness. They even managed to get them all to come to evening services with the promise of a disco afterwards which proved very successful! I became a regular at the church whenever I could and really enjoyed the spirit that spread to the whole area.

Business was always uppermost in my mind though, and I began a pattern which repeated itself for many years until I became the owner of a string of shops and premises across London and the North. I would buy one, then use it as security on the loan for another, and so on. It was a time of enormous risk, as if one link in the chain broke I could be in deep financial trouble. But I loved the thrill of it, the knowledge that everything could all go wrong but somehow managing to just about get away with it. The urge for adventures and risk had followed me unerringly from the cockpit of my Lancaster to the counter of my shops and my business dealings, and I loved the excitement.

I even branched out into hosiery! After talking to my cousin Jean's husband, a man called Fred Turner, about the money which could be made in the stocking business, I took a punt on buying up my own factory in partnership with him. I would need to borrow the money, and made an appointment to meet a bank manager called Mr Edgar who, I was told, dealt with large investments outside London. Arriving on time at the Westminster Bank's headquarters in Lothbury I was shown to a waiting room where I cooled my heels, having already passed an office with his name on. Eventually I was invited into a different office with a different manager, who intended to interview me. By this time I was very angry at the way I was being treated so I marched out of the office to the one bearing Mr Edgar's name, opened the door and went straight in without knocking. He was understandably taken aback, and even more so when I grabbed him by the lapels and shouted 'Who do you think is the bloody customer around here? I've travelled from Derby to see you and I will not be fobbed off with a minion!' The result was that – after I had cooled down – he listened to my business case and approved the loan. Fred put up his expensive car as part of the guarantee in exchange for shares.

It was quite a challenge though, as I had no experience of the machinery or processes involved in making stockings. Fred was in charge of the factory side of things, while I looked after the money. For a long time we produced far too many substandard items known as seconds, and I wondered what to do with them all until a rather shady market trader known as Stoney agreed to take them off my hands and sell them from his stalls. The whole enterprise teetered between success and bankruptcy.

Fred left because he couldn't pay his considerable private expenses with the amount we were making, having to fund his posh car, large house and children's boarding school fees. He was a lovely man, but out of his depth in what we were doing.

I also had a run-in with one of the people employed as an 'expert' in manufacturing, a Mr Jennison. Pieces of machinery were going missing, and with some simple detective work I laid the blame firmly at his door. The following day – a Saturday – he turned up for work early, but not as early as me. I was waiting for him in the canteen, and caught him red-handed with some of the stolen merchandise. The strain I was under made me unwilling to listen to apologies, and I hit him just as hard as I could on the jaw. Not surprisingly he passed out, and I had a sudden moment of fear that in my anger I had killed him. The lady who ran the canteen obviously thought so too, as she ran straight into the finishing room shouting 'Mr Trent has killed Mr Jennison!'

I called a doctor straight away, but luckily for me he quickly came to with nothing but a sore jaw. While he had brought it on himself I was sad to think that I had reacted so strongly. The nervous energy I had from constantly living on the edge of ruin was obviously getting to me, but still I couldn't get enough of the thrill of risk and danger.

I finally managed to sell the factory and its expensive machines in a few dodgy deals, even selling the fluorescent tubes from the knitting shop. Selling the machines was the most dangerous part of the process. I borrowed money from a lender's to lend the eventual purchaser a considerable part of the price in a very risky arrangement, which left me exposed for thousands of pounds. The deposit for the loan I paid myself from savings I had hidden under the stair carpet! I'm sure a lot of what we did was bordering on illegal, but when your back is against the wall you have to fight to stay alive: a feeling I was very used to. Everyone was happy at the end of the deal, and I was able to turn my back on stocking making and concentrate on my newsagents.

As the number of shops grew, I became increasingly aware that they weren't always making the money they should have been. The polite term for what was possibly happening was 'shrinkage'. I called it nicking. Without the incentive to make money for the shop, some managers were enhancing their wages by trading some of the stock for themselves. To combat this we set up a stocktaking system under the guidance of Les Pearson, a man who had worked on a similar system for the Fourbuoys chain of shops. It was time consuming work but eventually we got things worked out the way we wanted them. Finally we set up a 'model' shop where we knew exactly how much profit it should make, and set a trustworthy manager to run it. The deal was that if he made the profits we thought he should over two years, then he would be allowed to buy the shop on the never-never. It worked very well, and soon the manager had his own shop.

Over the years, my enthusiasm for buying and selling never waned and I became better at it. From my first shop in Chaddesden, I went on to own property in cities across the country. While there was always an element of risk and the value of the deals steadily went up, I learned fast and made a success of it.

After running my chain of shops for some time, I found that the speed with which we were buying and developing new properties was running away with me. On average we were buying, refitting and opening another branch every eight weeks!

Unfortunately it had an inevitable result for Cherry and I, and our relationship fell victim to my desire to get the next deal done, rather than spending time with my family. I decided that something had to be done – especially as the tax man was starting to get very interested in my business, saying that I was now making my money buying and selling shops, and not actually selling things to customers. We decided to sell the rest of the shops to their managers on the never-never. My lawyers, having consulted experts at Lincoln's Inn, told me that none of them could produce a document that any solicitor would advise a shop manager to sign, but virtually all of them did sign because they trusted me. I'd already decided that I wanted to move to the beautiful island of Jersey – and just as we were coming to a decision about it the prime minister, Mr Wilson, announced he would be introducing Capital Gains tax, but NOT retrospectively. It had come to a dangerous point where lack of control over shrinkage meant I could lose everything, and selling up was the best solution.

Jersey beckoned, a beautiful place in the middle of the sea where I could enjoy my new love - of sailing.

CHAPTER NINETEEN

A NEW CREW

When I left Bomber Command, I left behind some of the strongest bonds I had ever felt. The crews I had flown with, particularly at 625 Squadron, were a very tightly knit bunch who worked hard for each other for the good of the mission, every one of us doing his job meticulously for the good of the rest. I hadn't realised how much I missed that until I discovered sailing.

While my line of shops was still under development, I moved for a while to Thorpe Bay, where I was invited to try crewing a boat for some friends. At first I crewed with a chap known as Puddles, and we were last in every single race until one memorable day when we passed the competitor in front who promptly resigned, thus ensuring we still came last! I improved though and found myself in a 505 racing dinghy with Brian Bennett – Sterling Area Controller of the Banks of England – and John Ayshford, who was an air attaché to NATO. I was quickly absolutely hooked, as sailing is very like flying an aircraft. You have to keep a meticulous eye on the conditions, plot your course very carefully, watch out for dangers and threats, and of course rely one hundred per cent on the rest of the crew. I remembered clearly my childhood interest in *Dinghy Sailing for Boys and Girls*, and before long I was racing hard with Brian and John before having my own 505 built for me. We still hold the record for the cross-Channel race from Folkestone to Boulogne, an event which was called off soon after we got into harbour because of a force nine wind developing which could have caused chaos and even loss of life if it had arrived sooner.

Typically of me, I wanted to go bigger and better and it wasn't long before I was crewing an ocean-racing yacht called Jabula. I loved the design so much that I commissioned a sister ship, designed again by Alan Buchanan and built by Bill Sutton. To overcome a problem with Jabula and greatly strengthen the hull Bill decided to laminate the whole of the centre line timber (i.e. stem, wood keel and horn timber) in the boat with fairly large strips of oak all glued together into a centre piece over several weeks which provided an extremely strong base on which to build the hull. I christened her *Vae Victis* (Woe to the Conquered) and in the next few years she became famous.

We won virtually every race we entered, including Yarmouth to Santander. The thrill of pushing the boat as hard as she would go, every man working every inch of sail or turn of the wheel to drive us harder was, at last, a replacement for the thrill of flying. Again, like flying, your eye was on the compass, the weather, the wind, everything which could affect your voyage. On one occasion the racing fleet was driven towards a lee shore by a strong wind; one boat was thrown ashore, another went missing, and another had a man lost overboard. Together with my crew that included three former RAF pilots we managed to beat our way off shore into the wild Bay of Biscay and complete our voyage. Once more I was plotting courses, taking risks, confronting the elements and working in a dedicated team: and I loved it!

As our ultimate accolade, the world famous maritime photographer Beken of Cowes included *Vae Victis* in his book of outstanding yachts called *A Hundred Years of Sail*. That was an honour indeed, and I was very sad to sell her when we moved to Jersey.

The move to Jersey brought about several changes. After selling the shops on the 'never never', I was short of ready money so I had to look at opportunities to invest gradually. We found a house in Grouville, to the east of the island, and I found some lodging houses which might be worthwhile investments. They all paid their way quite quickly, as the tourism industry was just starting to boom, and I soon started making far more than I had to pay out to service my loans. Once we were settled,

I had the time to go out sailing again – and Jersey, as a small island, was absolutely ideal as a base.

This time I sailed with family and friends, and took part in a few local races. By now, I had a new family. Cherry and I had drifted apart, due I must say to my obsession with building my business and sailing at every opportunity. The hoped-for reconciliation had not materialised. I met Ann Ovenden at the Royal Channel Islands Yacht Club, where she had become secretary while I was helping as treasurer. She was a married mother of three children. For some time our relationship was entirely platonic, but when I came back from a three-month trip around the world, I met her again and we kissed … something had started which proved to be unstoppable. My relationship with Cherry was already untenable, but I knew that had been nearly all my fault. I agreed to everything her lawyer asked for in the divorce, and once more I was a bachelor.

There remained the awkward situation between myself and Ann, and I decided I had to give them some space. I spoke to both Ann and her husband Brian, and said that I would go away to Canada while they tried to sort out their own marriage. If it wasn't working out, I left a phone number for Ann to call.

Canada was wonderful, and I spent several weeks with family over there. We hunted and fished, and I even went looking for businesses. I wasn't convinced that Ann would finally be mine, and even started to consider moving to Canada for good to be with my family. One of the businesses I looked at was a camp at La Ronge, a vast camping and hunting area with its own aeroplane for ferrying in wealthy American tourists who wanted take advantage of its enormous open spaces. The kite was a strong incentive!

I stayed with Percy Trent and his extended family, moving from one home to another, hunting deer, playing endless games of cribbage, meeting local Inuit people and making ice rinks in the garden. Many of the Inuit could play crib as well as the rest of us, after Uncle Percy taught them! It was an idyllic life, but not one which I could continue forever. I made arrangements to see some properties in Winnipeg with a view to setting up business, but then at six o'clock one morning I was woken to be told there was a phone call for me. Percy's daughter Mary came down the stairs in her dressing gown to the cellar room where I was sleeping.

'Ken,' she said, 'It's a lady called Ann on the phone. She says she's getting divorced and really wants to speak to you.'

Needless to say, I was on the first flight back to Jersey.

The three of us – myself, Ann and Brian – came to a very amicable arrangement over their separation and responsibilities for Ann's children, and we remained on friendly terms. The girls decided they wanted to stay in the house with their mum, and I made arrangements to leave them all financially secure. Ann and I have never looked back, especially as I tested her character quite severely early on when I insisted she come sailing with me! While all this was going on I had a new boat built, a one-tonner called *Wee Victis* (named after my favourite *Vae Victis*!)

A five-week trip through the waterways of France was wonderful to cement our family together, although it did demonstrate that little *Wee Victis* wasn't really suited to the kind of sailing I wanted to do. She wasn't necessarily suited for socialising either, as one poor chap found out to his discomfort. We sailed her to Cowes to take part in some racing and ended up hosting a bit of a party after drinking the neighbouring yacht dry. This chap needed to relieve himself of some of the gin, so made his way to the back of the boat … moments later there was a great big splash as he found out the hard way that there was no guard rail!

I eventually sold *Wee Victis* and bought a boat which cost thousands to refit but was to prove a worthy companion: the *Belle Poule*. And what adventures we had in her! I bought the crew – Ann and our friends – T-shirts with the name of the boat emblazoned on them, only to face a mutiny when we made a trip to France. It turns out that *poule* is French for a 'lady of the night', and they had been greeted with laughter when they went ashore in that country for the first time!

With Ann and the children we sailed through Paris, to Corsica and beyond, my novice crew learning all the time, and had the company of a school of porpoises near Gibraltar.

Another boat, *L'Autre Femme,* took us on similar trips after I sold the *Belle Poule,* and I really couldn't imagine being without the excitement and simple satisfaction of mastering the wind to take me halfway across the world.

I became friends with a local couple in Jersey, Barry and Steph Sallows. They were waiting for a break in the terrible weather before sailing to the Canaries, and at a goodbye party, moistened by gin, I offered to go with them as crew. While they made the first part of their journey I settled my affairs at home then flew to join them at Lisbon. Naturally, Ann was included in the deal and the adventures we had on that trip finally cured her of the seasickness which had plagued her until then. Barry's genius as a sailor manifested itself many times as we fought our way to the Canaries. I was below preparing dinner when there came a loud *BANG* from above. I ran on deck to find that the foremast had broken in two, and we were being pushed fast towards the African coast. Somebody had to crawl out over the swinging bowsprit over the front of the boat to cut away the forestay – and Barry looked miffed when I politely suggested that as it was his boat, he should do it himself!

He decided the only solution was to cut the mast away, and did so quickly with a hacksaw. His genius with quick repairs meant he could fix it very neatly with wood from the leg we used to prop the boat upright when the tide went out, and he did it so well that you could hardly see the join. On another occasion while crossing the Atlantic he used two blocks of teak which we used for rubbing down the deck to re-fashion a broken link between the steering gear and the rudder. I loved the excitement of facing challenges and finding solutions in a crisis.

On another voyage we sailed all around the Mediterranean and up towards Sardinia, where I was inspired to see the site where Nelson had sailed out to meet the French before the Battle of Trafalgar. What stunning seamanship he had shown, to get a whole fleet of warships out of the bay of Isola Maddalena. I followed a very similar course to him, and found it very challenging even in a small modern yacht.

Our journey took us on from Gibraltar towards the Caribbean, a long voyage made possible by the addition of a deep freeze to stow a lot of fresh food. That deep freeze nearly cost me dear though. While in Gibraltar we needed to get a spare part for it from the supplier, which was some distance from the port. When I managed to find my way to the building I found it fenced off, with a small gate onto a path leading to the doorway. All over the place were signs saying 'Beware of the Guard Dogs', and with very good reason. Two savage looking Alsatians were prowling the ground between me and the door of the freezer supplier, one on the end of a long piece of rope and another which was running free. Both were growling and barking in a very convincing attempt to persuade me to bugger off quick. But I really needed to get into the building to get the part we needed for our freezer as without it we wouldn't be able to carry enough supplies to keep us going. 'Right,' I thought. 'Just do it.'

Opening the gate, I deliberately walked straight towards the dog on the rope, which was making the most noise, but avoided looking it in the eye. When I got within touching distance it suddenly went quiet, even docile; and the other calmed down too. I followed their own tracks to the door, left a message about the part I required, and walked slowly, palms sweating, back to the gate with the dogs trotting attentively by my side. Gratefully I closed it behind me, only for them to recommence their growling at the other people on the street. One chap approached me.

'You don't want to go in there mate,' he said, 'those dogs put someone in hospital last week – he's in a terrible state.' Perhaps if I hadn't been able to summon up the grit I'd felt when flying over Germany the same fate might have befallen me.

We finally arrived in Barbados in the middle of December, and joined the locals in celebrating Christmas, which was a wonderful occasion of singing and socialising. Not everyone was so friendly though. After setting sail for St Vincent, we decided to pull into a very tranquil bay in Dominica to rest for a while. After dropping anchor I went ashore and tied a line to a tree to keep us at the right angle for the wind to blow through the boat, keeping us nice and cool. We spread out some food on the deck, and began to enjoy the peace and tranquillity. Steph was reading aloud from an information manual for sailors visiting the area, and just as she got to a section which read: 'Last year some locals managed to get on board a visiting yacht, and one of the crew was killed', a whole bunch of suspicious looking chaps came out of the undergrowth and headed towards our boat with mischievous looks in their eyes. Steph's voice became more piercing as she drew my attention to what was happening. I dived below, pulled my shorts on, grabbed the gun I kept for such emergencies, and raced back up just as I heard the same piercing voice shouting 'Don't shoot them Ken!'

There were nine of us, and we agreed that if anyone tried to get onto our boat we would tread on their fingers. 'Smile,' I said, 'And be nice, but nobody gets on board.' I gritted my teeth and tried to appear confident and strong. Just do it. As well as concern for our health, I also wanted to get my long and very expensive rope back! I could only do that by going back onto the shore, which meant getting rid of the threatening crowd. I noticed one of them had a very large grouper fish that he seemed to want to sell – although he named a quite exorbitant price. Feeling we had little choice, I agreed, provided he untied the boat and let us sail off. It worked out to everyone's satisfaction; he got his money, I got my rope back and we enjoyed a slap-up dinner.

Our next destination was to be the British Virgin Islands, where we got into more trouble. Charlotte Amalie was a haven for pirates centuries ago, and I don't know whether much has changed. I went ashore to visit the large supermarket and also to arrange my American visa. But on my return I found a young chap holding on to the rope of my dinghy, while another was at work with a pair of bolt croppers trying to cut the wire which secured it to the harbour. Again I had to think 'just do it' and take fast action. Since he was below me in the dinghy and I was up on the quay, he was just the right height for me to kick him as hard as I could in the face while turning to defend myself against the other chap. Luckily he was running away, but the one with the bolt croppers took exception to being kicked and came up to attack me. I managed to dodge his wild swings at my head with the bolt croppers before, thank goodness, he too ran off. On getting back to the boat I found I was shaking like a jelly and needed a lie-down and a large amount of gin to affect a full recovery. After all, they were fit young guys, while I was a seventy-year-old man! Strangely enough, just a week later we were in the British Virgin Islands when I met a bloke at the harbour with his face all wrapped up like the Invisible Man. Despite the bandages, something about him was familiar and I leaned across the railings of my boat with a smile.

'Hello,' I said, 'Were you in Charlotte Amalie last week?'

'Oh, man, that was all a mistake!' he said, 'I was just trying to save your boat from someone trying to steal it!'

'Yeah right!' I thought …

On the subject of gin, when we sailed to St Bart's we felt we needed to stock up on basic provisions and knew there was a supermarket ashore. We landed and headed there, to find bottles of gin at the ludicrously low price of fifteen francs a litre. We bought the shop's entire stock of it there and then. After all, we were on a two-year voyage with nine of us on board and we didn't want to run out …

Our trip went on to Cape Canaveral where we saw the space capsule, and Bermuda via some inland waterways before finally setting sail for Jersey and home. By now most of my crew had flown off already – the girls to university, and Barry and Steph back to Jersey to get ready for the season.

The boat was singing, and we made very good speed. As we were leaving American waters a boat appeared behind us on the same course and appeared to be gaining on us slowly. I prepared my gun just in case. It got closer and closer, bigger and bigger, until we got a message on the radio: 'This is the US Coastguard. Please shorten sail and slow down so we can come alongside and inspect you.' What a compliment! Our sailing boat was travelling too fast for the coastguard's motorboat to catch up! When it eventually did so, one of its crew fell into the sea as he tried to come aboard and we had to go back to rescue him.

The way home called on all my experience as a sailor and also the fortitude and skills I had learned as a pilot. For fifteen hundred miles we sailed across open ocean, with no land to fix on and no satellite navigation. The only way to be sure of where we were was to use an old-fashioned sextant and take sightings of the sun and the stars until we came close to home again. Unfortunately when we arrived at the mouth of the Channel there was very thick fog and we were effectively sailing blind. Added to that our main engine had shut down because the water pump had failed, AND our radio had decided to stop working. It was just like flying over Germany lost in heavy cloud with no signal to help us home. We kept going; we couldn't simply stop, trusting in our navigation and seamanship not to run ourselves aground. Of course there was no guarantee that we wouldn't be hit by another ship, as the Channel is one of the most congested waterways in the world. Just as I had done in the cockpit of my Lanc, I held my nerve and watched the compass in a world of white, while the rest of the crew kept a keen eye on the sails and the wind. The fog was so thick at times that we could have run into rocks or shallows before we had time to slow down or change course, and the silence was eerie. Hold your nerve and just do it ...

'Hey Skip, what's that?'

Somewhere ahead of us a light was blinking. We sailed close enough to recognise it as a buoy marking rocks twenty miles off the west of Jersey, the first sign of land since we left America. We were nearly home, but still had to negotiate the treacherous rocks on the approach to our little island. The next fix we had was the lighthouse at Corbière, but by then the wind had dropped right off and the tide was slack. To try to achieve some forward motion we put the dinghy into the water next to us, lashed it to the side and tried to use the power of its engine, but to no avail. It also made too much noise, as we were all straining our ears to hear any other vessels or foghorns. Then I had a brain wave, and used my mobile phone to call Barry. He commandeered a boat from somewhere and sailed out to meet us as our tired yacht was finally pushed by the tide back to harbour.

What a trip – a perfect example of the thrills, excitement, comradeship, tranquillity, friendship and challenges which sailing offered me.

I have seen the sun rise over the Channel after a freezing stormy night, watched Barbados emerge from the early morning mists after three weeks in the open ocean, partied with the Rolling Stones at Basil's Bar on the island of Mustique and seen whales leaping from the water yards from our boat throwing cascades of glistening water into the sunlight.

I was so lucky to find a hobby, obsession even, which in some way replicated the feelings I had felt in the days when I flew Lancasters. It wasn't the only hobby to give me plenty of danger and excitement though ...

When they were young, the girls decided they would like to learn to ride. It was something I was delighted to encourage them in, and I loved the joy it brought them. We bought a pony called Bracken for Carol on her eleventh birthday, and it wasn't long of course before I had to have a go because it looked like a lot of fun seasoned with a fair sprinkling of danger!

Just months after marrying Ann and having our first proper sailing holiday together, I had my own horse and my first riding lesson, with a wonderful man called Mick Finnis. If I thought my flying instructors in Canada had been strict, they were nothing to Mick, who had no reservations whatsoever in describing your shortcomings even though you were paying for his attention.

'Get you on the saddle of that b****** horse, now b****** well sit down, canter, change the rein, wrong leg, give me strength, you never listen, and if you don't listen you'll never learn, b****** impossible to make a rider of you!' I loved his no-nonsense approach, which he employed with women as well as men, and managed to learn fast in-between picking myself up off the floor and dusting myself down. While sailing rewarded patience, cunning and clever planning, horse riding was all adrenaline and speed. It wasn't long before Ann learned too, and the two of us became firm fixtures in the local drag hunt. What a buzz that was, racing along over the uneven ground, aiming for a place on a high hedge to jump, pounding up to it and launching the horse into the air, crossing your fingers that it would land you safely on the other side. The rush of the hunt kept me going in the winter months when sailing wasn't on the cards, although it did result in both of us becoming fairly regular visitors to the local hospital with various breaks and knocks. On one occasion a horse called Yobbo I was riding reared, and I fell so hard that I was knocked spark out and not breathing. One of the other riders ran to me and pulled my tongue out of the back of my throat so I could start breathing again. Apparently they all thought I was a goner, until I woke up and spent the rest of the night asking the same question over and over again and telling the doctors there was 'Nothing wrong with me!'

I suppose I should have learned my lesson, but I've never been very good at that ...

Just a couple of weeks later I went to ride a horse called Patch just before going off on a sailing trip. He was quite frisky, which should have warned me to go easy, but of course I jumped on – and he was off. He bucked like hell and galloped off towards the road as I tried to pull him around to head for a safe grassy bank. It was to no avail, and as he charged full pelt at the road I slipped off and landed hard on a broken pallet board. It shattered my pelvis, a serious injury at the age of sixty-eight, and I was hospitalised for weeks. My cousin Lily, known to all as Lilo Lil, put a sign outside my room which read 'Sex Clinic' with an arrow pointing within. I finally recovered, but it was a long process and I would never be able to ride again.

That blow was nothing compared to the sorrow which hit our family in 1988. Our daughter Linda, a lovely girl full of life and love, was taken from us by viral pneumonia. She had just qualified as an architect, and was a kind, caring and courageous girl of whom we were all very proud. We arranged to have a stained glass window put into our church in her memory.

Life was catching up with me. For years I had lived my life on the edge, running businesses only one step ahead of bankruptcy, sailing to the limit of the world's oceans, and risking my life jumping blindly over hedges and ditches on horseback. Retirement and a quiet life beckoned – but what I didn't expect was to be drawn back five decades to my time in the RAF.

CHAPTER TWENTY

BACK IN THE COCKPIT

It began in 1994 with a phone call which came totally out of the blue.

'Ken Trent?'

'Yes, who's speaking?'

'DFC and Bar?'

I was taken aback by that unexpected question.

'Yes, who is it?'

'My name is Gary Godel. There's a Lancaster bomber on display at the airport for Battle of Britain Week. Would you like to go and see it? There's a good chance I can get you aboard.'

All the yes's came pouring out of me very quickly, and I felt a huge sense of amazement and anticipation. The war and Lancasters had hardly entered my mind for fifty years, and suddenly it all came flooding back. Nobody had ever asked me about my medals before, and for the first time I felt the pride of being able to say yes, I have the DFC and Bar, and pinning them to my chest to show people.

I arrived at the airport with Gary and there she was, the *City of Lincoln*, squatting on the tarmac in that old familiar way, the only flying Lancaster bomber left in Europe. Gary is a recognised RAF historian and was as good as his word, and the Battle of Britain Memorial Flight crew seemed very pleased to see me as I climbed up the short ladder into the fuselage of a Lanc for the first time in half a century. The smell of metal, leather and oil was still the same, the dark green interior was just as I remembered it, and I felt as though I was coming home. It was a little harder to make my way forward over the main spar and into the cockpit but I found myself remembering everything, as without thinking I reached up for the pilot's handhold and heaved myself up into the seat. Emotions began to get the better of me, and I choked up as an interviewer started to ask me questions. It was a wonderful moment, yet full of sadness as I remembered Joe Cunliffe, John Powell and all my other friends who hadn't landed yet.

Later, Gary asked me why I was only wearing my DFC and Bar, and none of the other medals to which I was entitled. The truth was that I had never had them. After the war I had been determined to put it all behind me, to get on with my life and look ahead; I always used to say that the past was dead and tomorrow was the future. But because of the interest shown by him and many others who I met that day I started to feel a real pride in what I had done, and felt for the first time that I wanted to have them on my chest for the Service of Remembrance on 11 November. They duly arrived, and I experienced the fantastic pride of wearing them among my contemporaries. I have worn them proudly ever since on suitable occasions.

With Gary's encouragement I joined RAFA, the association for Air Force personnel, and enjoyed meeting others who had served in the war at our monthly meetings. I even joined the associations for 625 and 617 Squadrons, which led me to some reunions with old friends. In fact, there had been one or two reunions on our old airfields just after the war, and I remember belting around our old runways in a car with Steve after a few jars!

As my interest in the old times revived, I began to enjoy the annual air shows in Jersey which often featured the *City of Lincoln*, one of only two airworthy Lancasters left in the world. One day, thinking 'just do it', I wrote to the Battle of Britain Memorial Flight (BBMF) and asked with my tongue in my cheek if there was any chance of a ride. Wonderfully, they replied very quickly inviting me to visit just before their next trip to Jersey. They paid for myself and my daughter Carol to fly over, and picked us up at the airport to take us to Coningsby. There on the tarmac was the Lanc, in beautiful condition, all polished up and ready for take-off. I remembered some of the kites I had flown, so patched up and full of holes, and was looking forward to being in such a well preserved model. They gave Carol a short flight in the Bomb Aimer's office first, so that she could experience it – and then it was my turn. I pulled on the flying overalls and white gloves they gave me with mounting excitement, and made my way up the ladder without stopping to have a lucky pee on the tailwheel; I think that would have been frowned upon! Down the fuselage, over the main spar with a little difficulty, and up to the cockpit I went, only to find a slightly different arrangement to the familiar layout. Instead of one pilot's seat and a fold-down chair for the navigator, there were two pilot's seats, with dual controls for the aircraft. I was itching to sit in one of them and have a go ... They passed me a leather flying helmet which was a bit too big, but I squashed it down on my head so that I could hear the intercom properly. I took a seat at what would have been the navigator's desk, and listened with glee as they started the engines and warmed them up.

'OK Ken, we are cleared for take-off ... here we go ...'

Memories were rushing back at me as he pushed the throttles forward, the second pilot reached out to back them up, and the kite leapt along the runway. They made a good take-off, and climbed slowly to a low altitude, just a couple of thousand feet. The sound was terrific, the view was marvellous, and the decades just melted away as we flew. I was interested to follow the crew's conversations. Instead of using a modern satellite navigation system, they worked everything out the old fashioned way with landmarks and compass bearings.

'Coast just ahead ...'

Sure enough, the twinkling blue of the English Channel beckoned. Then the pilot said something which made my heart leap.

'OK Ken, do you fancy taking her for a while?'

'What, really?'

'Yes, take the second pilot seat.'

Sure enough, the second pilot had got out of his chair and turned towards me with a huge grin. He gestured towards his vacant position, and I didn't need to be asked again. It was a bit of a squash to pass each other, but I was in place in a few moments and reaching out for the control column. My feet settled easily on the rudder pedals, and I felt the beating heart of the Lancaster again. I never doubted for a moment that I would be able to fly her.

'Are you comfortable? Good. You have control.'

'OK, I've got her.'

Oh, it was marvellous. To have the Lanc in my hands after all those years was an extraordinary feeling. Instinctively I reached down to trim the rudder, only to find of course that I was reaching with the wrong hand because I was in the second pilot's seat. Once I worked that out, it was easy flying. The control column felt alive in my hands as I followed the course on the compass in front of me, and after a few minutes of watching what I was doing the Skipper just relaxed and let me get on with it. The kite handled beautifully, just as I remembered. It was just like having an old girlfriend in my hands again fifty years on, one who was just as subtle and saucy and hadn't changed a bit. The sun was shining, there were few clouds, the engines were singing and all was right with my world.

All too soon we were approaching Jersey, but the pilot let me take her right on to the final approach before taking control back. I wasn't too upset at not being able to land her, because she is such a valuable and important aircraft that it would be dreadful if she were damaged. I watched with interest as he brought us down, and noticed that he kept the engines running until after we had landed. I always used to cut them as we came over the perimeter fence to drop us onto the runway more quickly, but despite that his landing was smooth and tidy.

It had been a wonderful experience for me, and every time I see the *City of Lincoln* I imagine myself back up in the cockpit with the controls in my hands. I'm sure I could still fly her now …

In the year 2000 I went to a 617 reunion at Petwood. Our old mess was being used as a hotel again, but the layout was still the same and I found my old room easily. It brought back so many memories – but of course what I most wanted to do was to find the Coulton's farm where I had spent so many happy days. Turning right out of the hotel I tried to retrace my steps of fifty-five years before but found it hard to recognise where I was. Hedges had grown up, roads had changed, and a golf course dominated a lot of the land in the area. I hoped that perhaps the family still lived close by, so went into the nearby village and asked around, inquiring in the shops if anyone knew Lucy or Joyce, or anything about the fate of the farm, but it was all to no avail. That blissful few months of my life in 1945 seemed to have been lost forever.

Sixteen years later, in the course of writing this book, there came another chance to visit Woodhall Spa. There was another 617 Squadron dinner, and my friend Chris came with me to help with his research. A few days before we left Jersey he recorded a short interview with me to be played on BBC Lincolnshire, recounting some of my memories but asking in particular for help in finding the Coultons.

I'd heard nothing by the time we left though, and we agreed that we would look for the farm ourselves. In fact it was the first thing we did when we arrived at Woodhall, before even going to our hotel. Chris drove us slowly around the lanes, and I was sure we were in the right spot as we passed a gap in the high hawthorn hedge leading onto a golf course. There was no way of knowing though, and I left feeling deflated once more.

It turned out to be a wonderful weekend though. We paid a visit to the Lincolnshire Aviation Heritage Centre which has a Lancaster as the central part of its great exhibition. Thanks to the help of the Panton family which owns the site, I could climb up into the cockpit once more; although my advancing age made it a real struggle to get over the central spar. Later, as I looked through their archive of photos I found one of Steve and his crew, taken at Kelstern during the war. I spotted him immediately, and it was an emotional moment to see his face again. My great friend had died some years before, and I still miss him dreadfully. We had stayed in touch after the war, and he even asked me to be godfather to his son Robbie with whom I am now very close. Together with his lovely family we have shared many adventures together.

Dinner at Petwood that evening was a formal affair, and we had been asked to wear black tie. For me, far more comfortable in sailing shoes and shorts, that meant rummaging around to find my old dinner suit. It was one I'd had made in 1948, which had twice been 'modernised'. When I tried it on it still fitted me like a glove and even the old buttons on the fly were still attached! The evening was great, a chance to catch up with some of the few who were left from the old days. I chatted to John Bell and Johnny Johnson, two veterans who, like me, can remember what it was like to take off in the cold night air heading for the dark dangers of Germany.

The following day we decided it would be a good idea to visit the Bomber Command memorial in Lincoln. It's a huge spire reaching up into the sky, as tall as the wingspan of a Lancaster, and surrounded by metal plaques with the names of dead crewmen engraved onto them. I'd been there when it was first installed together with many other veterans, and work was still going on to get it finished.

Unfortunately, when we arrived we found the unfinished road leading to the site was closed off with fencing. Signs explained that the monument was still under construction, that it was a building site and there was strictly 'No Admittance'.

We noticed that there was a gap in the fencing though, just about wide enough to get the car through. We sat there for a few moments debating until Chris said 'Come on – let's "just do it!"' As we drove down the dusty track we kept our eyes out for irate builders, but as it was a Sunday it seemed they were all at home. As we got closer I could see activity around the base of the memorial though, and we realised there were a lot of motorcyclists parked up just in front of it. Chris got out to talk to them while I got myself out of the car and into my wheelchair. Moments later he was back, all smiles.

'Ken, this is the Dambusters 2016 Charity Motorcycle Ride – they're doing a bike ride all around Lincolnshire to raise money – and this is Sue Taylor, one of the people who is creating the memorial!'

I had met Sue when the memorial was begun, and she seemed absolutely delighted to see me again. She was keen for me to meet some of the bikers, and we made our way to where they were, more than twenty of them, gathered around the base of the spire. As they saw me they all came over, and I could see them looking at the medals on my chest. Chris told them who I was, and there was a moment of embarrassed silence … I could see they all wanted to speak to me and maybe to ask some questions but were too shy to say anything, so I spread my arms out wide, gave them a big smile and said 'Hi Guys!' which seemed to break the ice. Soon we were chatting away, and I told them some tall tales from my wartime days. As we were talking, by wonderful coincidence the Dakota aircraft of the BBMF came flying over quite low – it was displaying over the memorial to mark the anniversary of the Dams raid.

'I've flown that kite.' I said.

'What, you used to fly Dakotas too?' they asked.

'No, I've flown THAT kite.'

It was true.

When I had flown across to Jersey in the Lancaster, the BBMF pilot chatted to me afterwards and said that he was due to display their Dakota that day over Guernsey. Would I like to come? I didn't need to be asked twice, and was soon up in my second vintage aircraft of the day. She was a lovely kite, responsive and reliable. I enjoyed the feeling of being in a display, and seeing the crowds of people lined up along the sea front, all waving and having a nice time. As we peeled away from the island, ever so casually, he said,

'We're going to do a little display over Sark. Would you like to take her?'

Of course I would! Again there were dual controls, so I took the stick and felt my way into flying her. Being a steady aircraft she was easy to master and I felt at home very quickly.

'Just take her around the island at 500 feet,' he told me.

I had a wonderful time surfing us around the little island, and started really yanking it around from wingtip to wingtip following the coast. She flew beautifully and I was enjoying myself immensely when a voice came into my earphones.

'Erm, Ken, you know you are supposed to be displaying at 500 feet?'

'Yup.'

'Can you see the altimeter from where you are?'

'No.'

I really couldn't. There was dual control but most of the instruments were over on his side and I hadn't examined them too closely. It was a lovely clear day after all, and I could see easily where we were.

'It's this one here. We're at 150 feet at the moment.'

So we were; and up on a wingtip too. Oops … I eased back on the stick and soon had us back up to the correct height again.

'That's the first time I've been in an aircraft and had to show the pilot where the instruments are!' he laughed. I was touched to think that he had so much faith in my flying that he hadn't tried to take control back or interfere. I was having such fun that I had slipped back into my old low-flying habits. What an experience it was, an unforgettable day which I loved recounting to the assembled crowd of bikers at the memorial.

A few more tales, and it was time for them to go. Some of them lingered though, to ask some last questions before leaving.

'It's an honour to meet you,' one said, 'You are a real hero.'

I often hear people say this to me now and it's very kind of them, but my answer is always the same.

'No I'm not.' I said. 'Look around you at all the names on these plaques. All these blokes who never made it back. Those boys are the real heroes here. I'm just one of the lucky ones who got away with it.'

I think they all understood what I meant. I'm very glad that more and more of the younger generation today are taking an interest in what we did all those years ago, and helping to remember the ones who haven't landed yet.

After a long chat, the motorcyclists were on their way. As they roared off down the track leaving a cloud of dust behind them, I took time to look around the metal plaques which surround the spire of the memorial. Each one has cut into it the names of all the bomber crew who lost their lives flying during the war, and it was very emotional for me to find Joe

Cunliffe and the others I had known among them. Sue found me some poppies left from their Remembrance Day service, and I left them on the plaques next to their names. I said a little prayer for all of them before we left.

While it was a marvellous trip, I still felt a sense of regret that we had been unable to find the Coultons or their farm. After seventy-one years, I still had that yearning to be reunited with the one place which had offered me such warmth, love and kindness in the middle of the danger and death of operations.

'OK Ken, if you don't mind we're just going to visit a friend of mine who lives in the village,' Chris said as we headed back to the hotel. 'They'd just like to meet you, shake your hand, get an autograph, that sort of thing. Is that OK?'

'Well all right,' I said, 'But let's not stay too long. We could have another look for the farm before we go.'

We pulled up at a little bungalow right in the heart of Woodhall Spa, about 300 yards from our hotel. As we walked to the door, Chris said 'Ken, I haven't been entirely truthful with you …' and knocked on the door. A smiling, grey-haired lady opened the door. 'Ken,' said Chris, 'this is Lucy.'

For a moment I didn't realise what he meant. I began to say 'Oh, hello …' when it hit me. This was Lucy, Bob Coulton's daughter, who I had last seen as a twelve-year-old girl seventy-one years ago. The appeal on the radio had worked. Awash with tears we threw our arms around each other, and I could hardly speak as the years between us fell away.

When our emotions had subsided a little we talked for ages, remembering those far-off days on the farm, and Lucy even showed me a letter she still had from my sister, thanking the family for looking after me and for sending them food when my mother was ill. That of course brought forth fresh tears. She told me that her mum and dad had died many years before, but her sister Joyce had gone only recently. They had all stayed in or around Woodhall Spa for years after the war, and had been very sorry to leave the farm. Eventually I realised that she might be able to help me in my quest to find the site of the farm itself. 'Of course,' she said. 'Shall I come in the car with you?'

Trembling with emotion and excitement, we made the short journey back to the road next to the Petwood Lodge. It turned out that the gateway in the hawthorn hedge we had looked at before was indeed the site of the old gate which I used to lean on, but the farm itself had been flattened to make way for the golf course. Leaning on the new metal gate with its 'Private – Keep Out' sign, we tried to work out where the farmhouse would have been, and the pond which I had seen her father bringing water from on the first day I had visited. Then we noticed that the chain which held the gate closed was in fact unlocked … 'Just do it,' I thought, and we were through.

As we walked arm in arm across the green, we were both transported back to the idyllic days of 1945. Lucy told me how they had always looked forward to me visiting, how she used to run inside and tell her parents that I had come back from a raid because she had seen me waggle my wings, and how they had laughed at the state of my uniform after a day's work milking cows. There was the old oak tree they used to climb, and here still was the pond where Bob Coulton dipped his buckets to fetch water on the day we butchered the pig.

As we stood on the very spot where we had first met, she told me they had never forgotten me. For years after the war they would talk about me over dinner and wonder what had become of me, whether I had been shot down or survived, and whether I would ever come back. It took me seventy-one years, but I'm very, very glad that I did.

RECOMMENDATIONS FOR HONOURS AND AWARDS
IMMEDIATE

Christian Names	:	Kenneth Lionel.	Surname	:	Trent.
Rank	:	Flying Officer.	Official Number	:	176283
Command of Group	:	No. 1 Group	Unit	:	625 Squadron

Total Flying Hours on operations............ 97

Number of Sorties.................................... 19

Recognition for which recommended...... D.F.C.

Appointment Held.................................... Captain-Pilot

Particulars of meritorious service for which recommendation is made:-

Flying Office Trent is the pilot and captain of a Lancaster aircraft which attacked COLOGNE during the afternoon of 28th October 1944.

Just before crossing the French Coast the rear gunner attempted to leave his turret. In doing so, however, he accidentally rotated his turret under power and trapped his legs and would almost certainly have crushed them.

The pilot instructed the Mid Upper gunner to try and release him but in the mean time the rear gunner's oxygen tube was broken and the rear gunner was rendered unconscious. The Pilot immediately feathered the Port Outer engine in order to stop the rear turret rotating any further. During the whole of this time the aircraft was flying over Cumulonimbus cloud and after feathering the engine the aircraft dropped into cloud. The rear gunner was eventually freed and placed on the rest bed and the engine was re-started but it emitted volumes of blue smoke
. Realising the great danger of fire breaking out the engine was feathered again but smoke still persisted and Graviner was operated.

Even after this trying experience and in spite of all these difficulties the Pilot decided to carry on and bombed the target from a height of 15,000 feet but at a speed of 140 m.p.h. Obtaining an excellent Aiming Point photograph.

On leaving the target area the aircraft descended to 1,000 feet over Allied territory owing to the fact the aircraft was unable to fly over cloud.

Whilst returning over the English Channel the Air Bomber observed Florescence and a flashing light. As it was getting dark the Pilot brought the aircraft down to 300 feet in order to investigate. He then proceeded to a Tramp Steamer in the immediate vicinity and the Wop/Air flashed a message that someone was in trouble and gave a position about 1,000 yard astern.

Three Motor Torpedo Boats were then approached and an effort was made to lead them to the light, one of the boats following the instructions. The Pilot then proceeded to the position of the light and fired distress cartridges. By now the aircraft had orbited for tewnty-five minutes and the Pilot decided he could not observe any longer having one engine feathered. The aircraft therefore proceeded back to Base, back plotting from the coast the position of the light and passing the information to Headquarters Bomber Command.

As a result of this excellent and persevering observation, a patrolling destroyer, in company with one of the Motor Torpedo Boats, searched the area and seven members of another Squadron were picked up.

This Pilot showed continued prescence of mind and superb captaincy and airman ship and for his outstanding perseverance and devotion to duty in pressing home a successful attack on three engines, and also being largely responsible in saving the lives of Severn members of aircrew, I strongly recommend him for an immediate award of the Distinguished Flying Cross.

J S MacKay
Wing commander, commanding
625 Squadron   R.A.F.

REMARKS BY STATION COMMANDER.

This Office has been with 625 Squadron for a short time only, having been recently transferred from 576 Squadron. From the very first, however, he made an immediate impression by his extreme enthusiasm and desire to be helpful in every possible way.

On this particular occasion his determination to carry on to the target on three engines, coupled with the skilful way in which he directed vessels to the aircraft dinghy, shows a magnificent spirit and may well have been responsible for saving the lives of the crew of the ditched aircraft.

For his fine performance , he is strongly recommended for am immediate award of the Distinguished Flying Cross.

R Donkin
Group Captain, commanding
R.A.F. Station,   Kelstern

REMARKS BY BASE COMMANDER

I Strongly endorse the above recommendations for the immediate award of the Distinguished Flying Cross.

Unreadable
Air Commodore, commanding
No 12 Base,   R.A.F.

REMARKS BY AIR OFFICER COMMANDING

Strongly recommended for the immediate award of the distinguished flying cross

Unreadable
Air Vice Marshall,
Air Officer Commanding
No. 1 Group,   R.A.F.

RECOMMENDATIONS FOR HONOURS AND AWARDS
NON - IMMEDIATE

Christian Names	:	Kenneth Lionel	Surname	: Trent, D.F.C.
Rank	:	Flying Officer	Official Number	: 176283
Command or Group	:	No. 1 Group	Unit	: 625 Squadron, R.A.F.

Total hours flown on operations...................... 185

Number of Sorties... 34

Total hours flown on operations
Since receipt of previous award...................... 88

Number of Sorties since receipt
Of previous award... 15

Recognition for which recommended............. Bar to D.F.C.

Appointment Held.. Captain-Pilot

Particulars of meritorious service for which recommendation is made:-

Flying Officer Trent is the Captain and Pilot of a gallant Lancaster crew, and is nearing the end of his first operational tour, having completed 34 sorties comprising 185 operational flying hours.

He has participated in attacks on heavily defended targets including DUSSELDORF, DORTMAND, HANOVER, COLOGNE(3), and ESSEN.

He has operated in very bad weather on several occasions, and often in the face of intense Flak and Fighter opposition, invariably rising to the occasion and displaying coolness and prescience of mind.

One of the most valuable features of this Officers operational record has been the example set by his clearly evinced enthusiasm for the destruction of the enemy in the face of the fiercest opposition.

This Office has now completed his normal first tour of operations, but such is his devotion to duty, he has volunteered to continue to complete a further five sorties.

On one occasion whilst participating in an attack on Cologne on 28th October 1944 he was instrumental in assisting to save the lives of seven members of aircrew who were located in the English Channel, this being carried out on only three engines. For his gallantry he was awarded an "Immediate" D.F.C.

His operational record is one of the most outstanding examples of devotion to duty, and I strongly recommend him for an award of a Bar to the Distinguished Flying Cross.

T Barker
Wing Commander, Commanding
14/1/1945   No. 625 Squadron,   R.A.F.

REMARKS BY STATION COMMANDER

The zeal displayed by this Officer is outstanding and he has rendered invaluable service by taking on many new crews on their first trip, for his fine example of courage and devotion to duty is strongly recommended for an award of a Bar to the Distinguished Flying Cross.

R Donkin
Group Captain, Commanding

14/1/1945   R.A.F. Station ,   Kelstern.

REMARKS BY BASE COMMANDER.
                I concur with the remarks of the Station and Squadron Commander, and endorse their recommendation.

Aubrey
Air Commodore, Commanding

18/1/1945   No. 12 Base,   Base.

REMARKS BY AIR OFFICER COMMANDING
                Strongly recommended for the non-immediate award of a Bar to the Distinguished Flying Cross.

Harris
Air Vice Marshall.

27/1/1945   Air Officer Commanding, No. 1 Group. R.A.F.